1980   Merry Xmas Byrne.

H. d. S.   P.

11D699370

THE PATRICKS
HOCKEY'S ROYAL FAMILY

THE
PATRICKS
Hockey's Royal Family

ERIC
WHITEHEAD

Doubleday Canada Limited, Toronto, Ontario
Doubleday & Company, Inc., Garden City, New York
1980

Also by Eric Whitehead

CYCLONE TAYLOR: A HOCKEY LEGEND

A number of the pictures used in this book were photographed from old family albums by Bill Cunningham of Vancouver.

Library of Congress Cataloging in Publication Data

Whitehead, Eric.
  The Patricks, hockey's royal family.

  Includes index.
    1. Hockey—Canada—History. 2. Hockey—United
States—History. 3. Patrick, Lester, 1883–1960.
4. Patrick, Frank, 1885–1960. I. Title.
GV848.4.C2W48   796.96′20971
ISBN 0-385-15662-6 (U.S.)
Library of Congress Catalog Card Number 79-6879

FOREWORD

In researching this book, I was deeply impressed by the enthusiasm the project evoked among the many people interviewed. The common response—in Montreal, New York, Boston, St. Louis, Los Angeles, Renfrew, Nelson, Vancouver, and Victoria, wherever the trail of the Patricks led—was that the telling of the Patricks' story was long overdue. There was a great desire on the part of everyone to help.

An equally impressive aspect of the research was the very strong bond of affection within the surviving family circle itself. In a chronicle essentially of sibling rivalry between the two principal brothers, Frank and Lester, with their respective families branching off in their different directions, there was plainly room for the petty jealousies, guarded comments, and weighted observations that are often part of such relationships. There were no such problems in this case.

In discussing the intimate family history, each family branch showed nothing but the deepest admiration and regard for the other, and whenever a sensitive matter arose it was tackled frankly and without concern for protecting a family "image."

The reason that the telling of this story has been so long delayed possibly lies in the fact that it is so complex, has so many leading characters, and is set in so many eras and places. Creating a story line from this scattered history, which begins with the emigration of Tom Patrick from Ireland in 1848 and descends through five generations, represents a very challenging proposition.

Fortunately, I had a good start on the challenge through my long and personal association with one of the senior Patrick brothers' most illustrious contemporaries, Fred ("Cyclone") Taylor, who died in the summer of 1978, in his ninety-fifth year. As related in my book *Cyclone Taylor: A Hockey Legend,* Taylor's path crossed and joined with that of the Patricks throughout their respective careers. He was thus a priceless source of intimate material and firsthand anecdotes. He too had a great affection for the Patrick family, and expressed it in a warm and revealing fashion right up to our final chat just a few days before his death. I also benefited from a personal friendship with Lester Patrick in his latter years, and, later with his sons, Muzz and Lynn.

Still, the catalyst of this particular undertaking was Boyd Robinson, a gentleman in his sixties who is employed in Vancouver as a cab driver. A man of both modest means and manner (whose daughter, Janice, is one of Canada's all-time best softball players, and a member of ten national teams), Robinson has long been obsessed with the need for a fitting biography of the Patrick family. It was his persistence and support, especially in providing access to an invaluable stock of early historical data collected by the Patricks, that made the writing of this particular journal possible.

For all concerned, including myself, the production of this book was a labor of love. There is the usual impossibility of giving proper credit to all who helped in a project such as this, but I will at least list the following, to whom I extend my sincere thanks for their generous co-operation and contribution: Muzz and Lynn Patrick and their cousin, Joe Patrick, Jr., who are, of course, part of this story and are typical of the wholehearted family co-operation in its preparation. Doug Peden, Muzz and Lynn's talented Victoria chum, who is now sports editor of the Victoria *Times;* Archie Wills, ex-editor of the *Times* and the chronicler of the Patricks' earliest West Coast exploits. Frank and Dean Miller, two of Lester's grandsons, who provided the family tree and a magnificent album of family photos dating back to the turn of the century and assembled by Lester in 1915.

One of the original Rangers, Murray Murdoch, and his first Rangers boss, Conn Smythe. Many of the latter-day Rangers, including Neil Colville, Clint Smith, Alex Shibicky, and Babe Pratt, who contributed substantially to the many hours of taped conversations during research.

I also gratefully acknowledge the assistance and co-operation of the New York Rangers Hockey Club and the staff at Madison Square Garden; the Boston *Globe, Ring* magazine, the British Columbia Sports Hall of Fame, and the hundreds of authors of the thousands of newspaper stories written about the Patricks.

I owe a very special debt to the memory of my late dear friend, Cyclone Taylor, who was the last surviving member of the Patrick pioneer era. In terms of its impact on the course of hockey history, plus its special inspiration as a unique family adventure, that era will likely never be matched.

ERIC WHITEHEAD

CONTENTS

Foreword   v
Prologue: A Fortune Lost   1

1   GROWING UP IN QUEBEC   9
2   THE NELSON ADVENTURE   41
3   THE BOARDINGHOUSE BOYS   69
4   THE REBEL EMPIRE   89
5   THE CHANGING GAME   119
6   TALES OF MANHATTAN   151
7   SEPARATE JOURNEYS   191
8   THE NEW BREED   203
9   FAREWELL TO BROADWAY   231
10   THE LAST CHALLENGE   249

Epilogue   265
Index   268

PROLOGUE

A Fortune Lost

June 5, 1909

For the eighth successive day torrential rains lashed the Kootenay mountain country that sweeps up through southeast British Columbia, and Crescent Valley, six thousand feet up the east face of the Valhalla Range, lay brooding in yet another sodden dawn. The valley, site of the Patrick Lumber Company sawmill, a ramshackle structure tucked into a bend of the Little Slocan River, was at the center of the storm that had already caused the worst flooding in the recorded history of the region. Swollen by a runoff from the slopes of the Kokanee Glacier that knifed through the sky to the northeast, the mountain streams were over their banks and tumbling wildly down toward their confluence with the main flow that ultimately empties into the Pacific, far out on the Oregon coast.

The mile-high valley that served as working headquarters for the Patrick family's timber holdings was isolated by the storm, but word of its ordeal had somehow filtered down to the office of the Nelson *News,* the area's weekly newspaper. In a story in the June 4 edition describing the widespread flood havoc along the thinly-settled tablelands of Kootenay Lake, the reporter added: ". . . but the greatest disaster to property seems to have occurred at the site of Joseph Patrick's lumber mill in the Crescent Valley. There were rumors yesterday that the mill had been swept away by the floodwaters of the Little Slocan . . ."

Things were bad on the Little Slocan, but not quite that bad. Not yet, at least. Although the mill had suffered severe damage, it was still intact. But now there was another threat, and the proprietor stood high on the riverbank keeping watch on the turbulent scene below.

Joe Patrick, a tall, handsome, square-built man in his early fifties, was surrounded by a crew of his employees, most of them loggers called out of the nearby camps to keep an all-night watch on the beleaguered mill. Chins tucked deep into their rain-soaked mackinaws, they looked on helplessly as the swirling currents surged against the crude earth-rock-and-timber dam that provided a quiet backwater for the company's logs. In this late spring, the captive booms contained more than 10 million feet of lumber, representing a quarter of a million dollars in prime cedar, hemlock, pine, fir, and larch. Throughout the stormy night the men had worked at strengthening the dam and anchoring the logs, but now there was nothing left to do but watch and wait.

By midmorning, the vigil was over. There was a dull crunching sound as the dam gave way. A moment later it crumbled into a mass of debris that slid swiftly downstream, followed by the logs, as the backwater spilled into the eddies. There was nothing to stop the logs now as they swept downstream toward the junction with the Slocan River and then the meeting with the broader waters of the Kootenay, twenty miles southwest of Nelson. From there, it would be a rapid run down the Kootenay to the town of Castlegar, where the Columbia River that begins in the snowfields of the Canadian Rockies snakes down toward the border on its long journey to the sea.

When the groaning mass of timber had finally disappeared from view, Joe Patrick turned to his men, nodded wordlessly, and watched as they just as silently turned and trudged off, headed back into the woods. Only four remained: Joe; Ed Delisle, the mill foreman; and Joe's sons, Lester and Frank; the two oldest of his eight children. Turning to his boys, both sturdy youths in their early twenties, Joe said quietly, "Let's go home."

Home, to the Irish-Protestant Patricks since their migration two years before from Quebec, was Nelson, four hours from the mill by horseback, four thousand feet down the mountain. Known as the "Queen City of the Kootenays" because of its idyllic setting on the west arm of Kootenay Lake, Nelson was a wide-open boomtown of 4,000 souls. Its thirty-two saloons were kept humming night and day by the lumberjacks who worked the woods, and by the miners and prospectors who probed the hills for lead, zinc, and silver, and panned the streams for gold.

When the three weary Patricks arrived back at their house on Edgewood Avenue, they found Nelson to be an isolated community cut off from the outside world by washouts that had severed the two railway lines serving the area. The roadbeds had been ripped out of the Canadian Pacific spur across the lake that connected with the trans-Canada main line, and the floods had washed out the Great Northern route that traveled to the U.S. border forty miles to the south, linking Nelson with Spokane, Washington.

Other than the Patricks, none of the townsfolk yet knew of the Crescent Valley spill. The first ones to learn about it would be the early evening patrons of the Manhattan Saloon, a thriving establishment favored for its massive mahogany bar and gambling room, where small fortunes were routinely won and lost at poker. The crowd at the bar got the word from a thirsty prospector just back from his silver claim. There, astride his pack mule, he had been sole witness to the awesome sight of Joe Patrick's fortune racing by on the churning currents of the Kootenay River.

Well before light the next morning, Joe, acting on a hunch born of a sleepless night, walked to the Great Northern station and had the telegraph operator tap out a message to the first stop across the border. This was Northport, Washington, a little community situated on the Columbia River a few miles below the juncture with the Kootenay. Within an hour the return message came tapping back from the Northport operator. YES STOP LOGS PILING UP BEHIND SANDBAR STOP NO MORE INFORMATION AT PRESENT STOP

That was all the information Joe needed. He hurried back home and routed Lester and Frank out of bed with orders to scour the town and bring back a dozen of the biggest, burliest loggers they could find. Joe knew that there would almost surely be trouble trying to lay claim to the runaway logs, but if even a small portion could be reclaimed for sale to U.S. mills in the area, it would be well worth the try. The dozen loggers were found and flushed out of their hotel rooms and boardinghouses. Some of them were plainly the worse for the night's wear, but after a fast breakfast and a ten-dollar advance, they were all aboard the two wagons that went trundling over the rutted trail to the border, at times axle-deep in mud.

Fortunately, the washout on the Great Northern track was located just a few miles below Nelson, and a train that had brought in a repair crew was just about ready to shunt back to Northport when the grimy caravan hove to. The freight pulled into Northport an hour past noon, and when the motley salvage gang arrived at the riverside Joe's worst fears were realized.

Some other people had apparently done some fast recruiting, and a rough-looking crowd of more than twenty lumberjacks were huddled on the shore near the Northport sawmill. Some waved guns as they engaged in a heated discussion punctuated with shouts and curses. They appeared to be drawn into three separate groups, and the subject of the angry debate was obviously the matter of the division of self-assumed "pirates'" rights to the huge mass of logs trapped behind a sandspit and a chain of giant timbers that snaked out to midriver.

This surface dam device was known as a fin boom because of the heavy iron fins that jutted out from the timbers, angled to snatch logs from the current and fend them in toward the shore. It worked well for the local sawmill that floated its logs down from upstream, and it had worked well for the Patrick runaways that had been declared fair game by scavengers along the route.

Joe calculated that there might be two million board feet of lumber out there, and regardless of the quarrel on the shore, it was clearly the property of the Patrick Lumber Company. The problem now was to convince the locals. After a hurried consultation with his crew, he ordered them out onto the logs to establish possession while he located the town sheriff and got him to deal with the menacing situation.

Out they went, led by Lester and Frank, who muscled through the baleful mob before anyone quite realized what was happening. They spread out across the logs, steadying themselves with pike poles, heavy iron poles about an inch-and-a-quarter in diameter, topped by a sharp gaff and a spike. In a pinch—a point that had surely occurred to the log boarders—they would make pretty potent weapons.

For the first time in many days, the sun had broken through the overcast, and it was now glinting warmly down on this strange river scene and the almost comic-opera confrontation that was not quite yet ready to turn ugly. Joe's sons stayed together, and with their battle stations established, they were clearly enjoying themselves, exhilarated by the experience.

They were a strapping pair, youthful editions of their father with his fine physique and rugged good looks. Lester, twenty-five, was tall and lean and in his caulked boots rode the logs with an easy, catlike grace. His aquiline features, set under a shock of wavy brown hair, were animated by flashes of a quick, boyish grin. Frank, two years younger, was equally tall and graceful but more thickly set around the shoulders. He moved a bit more deliberately and was less quick to smile. The pair communicated wordlessly via little glances and nods that were mute expressions of their closeness as brothers and of their special kinship as the eldest of Joe Patrick's children.

Both had already established themselves as hockey stars in eastern Canada before coming West; Lester as the rover and captain of the Montreal Wanderers in the famed Redbands' Stanley Cup Championship victories of 1906 and 1907, Frank as defenseman with the Montreal Victorias following four seasons as a brilliant all-around athlete at McGill University. The sturdy brothers were plainly more than just a couple of transient lumberjacks, but who that afternoon in Northport could have foreseen the future that lay beyond this little adventure on the Columbia River?

Who could have imagined that four decades later the Madison Square Garden marquee on Eighth Avenue would glow with the words LESTER PATRICK NIGHT, and that New Yorkers of every political stripe and social hue would jam the arena to pay affectionate tribute to the man they called The Silver Fox, one of the most admired and respected figures in tough, blasé old Manhattan? Or that with Lester's help and Joe's money, Frank would build a whole new hockey empire on the West Coast and change the face of the game with his special genius for innovation? Or that after closing shop in the West, he and Lester would have major roles in the establishment of the modern NHL, the rich new league that would know yet another remarkable generation of Patricks?

There was precious little hint of this sort of history out there on the logs, but a perceptive observer might well have sensed the con-

trasting personalities that would eventually cause the brothers'
paths to diverge, one headed up, one down. There could perhaps
have been a hint in the carefree manner in which Lester moved
over the logs, at one point laughing uproariously when one of the
hungover hirelings slipped and saved himself from being crushed
to death by scrambling wildly to his feet, cursing the Patricks and
defiling their ancestry. It might have been detected in the way that
Frank jabbed his pole into a cedar log and just stood stolidly and
silently facing the shore gang. Or was the younger brother even
then working on an idea, in this case some ingenious plan that
would get them out of this mess with their skins and at least some
of Joe's money?

Whatever Lester's mood, it was abruptly snapped by the sharp
crack of a rifle shot as a bullet ripped into a log at Frank's feet,
splintering the bark. Then a voice bellowed out from the riverbank. The exact words were never recorded, but they were quite
explicit and the message was clear: Get off the logs or be shot off.
And get off now.

The men on the logs froze and looked around uncertainly.
Frank shook his head, and that was enough for some of the uglier
trigger-happy customers on the shore. There was another rifle
shot, then the harsher bark of a shotgun, and then another as bullets raked the logs, sending wood chips flying into the air. There
were angry shouts from an elderly man who appeared to be the
mill boss, ordering the shooting stopped, but the mob was apparently enjoying its dangerous game. Three of his hired hands
had already leaped into the water as Joe Patrick came racing
along the riverbank, stopped with his back to the mob and
shouted, "Get ashore. This isn't worth getting somebody killed.
Get off those damned logs."

For this sternly religious Methodist, this was a rare bit of
blasphemy, but then Joe Patrick was in a rare grim mood as he
turned and faced the gunmen, standing defiantly with his arms
crossed as his men scrambled ashore.

A few hours later, after a meal provided by the apologetic sawmill people who stoutly disclaimed any part in the shooting, Joe
and his gang were on a Great Northern freight that was headed
back to pick up the repair crew at the washout. The logs were
eventually hauled up to the Northport mill, although the Patricks

never did learn how the proceeds of the fin-boom windfall were split, other than that several tough characters had enjoyed a pretty good payday.

As for the rest of the logs that had escaped from the Little Slocan, some were almost certainly intercepted along the route to the river mouth at Astoria, Oregon, but the bulk of the family's quarter-of-a-million-dollar timber harvest had just floated grandly out to sea. Joe, with his infinite faith in God and the Patricks, was not noticeably bothered by his massive financial loss. Nor, as he went on to rebuild the family fortune, would it be his last.

There is a footnote to that hectic afternoon that offers a curious insight into the relationship between the two brothers then and in the later years. Frank had been the last one off the logs that day, and the scene must have remained vividly in his mind, for he was to recall it many years later in a seven-part autobiographical series in the Boston *Globe*. The lengthy series appeared in the winter of 1935, during Frank's second term as coach of the Boston Bruins. In relating to Joe's urgent call to get off the logs, he wrote: "I've always thought that my father was afraid of losing Lester." The wistful implication that Lester was the favored son would surely have disturbed Joe Patrick, had he known of it. It had certainly not been supported by events in the past, nor would it be supported by events in the years to come.

1

GROWING UP
IN QUEBEC

Although the Patricks can trace their origins far back in Scottish history, the earliest known male member of the family was an Irishman from County Tyrone. He was James Patrick, a prosperous flax merchant in Cookstown. There is no record of his birth date, but it is presumed to be in the 1790s as Thomas, the fourth of his eight children, was born in 1818. It was this fourth child who was to become the patriarch of the new Canadian line of Patricks later perpetuated by his son, Joe.

When Tom Patrick was eighteen, he was sent off to study law at Dublin University, got his degree and returned home to work with a legal firm in Cookstown. A few years later, Ireland's always uncertain economy was crippled by one of that country's cruel potato famines and there was precious little work to be found for a small-town barrister. Tom was then thirty, married, with three children. His younger sister, Margaret, had left Ireland seven years before with her husband, Thomas Mitchell, to live on a farm in South Durham, Quebec, a rural community sixty-five miles west of Montreal. Thomas now decided to follow suit and make a new home in Canada. He left Ireland in the spring of 1848, went straight to South Durham, and also acquired farmland there. He immigrated alone, but within a year he had sent for his wife, Lucinda, and their three children.

Another seven children were born to Tom and Lucinda in South Durham, and one of these new Canadians was a son, Joseph, who arrived in 1857. That then was the beginning of the new breed of Canadian Patricks that produced Lester and Frank, the fourth-generation County Tyrone Irishmen whose exploits comprise the bulk of this journal.

The story of hockey's royal family and their wandering Camelot began in the autumn of 1881 when Joe Patrick left the family farm in South Durham, Quebec, and took a job as clerk in a general store in the nearby town of Drummondville. A handsome young buck of twenty-three, he had the pick of the young ladies in that lively community, and he chose the demurely pretty Grace Nelson, a local schoolmarm.

They were married in the spring of 1883 and their first child, Curtis Lester, was born December 31 of the same year. The birth of their second son, Frank Alexis, took place in Ottawa, Ontario, exactly ten days short of two years later, December 21, 1885. There is no record as to why Grace Patrick had made the five-hour train journey west to the nation's capital to have her second-born, and it can only be presumed that she had needed some sort of special care that was not available in Drummondville.

Tom and Lucinda Patrick frequently made the two-hour buggy or cutter trip from South Durham to visit their grandchildren and to try and talk Joe into coming back to the farm. Tom could never quite understand why Joe had left it in the first place, as he had been working his own section and doing very well selling his produce to the local merchants. Joe had, however, given a pretty broad hint of his ambitious and restless nature when at the age of twenty-one he had undertaken a curious money-making scheme that has become one of the family's favorite stories. Frank Patrick recalled the yarn many years later, in the series he wrote for the Boston *Globe*.

"In 1877, my father, being young and fired with the adventurous spirit of his parents, both of whom had migrated from Ireland, decided to raid the bean market in Boston, which was suffering from crop shortage. Talk about taking coals to Newcastle or the Mountain to Mahomet! But he was sure he could sell the beans to the Bostonians and make himself a tidy profit.

"So, he stored up a huge amount that had been grown and

flailed by the farmers around South Durham, and then set out with two wagon loads on the five-day journey to Boston. But by the time he arrived, the baked bean market had taken a sharp drop. He lost $800 on the venture. It took him a couple of years to recoup the loss, and he never did hear the last of it around home."

As in South Durham, Drummondville was a predominantly French-Canadian community, and the only visible concession to the few dozen English-speaking families was the Methodist Church in which Joe and Grace were married. Later, the Patrick children were the best-dressed, best-scrubbed members of the junior congregation.

Lester's earliest memory of his father was when at the age of four he sat in the wooden pew with his mother and young brother, listening more or less attentively as Joe, substituting for the sick minister, delivered the sermon. This, with the head of the house always on hand when needed to help spread the gospel of the Lord, would become a fairly common family experience. The head of the household was not only a devout Protestant, but also, with his rugged Irish charm, a born evangelist.

In 1887 the family moved to Carmel Hill, a village nine miles from Drummondville, where Joe bought a half interest in a general store. The village was in boom times because of the development of the Intercolonial Railway system, which later became part of the Canadian National Railway line between Montreal and Halifax.

Among Lester's earliest memories was that of "feeling quite important, hanging around the general store operated by my father. I started school a year after our arrival. I was enrolled in a French school because there were just not enough English-speaking families there, nor in most of rural Quebec, for them to maintain their own schools. I, of course, learned to speak French, as did the rest of the family."

Joe's partner in the general store was his cousin and boyhood friend, William Mitchell. He was the son of Tom and Margaret Patrick Mitchell, the first of the County Tyrone immigrants to settle in South Durham. Young Mitchell had just returned to Canada after trying his hand at railroading in Maine.

Supplying the railroad gangs that just happened to be run by a friendly Irishman named McGinnis, the Patricks' general store became the busiest establishment of its kind in the area. When the partners sold the business in 1892, they split net proceeds of $10,000, a very substantial sum in those days.

Joe used his $5,000 to form a lumber company and build a mill in Daveluyville, a town situated in a thickly wooded area sixty miles west of Quebec City. After a spring and summer stopover back in South Durham, he moved to Daveluyville with his growing family, which now numbered five. The new arrivals were daughter Lucinda Victoria, a third son, Edward Feather, and another daughter, Dora Carmel.

Joe's ex-partner also went into the lumber business, but he eventually turned to Federal politics, and in 1904 was appointed to the Canadian Senate.

The Patricks' stay in Daveluyville was marked by a tragedy that would haunt the family for many years and stay with Frank Patrick for the rest of his life. The sad event concerned the third son, Edward Feather, who got his unusual second name from that of his father's youngest brother, the last of his grandfather Tom Patrick's ten children.

For gifts on their first Christmas in Daveluyville, Lester and Frank were given their first skates. They were crude metal runners that attached to the soles of ordinary shoes and were clamped tight, more or less, by a lever. The excited youngsters left right after dinner to try them out. Lester was then nine, Frank seven, and Edward four.

In his recollections, Frank related the loving details of that hike with their father and young brother through the crisp, new snow to the river "four or five miles away." He told of how his father, impatient with his initial squeamishness, "literally threw me out onto the ice. My immediate reaction was to get up and run on the skates, which I did. And that, incidentally, is how I skated throughout my school, college, and professional careers, always more like a sprinter than a skater."

As his two brothers wobbled awkwardly about the ice, Edward, already nicknamed Ted, followed them, clapping his hands in glee. At one point he took a nasty spill, and Frank was the first there to pick him up and get him to laugh by taking a couple of comic pratfalls himself. The two of them laughed and played together during the long trek back home, with Ted traveling most of the way astride his father's broad shoulders.

From that day on, the two younger brothers were very close, and for the next few weeks of that winter in Daveluyville they were practically inseparable. Wherever Frank went, Ted would tag along.

Then, on a cold, bright morning after a heavy snowfall, Frank took Ted sleighing on the slopes out on the edge of town. Frank was pushing the sleigh when it ran loose across a logging road, and overturned. The spill occurred just as a horse-drawn logging sled appeared, running downhill. Ted was thrown into the path of the heavily-laden sled, and the runners went over his right leg.

It was a cruel accident that the family was loath to talk about in the years to come, and the exact details of what happened immediately afterward are not quite clear. There seems to be a general belief in the family that although the leg was badly crushed, it might have been saved by more skilled and prompt medical attention; that the severity of the injury had been underestimated by the doctor, and that he had delayed proper treatment too long. At any event, gangrene set in and the leg was amputated above the knee.

The trauma of that unhappy day left a scar on this tightly knit family that never completely healed. Frank was inconsolable, and no matter how often over the years he was assured that no blame could be attached to him, he couldn't or wouldn't shake the thought that he had somehow been responsible for the accident. In neither his nor Lester's record of those years is there any mention of the incident, nor even any mention of Ted's name. It was as if the youngster had never existed. There later seemed to be an obsessive need to forget the start of what ultimately became a troubled, unhappy life. Ted Patrick would become a very private chapter in the family journal, but he was then nursed back to health and was eventually fitted with a peg leg that was changed as he grew.

That year of 1892 brought yet another sad note. From South Durham came word of the death of Tom Patrick. He had passed away at the age of seventy-four, four years after the death of his wife, Lucinda.

In 1893 Joe expanded his thriving company into Montreal and

moved there to manage an office for the distribution and sale of various lumber by-products.

As Lester remembered it: "And so it was that we moved again, and that in October 1893 we located in Point St. Charles, which was then a railroad district of Montreal. We moved into a house right near the tracks. Had we been just on the other side, we would have been in the St. Lawrence River. I was enrolled in Loren Public School on Coleraine Street. I was to reach the mature age of ten in two months' time."

It was there in Point St. Charles that the Patrick brothers were first exposed to the game that would consume them throughout the rest of their lives. Although they had been raised in Quebec's spacious winterland of frozen ponds, lakes, and rivers, they knew very little about skating and nothing at all about hockey when they arrived in Montreal. As Lester said, "I had never even seen a hockey stick up to this time."

Montreal was then a bustling city of about a quarter-of-a-million souls in a community split into distinct English- and French-speaking sections. In winter, the city was a sprawling network of snow-packed roads and icy sidewalks, flanked by the broad, frozen stretches of the St. Lawrence River.

The city's sporting heroes in that cold winter of 1893 were the nine members of the Montreal hockey team that had just won a handsome silver trophy put up for the first time as a symbol of the national hockey championship. It bore the name of the donor, Lord Stanley of Preston, who was nearing the end of his term as the sixth Governor-General of Canada. The Montreal players who were awarded the Stanley Cup as champions of the five-team Canadian Amateur Hockey Association, the game's premier league, bore such long-forgotten names as Paton, Cameron, Irving, Routh, Hodgson, Lowe, Kingdon, and Barlow. But, allowing for a little ethnic license, they were the Richards, Beliveaus and the Lafleurs of their time, the roots of Les Canadiens. That first Stanley Cup Championship team was simply called "Montreal." There was no team nickname. Nicknames were for a slightly later age and the start of mini-dynasties such as the Montreal Wanderers, Shamrocks, and the Ottawa Silver Seven.

Hockey was the only game in town played at an organized senior level, and the Montreal players were its finest practitioners. But the roar of the crowd emanating from the downtown arena with its enclosed outdoor ice rink was just a distant echo to the Patrick boys and the rest of the kids out in Point St. Charles. They provided their own wonderful sights and sounds.

With each drop of the temperature in the clear, crisp mornings of November, the new kids on the block would rush out to join the neighborhood gang in a race across the tracks to the river. There they would test the strength of the slick new ice, boldly probing to its thinnest edge.

With the first big freeze, the gang crossed the ice to Nuns Island, where they hacked their hockey sticks out of tree branches. The stout weapons looked, in Lester's words, "like crooked shillelaghs. When the game began, the puck was usually either a block of wood or a tin can. And the game itself was just straight shinny all the time." It was not only "straight shinny all the time," but also rough shinny all the time, as the ten-year-old Lester learned in his first joyous outing on the river. No match for the older, bigger kids, he was knocked flat on his back in the first rush, trammeled by the warring tribes loosely designated as teams, and left to nurse his bruised ego as the hostilities swirled around him.

This sort of thing was to happen many times to the two new kids from the sticks, but they quickly learned the first rule of survival at that marvelously exuberant level of ice hockey in 1893: when knocked down, get right up again and go after the puck. Find it, rag it, learn how to control it, and how to coax it into the delicate art of the pass and the deft cunning of the shot. With all this done, so went the theory, the skating, that pure flow of movement that is the foundation of all the game's skills, would just naturally follow. It was a primitive school, but a gloriously exhilarating and rewarding one, especially for superb natural athletes such as the Patrick boys would prove to be.

Nearly three decades later, at one of the regular seminars in his Madison Square Garden office called to brief the attentive New York reporters on the various wonders of the new game in town, Lester would say, "Gentlemen, there is no hockey school on God's earth to match that so innocently contrived by youngsters out on a frozen pond, learning to play by loving to play, free, unfettered, uncontaminated by adults, and unspoiled by the egos of elderly gentlemen such as myself. That, gentlemen," he grandly intoned as the Manhattan scribes, some of them numbered among the most famous names in U.S. journalism, stirred respectfully on their chairs, "is what this marvelous game of hockey is really all about."

Back at the old school in Point St. Charles, a good deal of the neighborhood hockey was played on a vacant lot across the street from the Patricks' house on Guy Street. When the river ice was poor, a little sweet-talking to the chief in the firehouse a few blocks away did the trick, and the men were sent around with their hose reels.

As Joe Patrick expanded his business and founded the Pennsylvania Wood and Coal Company another family move was inevitable. An agency for anthracite coal was obtained, and several branch outlets were opened. The family affluence was growing significantly, or as Lester saw it, "I must assume that my father was prosperous to some extent, because—with each new child—we kept moving to a better residential area."

The better residential area in 1895 was Westmount, Montreal's toniest suburb. The district was so swank that some of its avenues were paved with macadam, the revolutionary new road surface that provided glorious relief from the dust and mud of Point St. Charles, and even much of downtown Montreal. It also heralded the coming age of the automobile, although Montreal was not yet ready to plunge into the era begun just that year down in Indiana, where a one-cylinder auto hailed as the first of the American gasoline-powered breed had hurtled along the Kokomo Turnpike at the breath-taking speed of six miles per hour.

The Patrick boys and their new buddies saw the blessing in a different light: It was great for street shinny, which was a summer version of ice hockey. Macadam was in a sense sport's first artificial "turf," and its immediate effect was to produce a record crop of skinned knees and elbows.

Said Lester, "We played street shinny in Westmount each year until the rinks froze, but most of our summers were taken up by another game: baseball. I'd never seen the game before, but we played it instead of the lacrosse we used to play in Point St. Charles. I guess the kids in Westmount figured they were too refined for a roughhouse game like lacrosse."

One of the "refined" kids who showed up to play ball one sum-

mer afternoon was a cocky ten-year-old named Art Ross. This
was a name that would dog the Patrick brothers for most of the
next half century in a strange mix of bitter rivalry and warm
friendship. It was a name that would come to mean to the Boston
Bruins almost what the name Lester Patrick would be to the New
York Rangers.

"In our neighborhood," wrote Lester, "Art Ross was Mr. Big.
He wouldn't have liked me to have referred to him as a rich
man's kid, but we certainly thought he was just that. He had the
baseball, the bat, glove, catcher's mitt and mask—he had everything. When he showed up, the game could start. He also had a lot
of talent. He was a fine athlete, even then." Among the other
youngsters who became part of the Westmount gang in games on
the streets and the corner lots were Walter Smaill and the Cleghorn brothers, Sprague and Odie, three others who would follow
the Patricks into big league hockey and onto the sport's honor
roll.

The baseball was played on a couple of vacant lots at the end
of the Patricks' street, and the cramped outfield posed a danger
for unwary passers-by. One afternoon, a ball propelled by the bat
of Arthur Howie Ross bounded into the path of a carriage, frightening the horses and causing them to bolt. They were quickly
brought under control, but not before the passenger seated in the
elegant landau was considerably shaken—the greatest injury being
to the gentleman's dignity. To the surprise of the ballplayers, the
carriage pulled up in front of the Patrick residence, and the passenger emerged, shaking his fist angrily at his assailants.

This gentleman was none other than Sir William McDonald, a
Prince Edward Islander who had become famed as Montreal's
leading eccentric. The then sixty-four-year-old McDonald's
number-one eccentricity was philanthropy, which he practiced
with considerable diligence. Having made his fortune in tobacco
through the huge company that still bears his name, he had already given away a great part of an eventual total of more than
$15 million, a good deal of it in endowments to McGill Univer-
sity.

The Patrick boys, who would one day enter the school that Sir
William had so liberally endowed, watched as he walked stiffly up
the path, banged on the door of their house, and was beckoned in-

side. Sir William was paying a social-business visit to Joe Patrick, whom he had met in a downtown gentlemen's club. He had been impressed by the young entrepreneur's charm and business acumen, and, as had been reported in the Montreal *Gazette,* he had expressed interest in buying into the thriving new Pennsylvania Wood and Coal Company.

There was a distinct irony in this meeting between Joe Patrick and the czar of the Canadian tobacco industry. The deeply religious Methodist from the Quebec hinterlands could abide neither tobacco nor alcohol, and would have neither in his house. But Joe was also a very astute and practical businessman, and it is unlikely that his personal morality had any bearing on the fact that nothing appeared to come of the meeting. At least no business arrangement was ever recorded.

Nor could Art Ross's errant fly ball be properly reckoned as a factor. Lester and Frank got home before Sir William left and they astutely forestalled their father's reprimand by apologizing to the gentleman on behalf of Art and the rest of the gang. The distinguished visitor finished his tea and departed suitably mollified and in good humor.

Lester was now playing hockey in the neighborhood leagues and at school, and was soon in demand all over the city as a "ringer" brought in for important games. Although he had just taken up the sport, he was already a few cuts above others of his age group in its skills.

He got his first look at senior league hockey in the winter of 1906 at the age of thirteen, when his father took him down to the Victoria Arena to watch a challenge match between the Winnipeg Victorias and the Montreal Victorias. It was a dull contest, won 2–0 by the home team, and Lester's only lasting impressions were of the size of the first big crowd he had ever seen—a packed house of 1,500—and the gaudy attire of the visiting westerners. The Winnipeggers wore bright scarlet uniforms, and the goalie also sported immaculate white cricket pads and a yellow toque. He and Frank saw much better hockey at the Arena later that season, and there were better games still when the two brothers eventually got into the act downtown.

When the new 2,500-seat Montreal rink was built in 1898, Lester got to practice there with his high-school team, and turned up as stick boy for the visiting teams from Ottawa and Quebec. He also turned up as a ticket hustler, operating a thriving scalping business with the aid of his buddy, Art Ross.

They would arrive at the Arena early for important games, buy reserved-seat tickets for thirty-five cents and sell them near game time for twice that sum and more. At a championship game in 1899 between Montreal and Quebec, Lester recalls "applying my savings to buying thirty-five-cent reserved-seat tickets and selling them at a dollar. I cleared nearly fifteen dollars. It was so much money that I was in a dilemma as to how I could spend it without having to explain to my father."

Although he was still too young to get in on his brother's action, Frank had the sweet pleasure of outsmarting Lester at one of the family's hockey outings. "It was in March of 1899, when the Shamrocks and the Victorias were playing the final game to decide the league's Cup representative. All the reserved seats had been sold long in advance, so my father, who had a reserve seat ticket, gave Lester and me each a quarter to buy rush seats. When we reached the rink, the doors to the rush section were locked, and there were just a few standing-room tickets left, at thirty-five cents each. We discussed the problem and finally I said, 'Lester, you give me a dime of your money and I'll get a ticket, go inside and find Dad and send him out to pay your way in.' He agreed and I went in. Well, I could see there was no chance of finding my father in that howling mob, so I decided that since I was in, the most sensible thing to do was stay there. I found a nice spot in the aisle and remained there for the entire game.

"Poor Lester. He was still outside, and all he could hear was the roar of the crowd. It was a very good game, and the Shamrocks won 1–0. I suppose it was a rotten trick to play on one's brother, but you can rest assured that Lester was never so easily fooled again."

Lester Patrick was not yet known as The Silver Fox.

Occasionally, young Ted would sit with his two older brothers in the rush seats at the Arena, making the steep climb to his seat on crutches. He had the peg leg, but it was awkward on steep rises. He would not then or would he ever accept help from his brothers to ease his infirmity.

Despite the handicap that obviously gnawed at him, Ted was

generally a happy-go-lucky child, growing into the youth who would be said by so many who knew him to be the most handsome and personable and perhaps most physically gifted of all the Patrick boys. As he approached his tenth birthday he became increasingly involved in the street games and developed a remarkable agility that made him nearly the match of less naturally talented youngsters. Nearly. But, of course, never quite.

He watched Lester and Frank grow increasingly skilled at the games they played and rarely missed one of their neighborhood league hockey games. But that was one game he could not play, and Frank recalls that this bothered young Ted more than anything else.

One day Frank came home from a hockey game and asked for his nine-year-old brother who hadn't been there to watch as usual. Nobody had seen him that afternoon. Joined by his anxious father, Frank went off to look and found Ted at a rink on a lot a few streets away. He was sitting on a snowbank at the side of the rink, bent over a skate, trying to strap and tie it to his peg leg. The other skate was firmly fixed. He had not seen the approach of his father and brother, and Joe signaled Frank to stop and watch.

The boy was obviously having trouble with his crude attachment, but after a couple of minutes he dabbed at his eyes and got to his feet to test the wobbly connection. He stepped onto the ice, took a couple of strides and went sprawling as the skate slipped off. He sat up, his clothes matted by the snow of many previous falls, and bent over the skate again, sobbing as he tugged at the bindings.

Joe Patrick took Frank by the arm, and they turned silently away and headed back to the house. Ted got back some time later, was served his late supper by his mother, ate it in silence, and went up to bed.

Two days later, Joe came home with a package and left it in Ted's room. Inside was a box with a pair of skates, one fitted with an ingenious sole-socket strap attachment. There was nothing said of the gift the next day when Ted left right after an early breakfast with the box under his arm. He stayed away for the rest of the morning.

Before the winter was over, he was playing hockey with the kids of his age. He of course played the game in his own terribly limited and dogged fashion, but for a while at least young Ted was tremendously happy. His laughter was a tonic to a household that understood the boy's deep frustration.

That winter also saw the advent of a new century, and the first spring of the new age brought the Patrick children their first awareness of what was even then known among English-Canadians as "the French problem."

The Patricks were not English-Canadians, nor, as Protestants from the North of Ireland, were they anti-English-Canadians. Having blended easily and well into Quebec's rural French-Canadian culture, they were about as nicely neutral as it was possible to be in the countryside's state of ethnic unease. Joe Patrick was not at all pleased when his oldest son broke the spirit of the neutrality.

At seventeen, Lester was the victim of his own innocence when he became involved in a riot between English and French Canadians in downtown Montreal. With him in this lamentable breach of the peace was none other than the Westmount neighborhood's Mr. Big, Art Ross. The riot reflected a severe split over the conduct of the Boer War, with the French part of the Montreal populace strongly supporting the Boers, and the English just as strongly pro-British. It was a highly emotional issue.

There had been violent French-Canadian demonstrations when Prime Minister Sir Wilfrid Laurier had proposed that a Canadian brigade be sent to South Africa to fight side-by-side with the British. In March 1900 the English-Canadians responded with wild jubilation when the Boers' four-month siege of Ladysmith was broken. British flags broke out everywhere, church bells pealed, and joyous mobs poured into the streets. At McGill, the English-speaking university, classes were canceled and more than a thousand students stormed downtown to join the celebration. Finding no British flags showing at the offices of the French paper, *La Presse,* the mob hammered down the doors and smashed the windows.

The Messrs. Patrick and Ross, lured downtown by the smell of excitement, were on St. James Street a little later when the unruly mob came roaring by, preceded by a young man waving a Union Jack and several others waving hockey sticks. It was the hockey sticks that did it. To the young adventurers from Westmount, flags were no big deal, but hockey sticks they could understand. This had to be their kind of mob. They joined the group as it streamed off toward Laval University, the city's French-speaking citadel of higher learning. (This was a recently established branch of the main establishment in Quebec City, and would later become known as the University of Montreal.)

Finding no Relief of Ladysmith celebration in progress there, the mob swarmed onto the campus and raised two Union Jacks—and the ire of Laval students who tried to haul them down again. The ensuing battle lasted for more than an hour, and it took a squad of fifty policemen to restore peace. Dozens of the combatants were hauled off in paddy wagons, and in one of these, nursing a bruised eye and a bloodied nose respectively, were Curtis Lester Patrick and Arthur Howie Ross of Westmount. They were later claimed by their parents and taken home in disgrace.

"My father," said Lester, "didn't speak to me for three days while I sweated over what punishment I would receive. I guess he figured that this was punishment enough, and on the fourth day everything was fine again. Looking back, I'm sure my father got a secret kick out of the episode, although at the time he seemed pretty angry. But he never stayed angry long. My mother helped. She was a quiet, gentle soul who always seemed to hover in the background, yet there is no doubt that she was a power in the household and had a great influence on my father. There was a very strong bond of affection between them, and although Dad certainly dominated the family with his warmth and his gregarious manner, Mother was the quiet strength behind it all."

The year following the Laval escapade, Lester enrolled as a student at McGill University, became the star center of the basketball team in his first semester and then moved straight onto the hockey squad. He was positioned at rover, the fourth forward spot in that era of seven-man hockey. When word of the heavy demand for the off-campus services of the talented eighteen-year-old in the city's tough neighborhood leagues got around, Lester was offered a tryout with defending Stanley Cup Champions, the Montreal Shamrocks. However, that posed a choice between the McGill team and the Shamrocks, and on his father's advice he declined the offer.

While Joe Patrick was enthused over the prospect of turning

out the family's first college graduate, his son was not. After just one year at McGill, with Lester showing more interest in basketball and hockey than in his studies, Joe took him out of school to work in the family's coal-and-wood business. He began as an office boy and after one year was made manager of one of the branch offices. Then came another change.

"In the spring of 1903, my father and his associates liquidated the Montreal business and I got the bug to go out West and be a cowboy. I was a few months past nineteen years of age. My father bought me a sixty-day return ticket to Calgary. He must have figured that I would be back long before the ticket expired. However, fate determined otherwise."

This sudden urge to go West and try life as a cowboy wasn't a complete surprise to the head of the family. Two years before, Joe had taken the two oldest brothers down across the border to Burlington, Vermont, to see a rodeo show. The big attraction was a twenty-one-year-old trick rider named Tom Mix who was making a name for himself in the traveling wild-west shows. At eighteen, he had fought in the Spanish-American War, then later in Asia, in the Boxer Rebellion. He must have made a strong impression on the seventeen-year-old from Montreal, for in the coming years Lester would see as many as possible of the four hundred Hollywood Westerns that would make the youth from Driftwood, Pennsylvania, the hero image of millions of Americans.

If Lester had any illusions of becoming another Tom Mix on his 1903 trip to Calgary, he was swiftly disenchanted. He arrived in the booming frontier town at the foot of the Rockies in early June and started hunting for a job as a ranch hand. He couldn't ride a horse too well, but he was willing to learn, and the Alberta ranchers were short of hands. However, his new career never got off the ground, and Lester never got on an Alberta horse, at least in earnest.

"The only job I could find," he said, "was one that would give me twenty dollars a month plus board, and it was pointed out to me by the foreman that the working hours were from sunrise to sunset. I was through with the life of a cowboy right there. I went back to Calgary and got myself a job with the Canadian Pacific Railway as a rodman and chainman on a survey gang."

Lester stayed with the survey gang until it was frozen out in the late fall. His return ticket having expired, the CPR gave him free transportation home to Montreal, but although he left for Montreal in November, he didn't get there until spring. He decided to stop off in Brandon, Manitoba, to look up three friends from Montreal who were playing with the Brandon hockey club, and was offered a job with the team for his keep and twenty-five dollars a month expense money. Lester wired home to his father for permission to stay, and got it.

"The record of that season will show that we won the Manitoba League Championship." The record will also show that the new Brandon cover-point (a free-wheeling defenseman operating independently of the other) rushed the length of the rink to score a spectacular goal in a game against Winnipeg. This tactic broke the unwritten law that said a defenseman should play defense only, and should never leave his beat to stray into the offensive zone. With that one audacious move against Winnipeg, Lester Patrick had become the game's first rushing defenseman, the first of a long line that ultimately led to the king of them all: Bobby Orr.

The record will further show that after winning their league title, the Brandon team challenged for the Stanley Cup and traveled East for a two-game series against the famed Ottawa Silver Seven. Although the Brandon cover-point performed brilliantly in his first test at the top, the precocious westerners were soundly thumped, losing by scores of 6–3 and 9–3.

While lavishing praise on Lester's overall play, the Ottawa reporters criticized him for "his tendency to wander off down the ice away from his position." But then they had no way of knowing that this was the way the game would be played in the future.

It was mid-March in that year of 1904 when the wandering prodigal finally arrived back home in Montreal after the short train run from Ottawa. He was greeted by the news that the family was on the move again. Joe Patrick was leaving to attend the lengthy business of winding up his lumber interests at the mill in Daveluyville, and the family was to go with him. That included Lester, who was needed in the mill office, but not Frank.

He had been enrolled in Stanstead College, a prep school in the Quebec town of Stanstead, on the Vermont border. He was being groomed for entry into McGill, hopefully to pick up where Lester had left off after his freshman year.

"Those days at Stanstead," Frank reminisced, "were among the happiest of my life. It was a beautiful setting for a school, and there are ex-Stanstead students now living in Boston whose friendship I've treasured through the years. The fathers of some were friends of my own father, who met many Boston people during his Drummondville lumber dealings. One of these was a Boston businessman named Frank Alexis Cutting, after whom I was named."

Frank made the Stanstead football team that autumn. Playing halfback, he was named captain and led the team to an undefeated six-game season. The seventh and last game of the year was a Thanksgiving Day exhibition contest against a city league team from Montreal. On the team was old friend, Art Ross, and older brother, Lester, who had recently returned to Montreal with the family.

Frank had viewed the reunion with mixed feelings. "I nearly keeled over when I saw that all the players were bigger and older than us. They were senior players about equal to those on a college varsity team. We were just a junior college, with a team that certainly rated no better than a college freshman squad.

"I got Art aside and said, 'What's the idea, Art? Do you want to murder us?'

" 'Sure,' Art replied, grinning. He went over to Lester and the two of them walked off to a waiting carriage, convulsed with laughter."

But later on there was a conference between the team captains: Ross, of the Montreal Independents, and F. Patrick of Stanstead. The visiting end, L. Patrick, was allowed to join in.

Captain Ross opened the discussion. "Frank," he said gravely, "I understand that this is a co-ed institution."

"It is," said Frank.

"And that the traditional highlight of Thanksgiving Game Day is the Stanstead Chicken Pie Social in the gymnasium."

Frank nodded again.

"Well," chuckled Art, "there you are."

"Where?" sighed Frank.

"That's what we're here for. A little fun. We can play football back home anytime. You get us into the Stanstead Chicken Pie Social and line us up with some nice co-eds, and we'll have a real good fun game out there tomorrow. Okay?"

"Okay," said Frank.

"Good," said Lester. "And to make sure we have a nice friendly game, and that I don't get too tired—I'll be the referee."

It may have been the first "fix" in the history of college football, but then the stakes were substantial. It wasn't every day that a couple of rambunctious kids from the old Westmount neighborhood gang got to attend a junior college Chicken Pie Social and dance with the co-eds. And whatever.

It was, in fact, quite an entertaining football game, ending in a 6–6 tie, and nobody got hurt. Afterward, a very good time was had by all.

After the football season at Stanstead there was hockey, and with Captain Patrick playing rover that meant another unbeaten season. It was a breeze for the Westmount old grad, and he dismissed the season lightly. "The only thing I remember about the season was that in a couple of games I got lucky and scored thirteen straight goals."

In Montreal, with the family back from Daveluyville, Lester was playing hockey, this time with the new Canadian Amateur Hockey Association entry from Westmount. The new team had Lester at rover and Art Ross on defense, but it was plagued by two things—terrible goaltending and the fact that the top player, Lester, was busy working for his father and was unable to attend workouts. In three games, against the Victorias, the Shamrocks and Quebec, Westmount gave up the horrifying total of forty goals.

Frank was enlisted to play defense when he arrived home for the Christmas holidays, but his brief two-game appearance served no historic purpose other than to mark the first and last time that he and Lester would play on the same team. The brothers went their separate ways in 1906, with Frank attending McGill, and Lester at work as a clerk with the Canadian Rubber Company, which was later to become known as the Dominion Rubber Company, one of Canada's richest conglomerates.

Joe Patrick had liquidated his Quebec business interests and was organizing a new company with an eye on new timberlands opening up in the West. In the spring, he took the train to the coast to start his search for new properties. That was the first tentative move toward the eventual establishment of a new hockey empire on the West Coast, and of the two oldest Patrick boys as the game's foremost innovators.

At McGill, Frank captained the varsity hockey team in a season highlighted by a victory over Harvard University in the first-ever international collegiate hockey game. In his memoirs, Frank brushes off this historic event with the comment, "Offhand, I don't recall much about that game in Harvard Stadium. I'm pretty sure we won by a score of 8–2, and that I managed to get a couple of goals."

The local newspapers had a little more to say about the game, as in these excerpts from the story in the Boston *Post:*

> The superiority of the Canadians in their national game was clearly demonstrated, and although Harvard fought hard, it never had a chance once the Canadians, led by the marvelous play of their cover-point, Frank Patrick, got going. A crowd of 700 watched in Harvard's fine new rink.
>
> For his third goal late in the game, Patrick, in the prettiest individual effort ever seen by local fans, maneuvered in spectacular fashion past mid-ice and then lifted the puck with a shot traveling so fast that the goalie never saw it until it hit the back of the net.

That game took place in mid-February 1906, by which time, back in Montreal, Lester was closing in on one of the biggest thrills of his young life. He had signed on with the Montreal Wanderers as rover, and it was his brilliant play that had kept the club in a season-long deadlock with the Ottawa Silver Seven at the top of the Eastern Canada League standings. At the same time, Lester was playing a full schedule with his company's team in the Manufacturers League and leading that club to the championship. There is a natural temptation here to question the caliber of a senior hockey establishment in which a young player can perform as one of its top stars while working at a steady job and also playing a full schedule in a junior league. Was the twenty-two-year-old Patrick that good, or was the top brand of hockey that bad? Is the quality of "big league" hockey of that era overexalted in retrospect?

The best answer to this lies in the fact that while the quality of performance in any sport is relative to its era, those pioneer hockey days produced a lot of outstanding hockey players by any time standard. Fair proof of this is in the statistic showing that from two senior league rosters of 1905–6, no less than seventeen players are in the Hockey Hall of Fame. They were put there four decades later by a Selection Committee whose familiarity with players covered pretty well the whole spectrum of the sport up to that time, and who set very tough standards, assessing talent for talent's sake. There seems little doubt that 1906 Eastern Canada League and Federal League stars such as Si Griffis, Joe Hall, Riley Hearn, Ernie Johnson, Lester Patrick, and the rest of that era's Hall of Famers would be as great today as they were then.

Frank was yet to earn his spurs as a full-time player in senior hockey, but even while a collegian he managed to stay close to the action at the top. During the previous season, while holidaying from Stanstead College, he had been called out of the stands early in a game between the Wanderers and the Ottawa Victorias to take over for a referee who had been injured in a collision. He did such a good job that when he was due in town again on a subsequent week-end he was asked to handle a crucial contest between Montreal and Cornwall, two teams that were in the thick of a bitter fight for the championship of the Federal League.

"That," said Frank, many years later, "was my most trying experience in hockey, as a referee, player, or coach. That particular game was a grudge match if ever there was one. The Cornwall players had taken a terrible physical beating in the Montreal rink the week before, and they had sworn to get even in their own bailiwick.

"Cornwall, Ontario, was a factory town, and the people there took their hockey very seriously. On the day of the game there must have been nearly 3,000 people jammed into a rink built to hold a little more than half that total. Walking onto the ice just before game time was like walking into a bear pit. I knew that I had a nasty job on my hands, and it didn't help to know that I would be the youngest and least-experienced person on the ice.

"The Cornwall players wasted no time laying on the wood, and I immediately began assessing penalties against them in an attempt to control the contest. This didn't sit too well with the fans, and when I sent one of the home-town boys off for opening a Montreal player's skull with his stick and the Wanderers scored a minute later, they all but tore the place apart.

"That one-goal lead held up, and when the game was over the

crowd stormed down onto the ice and came after me. They had my route to the exit blocked and I was all but surrounded. I don't believe I would have gotten out of there alive had it not been for one of the Cornwall players, Reddy McMillan, who came to my rescue, flailing at the mob with his stick and screaming at them to get off the ice.

"He rushed over and backed me against the boards and stood in front of me while he tried to reason with the mob. He told them that to get me they'd have to get him first, and they finally backed off. Reddy saved my hide. The whole game was a terrible ordeal, but that finish was the most frightening part.

"However, the very undesirable custom then in vogue was to have the referee dress in the home-team's room, and I had some pretty anxious moments before I got out of the Cornwall quarters. I think it was during this experience when the idea was born in me for the rule requiring separate rooms for players and officials. This eventually became law. It might even have saved a life or two."

In a follow-up to that episode, the Cornwall team officials asked Frank to return the following week-end to referee another grudge match scheduled for the home rink against the Ottawa Victorias. It wasn't quite clear as to whether this invitation was a tribute to the coolness and the courage of the nineteen-year-old collegian, or whether the Cornwall folks just wanted another crack at him, but Frank didn't bother to find out.

"I declined. Fortunately. A far worse riot broke out in that game. One of the Cornwall players, Bud McCourt, was killed. Ottawa's Charlie Masson was charged with assault, accused of having clubbed McCourt over the head with his stick. He was acquitted in a court trial."

With Frank playing his hockey at McGill, Lester was getting his own baptism of hockey violence, vintage 1905–6, as the bright new star of the Wanderers.

Two other new Wanderers that year were Ernie Russell and Ernie Johnson, a pair of fine young forwards already established as stars of the game. For Johnson, later labeled "Moose," this was to be the first of twenty years' association with Lester, many of these as a magnificent and tremendously popular defenseman in the Patricks' Pacific Coast hockey empire.

The new partnership got off to an auspicious start in the first game of the season, an 11–5 rout of the Victorias. Lester, on one wing, scored three goals for the Redbands, and Johnson, on the other, scored one. Unhappily for the big, good-natured Moose, his goal was against his own team. In attempting to clear in front of the goal, he had swept the puck more or less smartly into the netting. Despite this, he was hailed in the newspaper accounts as one of the game's outstanding performers, second only to Lester.

That was a relatively docile game, the Victorias having been definitely outclassed, but things began warming up a few weeks later in a contest against the one-time Cup holders, Montreal. Tied with the defending champion Ottawa team in the battle for the Cup, the Wanderers went into the Montreal game in great shape for a run at the Silver Seven, but came out in trouble, despite a 6–2 victory.

Early in the game, Lester was cut over the eye with a stick swung by one of his old Westmount buddies, Walter Smaill. He had to retire to the infirmary for mending, came back a few minutes later with a dozen stitches just over the eyebrow, but had to leave again because the wound was still bleeding and he was blind on one side. Teammate Billy Strachan was knocked to the ice during a melee, run over by a skate and departed with a severely gashed foot. Ernie Johnson squared off in a dispute with Montreal's Art Coulson and both went off for repairs, Coulson with a cut eye and Johnson with a broken nose.

But the next week all players were in the lineup as the Wanderers once again swamped the hapless Vics, 9–4.

The foregoing notation of these fairly average examples of exuberance in those early days is made merely because that second game set up one of the most remarkable confrontations in Stanley Cup history. And it starred the twenty-two-year-old from Westmount who had become the leader of the Wanderers in their quest for their first Cup Championship.

Having effortlessly brushed off the Cup challengers of Queen's University, the collegiate champions, and of Smith Falls, champions of the rival Federal League, the Ottawa Silver Seven faced the Wanderers in the real showdown. These teams had finished tied at the top of the newly formed Eastern Canada Hockey League, with identical 9–1 records, and a two-game total-goals series was scheduled to settle the issue. To the winner would go both the league title and the Stanley Cup.

For the first meeting in Montreal on March 15, 1906, the defending champions were 2–1 betting favorites, but the Wanderers obviously weren't listening to the neighborhood bookies. Their fans went wild as Ernie Russell got four goals, Pud Glass got three and Moose Johnson shared a pair with Patrick in the home-town 9–1 victory.

The next game was booked for Ottawa on March 17, St. Patrick's Day, and the holiday date looked like a good augury for the Wanderers' rover of the same name. But the team appeared to need precious little in the way of favorable omens. Eight goals down for the round following their shock defeat in Montreal, the Silver Seven appeared to be headed for little more than an exercise in futility, but you couldn't tell that to their fans.

There was tremendous interest in the game, and Dey's Arena on Gladstone Avenue was sold out to its normal capacity long before game day, and that was just the beginning. When rush tickets were placed on sale at Allen & Cochrane's Store on Friday morning, the plate-glass window was smashed in the crush of the huge crowd, many of whom had been waiting in line all night. The local gendarmes were called to restore order, and three fans who objected to this intervention were tapped gently on the skull and hauled off in a paddy wagon.

The inside of the rink had been practically gutted in order to squeeze in as many bodies as possible without suffocation. Temporary standing platforms were erected at one end and double-deck bleachers hoisted at the other. The grandstand press box had been torn out and a new one suspended from the rafters, a fact that brought howls of dismay if not downright fear from the reporters. Loose boards had been laid across the bottom of the press box, and a careless step could send a scribe hurtling between the two-by-fours and down onto the heads of the vice-regal party, who were seated directly below. In addition to the reporters' misgivings, the Governor-General himself, Earl Grey, was reported to be a little apprehensive.

Despite the fact that just 200 tickets had been allotted to the Montreal fans, more than 1,000 had made the journey up the Ottawa Valley in special trains, jamming the Ottawa hotels and providing a land-office business for scalpers. The top $2.00 tickets were going for $10, with no guarantee that they were genuine. The visitors were also hungry for betting action, but despite their big goals' edge and their high hopes, they were no fools. Mindful of the Silver Seven's awesome unbeaten record on home ice, Wanderers' fans were offering no better than even money. At that, $12,000 was covered in one pooled bet in the lobby of the Russell Hotel, with most of the Ottawa backing said to be New York money.

Controversy rose to fever pitch when it was rumored that the Silver Seven had "borrowed" the brilliant young Smith Falls goalie, Percy Leseur, and would play him regardless of any protest against the illegality of this late addition to the roster. Another report had it that another "ringer," Kenora's Tom Phillips, one of the best forwards in hockey, was locked in a room at the Russell Hotel and would also start for the Silver Seven. Only the first rumor turned out to be correct.

At game time on Saturday, the rink was jammed with humanity, with clusters of intrepid youngsters all but literally hanging from the rafters. In an arena built to hold 3,000, more than 5,400 were shoe-horned inside. Another 2,000 were hammering on the doors to get in.

It was against this setting that developed what the *Sporting News* several years later in sober retrospect described as "The Greatest Hockey Game in History." Now, if all the Greatest Hockey Games in History were laid end to end, they would stretch from here to any far-flung fan of your choice, but there can be little doubt that this one was at least a contender for the title.

A deafening roar greeted the home-town team as it skated onto the ice for the two thirty-minute halves that would decide the championship. The Silver Seven were plainly fired up and a mile high and ready to slash into that eight-goal deficit. Twelve minutes after the puck had been dropped, Lester Patrick came cruising down the ice behind Moose Johnson, took a pass from his buddy, tucked the puck deftly behind ringer Leseur, and the deficit had grown to nine.

The Ottawas had just forty-eight minutes left in which to salvage some measure of respectability, and five of those minutes were gone before the first faint glimmer of hope surfaced. At that point, Ottawa's Frank McGee, the marvelous one-eyed forward who had scored fourteen times against Dawson City in that fore-doomed Yukon outpost's incredible Cup challenge of 1904, made it 1–1 on the game, 10–2 on the round. Then Harry Smith narrowed the gap with another goal, and McGee struck again just before half time.

As the teams went to their dressing rooms the round stood at 10–4 for Montreal. The faint hopes of the Ottawa fans stirred to such an extent that midway in the intermission one of them fell off the back of the double-tiered bleachers. Miraculously, he was un-injured, having quite apparently been well fortified against such a mishap, and thus suitably numbed.

The fellow had barely scrambled back to his perch when the puck was dropped to start the second half, Harry Smith got the draw and raced in alone to beat the Wanderers' goalie. The build-ing was still shaking when "Rat" Westwick took a pass from Har-vey Pulford, and suddenly Ottawa was just four goals down.

Thirty seconds later the magic number was three as Westwick scored again.

The din was such that it could have been heard throughout the entire Ottawa Valley, and there was no doubt about it, the Wan-derers were on panic street. Right after the last Westwick goal, Lester Patrick bent over his skate and was taking an inordinately long time fiddling with a shoelace while the referee waited to drop the puck. It was just time enough for his teammates to cluster around and formulate a strategy to stop the flood of goals.

The strategy was simple enough. Whenever the Silver Seven came down with the puck, the Wanderers would sag back and form a barricade in front of their goal, and as soon as one of them got possession he would flip it over the boards and into the crowd. The ploy incensed the Ottawa fans and baffled the Ottawa players, but just temporarily. After eight minutes of uproar, Harry Smith scored, and repeated two minutes later.

It was now 10–9 on the round, with ten minutes to play. Then it was 10–10 as Harry Smith swept around Patrick, was cross-checked by Billy Strachan at the goal mouth and then tumbled into the back of the net with the puck. The roar that went up from those Ottawa fans has perhaps not been matched in decibels before or since. Reported the *Sporting News:*

> The madness was such that Governor-General Earl Grey, quite an elderly man and not known to be athletic, was said to have leapt four feet in the air, and one fan who had not spoken to his wife in years rushed up and kissed her.

The place was bedlam. The ice was littered with everything the fans could tear loose, and hundreds of them poured onto the ice, stopping play as the bemused Wanderers huddled behind their own goal net. During the lull Earl Grey fought his way to the boards to lean over and shake Harry Smith's hand and smack him on the back with somewhat less than lordly grace.

This was the light side of what swiftly evolved into a small tragedy for the fans and their team that had come so far against seemingly incredible odds.

With both teams suffering from extreme fatigue, it was Lester Patrick who sensed the kill as the Ottawa forwards labored deep in the Montreal zone, drawing their defensemen with them. He got the puck, flipped it to Moose Johnson on a break, and a moment later beat Leseur with the goal that burst the Ottawa bubble. There were then just ninety seconds to play, and just before the whistle, Patrick, now plainly the coolest man in the arena, scored again to end this *Sporting News* pick as The Greatest Hockey Game in History.

The Wanderers had won the round by a goal count of 12–10 and with it the Stanley Cup. It was to be the first of five Cup championships for Lester Patrick as player, coach, and manager, in three different leagues.

Ernie Johnson, Lester's sidekick in three of those victories, fashioned his own little trophy in that frenetic win over the Silver Seven. Late in the game, some time after His Lordship had leaned over to congratulate the hero of the moment, Harry Smith, there was a scuffle along the boards during which Ernie, with one swipe of his stick, neatly dislodged the Governor-General's stovepipe hat. A fan, presumably of the Wanderers, had picked up the topper and scooted off with it amid the confusion. After the game he came to the dressing-room door, asked for Ernie, and presented it to him as a token of his esteem. There is no record of Ernie having

worn the chapeau into the shower, or indeed if there was a
shower. But it had to be conceded that he had scored a unique
and soul-satisfying hat trick.

At the league meetings prior to the 1906–7 season, there was a
bitter fight over the matter of hockey players' salaries, not just
over how much a player should be paid, but whether he should be
paid at all. On hearing a report that the Wanderers had actually
gone out and signed players to professional contracts—three of
which were said to add up to the staggering sum of $2,000—the
Shamrocks' president, John McLaughlin, roared his indignation.

"Clubs that pay their players should be thrown out of the
league," he stormed. "They are parasites. We have never paid any
of our players, and we don't intend to start now."

"You, sir," sighed Jim Strachan, president of the Wanderers,
"are a nincompoop and a numbskull. You are behind the times."

All of this was of considerable interest to Joe Patrick, who was
of the avowed belief that a person playing a game is doing just
that, playing a game. And that if you are playing a game, it is un-
Christian to be paid for doing so. He had impressed this philosophy on his sons, and Lester, although now well past the voting age
and quite capable of making up his own mind, was content to play
as an amateur. When the Wanderers provided details of their controversial payroll, Lester was one of four players so listed.

Those noted as professionals were the new goalie, Riley Hearn,
the new cover-point, Hod Stuart, and veterans Pud Glass, Ernie
Johnson, and Jack Marshall. Stuart, Glass, and Johnson were said
to be the money-mad hirelings who had ripped off the hockey establishment for salaries totaling $2,000. Here was the first har-
binger of the wondrous Age of Alan Eagleson. That $2,000 split
three ways for a 10-game season works out at somewhat less than
what several of Al's clients are now each paid per game over the
eighty-game NHL schedule.

On the other hand, in Montreal circa 1907, $2.00 would buy
you a good pair of shoes, you could get a gourmet meal for
seventy-five cents, and board-and-room "for a respectable single
man with nice habits, no drinkers, please" could be had for $22 a
month. For Lester Patrick with his $75 rubber company monthly
salary, free board, and sarsaparilla at a nickel a bottle—the extent

of his drinking excesses—life was a breeze. He may have been the last of big-time hockey's happy amateurs.

There were other players who were less fortunately situated, and needed hockey to help scrabble out a living. As, for instance, Hod Stuart, the new man just up out of the rough-and-rowdy International League in Northern Michigan and Pennsylvania, copper-country circuit that had become hockey's first fully professional establishment. In a sense, although he played it as hard and tough as anyone else, hockey to Lester Patrick in those days was just a plaything. Not so for folks like Hod Stuart, whose earnestness and earthy simplicity is revealed in a letter he wrote to the Montreal *Star* dated December 13, 1906. It airs his dissatisfaction with life as a defenseman for the International League team in Pittsburgh, and his desire to better himself with the Wanderers, if the price was right:

> They don't know how to run hockey down here, they appoint the dumbest and most incompetent referees they can find. Last season they had Chaucer Elliott who was not too bad, and Doc Gibson, who was.
>
> This year they are all rotten and I am coming up to the Wanderers if things go okay. I can get more money here, but I want to play hockey not shinny such as the OHA [the Ontario Hockey Association] puts up. They get men to referee here who never saw hockey before coming here and they practice the OHA brand every chance they get.
>
> I will let the Wanderers know whether I am coming up or not this week. They could not offer me enough money here to make me go through what I went through last year in this league. Everybody had a slur for me, and I daren't lift my stick up off the ice. I never lift it off the ice except in shooting and never check a man with my stick. Otherwise, they would get me.
>
> Yours sincerely,
> Hod Stuart.

Hod joined the Wanderers for their first game two weeks later, and this diamond-in-the-rough—a doggedly tough and tenacious defenseman—struck up an instant rapport with Lester, the new team captain, the player of grace and style. During a season in which the Wanderers were undefeated in league play and swept to their second straight Stanley Cup title, the oddly matched pair were inseparable.

If there was ever a "team policeman" in those days to equate with today's designated "hit man," it was Hod Stuart. There was graphic evidence of this in the Wanderers' third game of the 1907 season, against arch-rival Ottawa. Known as the Silver Seven when they had lost their Stanley Cup Championship to the Wanderers in that bitter series in March of 1906, the Ottawas were now known as the Senators, and they were out for blood in this return engagement.

Played in Montreal before a record crowd of 4,200, the game was subsequently described in the Montreal papers as "a saturnalia of blood-letting"; "the most sordid exhibition of butchery ever seen in hockey"; "an exercise in primitive savagery." Another reporter saw it as "quite literally, a bloody disgrace." Montreal *Star* headlines screamed for "Six Months in Jail for These Criminals." Of course, the *Star* demand referred to the Ottawa players, and reasonably so, as accounts of the game indicate that the Wanderers spent most of the time trying to defend themselves from violent attack, and not always succeeding.

Ottawa's Baldy Spittal and the Smith brothers, Harry and Alf, were named as the principal villains. One of Harry Smith's many violent sorties was against Ernie Johnson, who had certainly not been nicknamed "Moose" because of his delicate nature. Harry came at the Moose head-on, away from the play, slammed him across the face with his stick and broke his nose. Brother Alf is said to have accosted Hod Stuart in similar fashion with a crack across the forehead that sent Stuart thudding to the ice, unconscious. Baldy Spittal was reported to have deliberately attempted to crush Cecil Blachford's skull by striking it with a vicious blow with his stick held in both hands. Yet the most vicious and potentially dangerous incident was the one that never quite happened, thanks to Hod Stuart.

Late in the game, Lester Patrick, playing with great cool and poise despite the physical beating being absorbed by the whole team, flipped in a goal that made it 4–2 for the Wanderers. And now he was down on his knees, dazed and helpless after a crushing body check from the blind side. He was trapped by two Ottawa players who homed in with their sticks, plainly intent on administering a lesson in submission. They were slashing at him with their sticks when Stuart, just back on the ice and barely recovered from his own ordeal, came roaring to the rescue. With blood still oozing from the hastily stitched gash on his forehead, he waded in and took on all four assailants. A moment later, with the rest of the players joining in the fray, there was a mass melee behind the Ottawa net. Patrick remained on his knees and, in fact, didn't know what had happened until told in the dressing room after the game. Hod Stuart had already left the room for more stitchwork.

When the Senators returned to Montreal two weeks later for a game against the Victorias, both Smith brothers were arrested, charged with assault and tossed into jail. They were bailed out in time to help beat the Vics 12–10. Later, the Smiths and Baldy Spittal were tried in court and two, Alf Smith and Spittal, were each fined $20. Such were the meager wages of sin.

The week after that gory affair, the Montreal Arena was the site of a sentimental homecoming starring Art Ross, the one-time Mr. Big of the Westmount gang, who had gone West to make a name for himself as a defenseman with Brandon of the Manitoba League. He had now suddenly turned up in the lineup of the Kenora Thistles, 1905–6 champions of the Manitoba League. Borrowed from Brandon for the Thistles' Stanley Cup challenge series against the Wanderers, Ross was exposed as a genuine "ringer," but there was no protest from the Wanderers.

That may have been their first mistake. Their second was in underestimating the Thistles, who had built a powerhouse with the addition of two of the game's brightest young stars and certified future Hall of Famers, Si Griffis and Tom Phillips.

The cheers from the big Westmount delegation on hand to welcome back the prodigal son had barely died down when Phillips scored the first of his four goals in a stunning 4–2 Kenora victory. In the second game of the two-game total-point series, Lester Patrick outduelled Ross with his brilliant rushes and scored three times for the defending champions. That fine effort was nowhere near enough as the Thistles closed out the series and took the Cup when Phillips notched three more goals in an 8–6 win that left the Wanderers' fans, and their team, in a state of shock.

At the conclusion of their unbeaten season, the Wanderers challenged the Thistles to a rematch. It was scheduled for late March, and because the rink in Kenora was far too small for such a big series, the showdown was moved to Winnipeg.

Ross the ringer was not with the Kenora club that arrived in Winnipeg for the rematch. Two others of the same devious ilk, Ottawa's Harry Smith and Harry Westwick, were. This move was roundly condemned by league officials, who threatened to forfeit the series to the Wanderers if the imports were used. However, in the quaintly disorganized and carefree manner of the times, the Wanderers ignored the edict, made no protest, and the illicit recruits played. But not well enough.

Before two crowds of 6,500, the largest ever to attend a hockey contest in Canada, the Wanderers won the first game 7–2. That margin was quite enough to offset the 6–5 comeback by the Thistles in the second contest of this total-goals series. The Redbands had the Cup back, and nobody in the record throng was more pleased than Joe Patrick, who had interrupted his West Coast search for new timber properties to make the long train hop to Winnipeg.

Actually, Joe Patrick's search was over, as he had just settled on a deal for a large tract of timberland in the Slocan district of British Columbia, and planned to take the family out there in the spring. The family now numbered eight children. Myrtle Eleanor had arrived in 1895, Guy Waterson in 1899 and William Stanley in 1900. A baby girl had died five years later, in June 1905. Frank was still at McGill, about to enter his senior year there, but Joe wanted Lester to quit hockey and come West with the family.

Joe went back to British Columbia to get the new home ready, and Lester returned to Montreal to think things over. The decision was made for him by a poignant turn of events that are best related in his own sparse, direct style:

"My father told me that the family home was to be transplanted to Nelson, B.C., a beautiful little city of about 5,000 people located on Kootenay Lake. I had left the rubber company and was now working for a realty concern. I was urged to play one more season of hockey by Hod Stuart, whom I revered as a friend. Hod was twenty-seven and I was twenty-three. I respected his wishes and his advice, so when the family took the train for Nelson in April 1907, I stayed behind.

"In the month of June that year, my heart was saddened by

news of the death of Hod, my pal and idol. Impulsively, he had dived into shallow water in a lake near Belleville, Ontario, and had broken his neck and died instantly. He had been working in Belleville on construction work with his father.

"In early August of 1907, my father came East from Nelson to confer with his associates regarding policies for the new company in Nelson, which was known as the Patrick Lumber Company. He persuaded me, with little effort now that Hod was gone, to resign my Montreal job and join his new company. I was to forget hockey. Reluctantly, I acquiesced, and I arrived in Nelson on Labor Day of 1907. I was sure that all of my hockey days were now behind me."

How wrong he was.

2

THE NELSON
ADVENTURE

It was in the twilight of what had been a fiercely hot Sunday that Lester Patrick, leaning over the bow rail of the stern-wheeler *Kuskanook,* got his first glimpse of the new family home in British Columbia. He had taken the rail link from the CPR main line through the Rockies down to Kootenay Landing at the south tip of Kootenay Lake, then boarded the *Kuskanook* for the run to Nelson, twenty-nine miles north and another twenty-one miles up the lake's west arm. Now, as the stately vessel slid along the waters of the west arm, Lester could see the lights of Nelson flickering softly in the distance.

It was a setting to warm the heart of the most imaginative Broadway producer, let alone that of a romantic such as this twenty-three-year-old off on his latest adventure. On three sides, to the west, north, and east, rose the towering ranges of the Valhallas, the Monashees, and the Selkirks, still snow-tipped in this late, hot summer. Above them all spread the jagged peaks of the Kokanee Glacier, now a rosy-white sheen in the gathering dusk. There was the silvery jangle of a bell in the ship's pilothouse as the captain, resplendent in summer whites and gold braid, signaled the engine room to lower speed, and moments later the faint strains of band music could be heard above the rhythmic swish of the paddle wheel.

It was Labor Day holiday week-end in Nelson, and that meant that the crowds would be down at Lakeside Park, listening to the City Band and strolling the waterfront in their best Sunday finery.

Lester already had a curiously mixed impression of what—with obvious merit—was so grandly called the Queen City of the Kootenays. Idyllic it certainly was there in its picturesque valley setting, but another view of life in this paradoxical Shangri-la had been provided by a fellow traveler who had boarded the train back at Medicine Hat, Alberta. Although this gentleman's name is long forgotten, Lester recalled him many years later as "a pleasant enough gentleman" from some Calgary law firm who was making the trip to Nelson to defend a client in a murder case. The client, a middle-aged prospector, had strolled into Nelson's Manhattan Saloon late one evening, calmly produced a revolver, and shot two patrons dead. There had been no apparent reason for the shooting, and indeed the incident caused no great stir in Nelson other than temporary damage the Manhattan Saloon's thriving bar trade.

Lester was still at the rail when the *Kuskanook* nudged into the wharf, an exercise viewed by a crowd that had come over from the nearby Lakeside Park to partake of a favorite evening pastime: watching the boats come in. Behind the crowd, horse-drawn carriages were lined up, their drivers up on their seats, shouting out their fares and extolling the virtues of their favored hotels and boardinghouses.

Joe Patrick was at the foot of the gangplank when Lester disembarked, and he took him directly to one of the waiting hacks, the best and shiniest of the lot. As the Patrick house was just minutes away, they could have walked, but Joe liked to go first class, and always did, especially where his sons were concerned.

Grace Patrick had prepared a late supper for the prodigal son, but it was a subdued gathering. The girls, Lucinda (eighteen), Dora (fifteen), Myrtle (twelve), were there, as were Lester's two youngest brothers, Guy and Stan, now eight and six years old respectively. Ted, the seventeen-year-old, was missing. He had gone for a walk, his mother quietly explained, and he was a little late getting back. Lester sensed that there was more to it than that, and there was.

There had been a hint of trouble even back in Montreal, where Ted had sometimes gone off on his own into the downtown area after school and balked at returning to classes the next day. Lester himself, busy with his job and his hockey, had put it down to the boy's natural restlessness, and perhaps the fact that he had missed Frank after the older brother had gone off to Stanstead College. But the real fact, although Joe Patrick couldn't bring himself to say it in as many words in a private chat with Lester after supper, was that Ted was drinking, and had been for the past year.

Here in Nelson with its many saloons and swarms of miners and loggers in town for week-ends of carousing, there was ample opportunity for the boy to get liquor and drink on his own. Nelson old-timers, who were then little more than Ted's contemporaries, long remembered seeing "the kid with the peg leg" wandering the streets alone, shunning their companionship. To Joe Patrick, the God-fearing Methodist who couldn't abide alcohol, the knowledge of his son's weakness was a terrible blow, as it was to the rest of his teetotal family. But that night Joe did no more than mention it to Lester, and they stayed up chatting until Ted came home. He seemed cheerful enough and genuinely pleased to see his brother, but there were moments when he was guarded and withdrawn, and the reunion was brief and uncomfortable. But next day before lunch it was Ted who took Lester on a walk through Nelson, bubbling with good spirits as he talked of the local sights and the town characters. Characters like the "Gunnar from Galway," a brash, bald-headed Scot who sported a bowler hat and got his name from saloon patrons who were regaled by tearful renditions of the poem "Gunnar from Galway" whenever he got sloppy drunk, which was not infrequent. He was also said to have walked off with a fortune from the sale of shares in a silver-mine claim that turned out to be worth less than the Gunnar's battered derby.

Another character was an Englishman named Coal-Oil Johnny because of his trade in empty oil cans. He bought and sold the five- and ten-gallon cans that were common in this area where coal oil was used for cooking and heating, built up a prospecting stake, then disappeared into the wilds of nearby Elephant Mountain. Some time after, a bright white light appeared late each night far up the side of the mountain, the mystery of which wasn't solved until the night Coal-Oil Johnny came to town for provisions and a few whiskies, fell off the wharf while loading his boat, was rescued from drowning and rushed to the hospital. There, he

explained that he had been corresponding with a mystic in Montana, and that the lady had directed him to the site of a hidden
gold mine on Elephant Mountain, with orders to dig only at night.

These were young Ted's favorite stories, sworn and attested to
by the local elders, and when they turned off dusty Baker Street
with its one-track streetcar line, he gravely pointed to the swinging
doors of the Bodego Saloon, where the Gunnar From Galway had
exhibited his magnificent silver-ore sample from the mine that
never was. They went into the plushly appointed lobby of the
white-frame Hume Hotel, with its vaulted ceiling and elegant stair-
case, then stopped to check the prices-board outside the nearby
Klondyke Hotel: "First Class Rooms for Ladies or Gentlemen;
$1.00 and $1.50."

They turned up Lake Street, the thoroughfare famed, as coyly
noted in chronicles of the era, for its "sensuous pleasures." However, at this relatively early time of day the second-story windows
were still curtained, and the ladies had not yet made their usual
smiling appearance at the sills.

Viewing yet another aspect of civic culture, a stop was made at
the big, ugly frame building that luxuriated behind a sign that read
"Sherman Opera House." And on the billboard was the message:

—SHOWING THIS WEEK—

"THE MINSTREL MAIDS"
Adults 50¢ Children 25¢

If "The Minstrel Maids" seemed pretty sparse fare for an opera
house, this, as Ted explained, was not always so. The primitive
five-hundred-seat auditorium, condemned as a fire hazard the day
it was finished, had hosted such operatic giants as Europe's Mad-
ame Schumann-Heink and Australia's fabled Melba. For Melba—a
full house with the front rows jammed as usual with the local
socialites—tickets were priced at $10, a week's wage for the aver-
age working stiff.

Lester marveled at the vitality of the boy hobbling along at his
side at a pace that at times seemed painfully agitated. He himself
welcomed the rest on a bench in Lakeside Park, which was already half-filled with holidaymakers enjoying the hot sun and

awaiting the start of the Labor Day Sports Program, featuring the Annual Hose & Reel Competition, between "The Boys of the Nelson Fire Department and a Team from Castlegar."

Just offshore, the lake was jammed with all manner of vessels from rowboats to gas-powered speedboats and luxury cabin cruisers. One of the latter was an eight-bunk beauty named *Laugh-a-Lot,* imported from the East by the local bank manager. Ted had been aboard it once with his father, and it was, in fact, on the *Laugh-a-Lot* that Joe had finalized the financing for his mill up in Crescent Valley. Beyond the boathouse, the five-hundred-passenger *Nanooskin,* queen of the fleet of four stern-wheelers that plied the lake, lay berthed as its dining salon with its rich silver and crisp white linen and the main salon with its grand piano and potted palms were being prepared for the afternoon cruise.

No doubt about it, Lester mused, this little mining community on the edge of the British Columbia wilderness was a stunning blend of the bawdy and the beautiful.

On the walk back to the Patricks' spacious five-bedroom frame house on Edgewood Avenue, Lester could not help but wonder at the distance in miles and lifestyle that now lay between him and the brief glory days as captain of the Wanderers, hockey champions of the sport's limited world.

The distance seemed even farther the next day as he and his father headed into the mountain country beyond Slocan City, forty-five miles northwest of Nelson. Joe needed help in staking out the limits of the timber claims that would stock the Patrick Lumber Company sawmill now being built on the Little Slocan River.

Led by a guide, the little party rode pack ponies into the dense forest country, marking logging campsites along the way. They carried a ten-day ration of bacon, beans, and bannock, the latter a dry biscuit made of baking powder, flour, and salt. The ration lasted only seven days, thanks to a bear that was apparently partial to bannock and had dropped in for a midnight snack as the party slept during the journey home. It was Lester's first modest test of survival in the wilderness, and he passed it with flying colors.

Fanning out with Joe and the guide to pick off a grouse or two to restock the larder, he came across a cabin at the edge of a clearing. The proprietor, who obligingly put away his rifle as

Lester approached, was a bearded recluse named McDaniel, who until just recently owned a substantial ranch in the valley. Lester politely explained his intrusion, introduced himself, and glory be, the bearded gentleman not only knew the name but proudly announced that he had been in the Montreal Arena on an afternoon two years before when Lester had scored three goals against Quebec. Lester didn't rightly remember that hat trick, but he had no quarrel with the idea, and that night there were three guests at a fine dinner of venison.

The only person who did not seem to enjoy the repast was McDaniel himself. It turned out that the feast had been made possible by McDaniel's own young pet deer, which had been accidentally shot two days earlier by a trigger-happy house guest who might also have been a bit high on his host's dandelion wine.

However, with full bellies and extra rations provided by McDaniel, the Patricks' safari made it safely back to Slocan City and then down the mountain to Nelson. Put to work in the Patrick Lumber Company office in Nelson, Lester helped with the mill construction on week-ends, supervised the arrival of twenty French-Canadian lumberjacks Joe had imported from the woods of Quebec, and by the first snows of late November was back in the hockey business. Visited by a delegation from the Nelson team of the Kootenay League who had read of his Montreal exploits, he was asked to aid the local cause. It was like asking a bedouin roaming the sands of the Sahara if he'd like a sip of cool water.

The first game was in early December, a City League contest against the Thistles. Patrick's team, the Victorias, won by the score of 5–0. The new rover, late of the Montreal Wanderers, scored all five goals. The five hundred fans who jammed the rickety uncovered stands of the outdoor rink were delighted with their first look at the new boy from the big city.

A week after that debut Lester got a letter from Edmonton asking him to join that town's hockey club for a Stanley Cup challenge series against the Wanderers. Edmonton had earned the right to challenge the previous season by winning the Western Canada championship. As their regular roster stood little chance against the powerful Wanderers, the Edmonton management had decided to bring in a few late additions, of whom Lester was one. When Joe Patrick gave grudging permission for three weeks' leave

of absence from the company office, Lester wired his acceptance
and got to Montreal in time for a few days' practice before the
start of the series.

It was like old-home week. All of his old Wanderers teammates were there, including, of course, Moose Johnson. In fact,
the only name missing from the Wanderers' lineup was that of
Lester himself. He had been replaced by none other than Mr. Big
of the Westmount street gang, Art Ross.

Lester knew several of the Edmonton players, but only because
they had been imported from other clubs in what was recorded as
the all-time high for ringers on a challenge team. Bert Lindsay
(who would father Terrible Ted of the future Detroit Red Wings)
had been brought up from the International League to play in
goal; the lightning-fast Didier Pitre of the Kenora Thistles was
acquired to play alongside Lester on defense; the Ottawa star,
Tom Phillips, took over at right wing. The only Edmonton regular
who was not replaced was the rover, Fred Whitcroft.

The fact that this sham lineup was not challenged by league
officials or protested by the Wanderers merely points out the
quaint informality of the times, or, if you will, the laxity of the
game's governorship. At that, the Wanderers' unconcern over the
supposedly illegal imports became understandable when they
turned back the challenge with relative ease, winning the two-
game set 7–3 and 7–6. Although he scored just once—in the second game—Lester Patrick was the best of the Edmonton team, and
he easily won his first head-on duel with Ross.

After the second game, the two old friends had late supper together, and an interesting conversation, recalled word-for-word
many years later by Lester, ensued.

"Lester," said Ross over coffee, "how much did they pay you
for the series?"

"Just expenses," said Lester. "Why?"

"Why?" snorted Ross. "Do you know what kind of money
we're getting now in the East to play hockey?"

As a matter of fact, Lester did know. This was the first year of
full professionalism in the Eastern Canada Hockey League, and
players were averaging less than $600 for the season. Ross himself
had held out for what was considered the outlandish sum of
$1,600, but settled for $1,200.

"I got four hundred dollars for this series," said Ross. "In advance."

He reached in his pocket, pulled out a wad of bills and counted them out on the table.

"And I was cheated, too. Phillips got six hundred from Edmonton and played less than half a game. Lester, you are a dumbkopf."

Art allowed the dumbkopf to pick up the check. After all, Lester was getting expenses.

When Lester got back to Nelson, Joe asked him how much the trip had cost, rail fare, meals, hotel, and all.

"Sixty-two dollars," said Lester.

"How much expense money did you get?"

"One hundred dollars."

"Then you owe Edmonton thirty-eight dollars."

Lester sent a check for that amount. "That," he mused many years later, "must have been the first and last time in history that a hockey player ever returned any part of his expense money."

Back East, Frank Patrick kept the family slate unsullied by professionalism by signing on as an amateur with the Ottawa Vics, mainly because he was committed to another season of college hockey at McGill, where he was now in his senior year.

An undistinguished team, the Vics finished fifth in the six-team Eastern Canada Hockey League as Frank, with eight goals in eight games at defense, missed the last two games of the schedule when he suffered a torn shoulder ligament. But he was also on call as a referee, and was not only the league's youngest, but considered one of the best. When the Ottawa Senators (formerly known as the Silver Seven) protested the choice of Patrick for a very important game because of his age, the ECHL president rejected the protest and called him "the most competent referee we've seen in the league all winter. Nobody does a better job of taking charge and keeping a game under control."

A game typical of the young ref's no-nonsense style was one he recalled between the Wanderers and the Toronto team of the new Ontario Professional League.

"It was a Stanley Cup challenge match," Frank explains, "and I knew it would be a tough assignment because of the temperamental nature of some of the players who I knew would take advantage of me if they could. The Wanderers were rated a much stronger team than the Toronto challengers, but they were having a rough time hanging on to a 4–3 lead with just a few minutes to play, when one of the Toronto players was injured.

"The procedure then was to call a time-out to give the injured man a chance to recuperate, so I stopped play. During this brief respite, Riley Hearn, the Wanderers' goalie, skated over to the boards and stood there with his teammates Art Ross and Walter Smaill chatting with their girl friends, who were in the front row of seats. When I blew the whistle to resume play, the trio paid no attention. I blew the whistle again, twice, but the prima donnas kept right on chatting with the girls and paid no attention to me at all. I guess Art Ross still remembered me as the younger kid on the block and wasn't going to be pushed around by any young whippersnapper. I was a little annoyed.

"The play was to be resumed down near the Toronto net, and I thought to myself that I would drop the puck for the face-off and by the time the play moved toward the Wanderers' goal, Ross, Smaill, and Hearn would be back at their positions. Newsy Lalonde, as smart and crafty a player as ever lived, was the Toronto center. I dropped the puck, he got the draw and before anyone could say "look out" he had fired it the length of the ice and clean as a whistle into the empty net.

"The warning screams of the Montreal fans as Newsy got the draw snapped Ross et al out of their seance, but it was too late. The sight of the three of them standing there waving their sticks as the puck went flying by was laughable to all but the Wanderers, the Montreal fans, and myself. There in front of the home crowd, I was on the spot for fair, with the score now tied.

"The Wanderers clamored around me screaming that the face-off had been illegal, but I stuck to my guns and allowed the goal. I don't know though what might have happened to me, a fellow citizen of Montreal, if Toronto had managed to score again. You can be assured that I breathed a lot easier when the Wanderers went right out and got two quick goals to clinch a 6–4 victory. I must say however, that the play by Lalonde was the smartest, most astute bit of hockey I ever saw. That's the way Newsy was."

And, of course, Newsy, in the not-too-distant future, would play for Frank Patrick, hockey's first (with Lester) owner-coach-player. Not to mention league president to boot. So would another player of that season of 1907–8, a tough, wily little bolt of lightning named Fred "Cyclone" Taylor of the Ottawa Senators.

At twenty-three, Taylor was fresh from two brilliant seasons with Houghton of the six-team International League that had just closed shop after a brief but turbulent life as the game's first fully professional circuit. In those two seasons, he had dazzled the fans in the tough Michigan copper country with a blinding speed that was matched only by his remarkable stick-handling. He was the player about whom Lester Patrick would one day, after ending his long reign as boss of the New York Rangers, say, "There will never be his equal."

Frank may well have had a premonition that this man who had come out of Renfrew, Ontario, just a few miles from Ottawa, would play a big part in the Patricks' future, for he was in the stands to watch Taylor's highly publicized home-ice debut in a critical early test against the Wanderers. Taylor, a center at Houghton, had been switched to cover-point, a more independent role that made better use of his great speed. A prime factor in the switch was the fact that the Ottawa forwards simply couldn't keep pace with him.

Taylor's debut and the christening of Ottawa's brand new Laurier Arena brought out a league record throng of 7,100 fans, and despite the fact that many of them had paid scalpers five times the legal price of their $1.25 reserved seats, they all got their money's worth and more.

The Senators shocked the defending league and Stanley Cup champions 12–2, and of Taylor's rookie performance, the Ottawa *Citizen* said:

> The contest brought to light a bright new star in the Eastern Canada Hockey League. For some time, Fred Taylor, a new member of the Ottawa team, has been in the limelight, not so much through his play as through certain circumstances regarding his signing that evoked much publicity. Until Saturday night, he was still looked on here as an unknown quantity . . .
>
> Taylor proved to be the sensation of the night. Such marvelous defensive play and individual work has never before been seen in Ottawa. He himself scored four goals, but was directly responsible for many more. Taylor arrived here with the appellation "The

Whirlwind of the International League" tagged on him. On his performance Saturday night, he can well be called the "Tornado of the
ECHL."

The sports editor of the rival Ottawa *Free Press* went one better
in the battle of the meteorologists. Following the vice-regal party
as it left the arena, he overheard the Governor-General say of the
new man's performance: "That number four, Taylor . . . he's a
cyclone if ever I saw one." The comment was reported in Monday's *Free Press* as Bryce wrote: "In Portage la Prairie they called
him a tornado, in Houghton, Michigan, he was known as a whirlwind. From now on, he'll be known as Cyclone Taylor."

And so he was. For more than seventy years.

As for Frank Patrick, high up in the cheap seats at that historic
unveiling, he was stunned by Taylor's performance. "I had never,"
he recounted, "seen such an explosive hockey player, nor one with
such skills. I was literally mesmerized by the man. I knew right
away that he was something special." So were sown the seeds of
the Patricks' lifelong association with the youth from Renfrew
who would reap more headlines than any other hockey player before or since.

Eight days prior to that Ottawa game, Frank had been in Montreal on a sentimental assignment as a member of the All-Star
team in a Hod Stuart Memorial Match staged in memory of Lester
Patrick's great friend who had died the previous summer in a
diving accident. The Wanderers, Hod's old team, provided the
opposition. The match, the first to feature a league All-Star team,
got a big buildup in the press and was sold out several days before
the January 2 date—which Frank almost didn't make.

In Toronto to visit old friends, he was booked into the King
Edward Hotel for New Year's Eve and was scheduled to leave on
the early morning train for Montreal. His room, as he would discover later, was just up the hall from that of another overnight
visitor, a Mr. Terry McGovern, of New York City.

McGovern was one of the great featherweight fighters of his
day, and had lost his world title several years before to Young
Corbett. Now a battle-scarred pug nearing the end of a particu-
larly gory career, McGovern was in town with that same Young
Corbett and a young man from the Bronx named Joe Humphries.
Joe was Terry's trainer, but his big day was yet to come as the

famed Madison Square Garden ring announcer of the late forties
who once finished his introductions for a $50-ringside-seat main
event with the immortal words: "And may the most woithy ad-
voisary emoige triumphant!"

In Toronto on that New Year's Eve of 1907, Frank was not
aware of his more or less distinguished neighbors until well into
the wee hours, when he was wakened by a racket in the hall. He
emerged from his room to see the night porter in heated discussion
with a man standing, more or less, in a doorway from which came
the sounds of a boisterous party.

The man at the door was McGovern, who was plainly in his
cups. And as the night porter, a Mr. Bert Beech, also learned just
seconds later, the one-time world featherweight champion still
packed a mean punch—mean enough to open a gash on the poor
man's cheek, and part him from several of his front teeth.

What had happened was that McGovern had called room service for food, and the night porter had been dispatched to explain
to the outraged guest that it was a little too late for room service.
The porter had tendered his regrets and McGovern had tendered
his, by lashing out with a left hook followed by a right cross.
Frank was still trying to revive the porter when the night manager
arrived to investigate the disturbance.

The next morning as Frank was about to check out, he was informed by a police constable that McGovern was being charged
with assault and battery and Frank would be required to appear in
court the next day as a witness. As the next day was also the day
of the big game in Montreal, Frank was in a jam. However,
McGovern arrived in the lobby looking appropriately sober, and
through his spokesman, Joe Humphries, agreed to leave the hotel
immediately and to settle out of court for any damages. The
charge was dropped, and Frank caught a later train for Montreal.

The Wanderers won 10–7 before 4,000 fans, and although
Ernie Russell scored five times for the victors, Frank, who bagged
a pair of goals for the losers, was named the outstanding player.
The proceeds of the game, $2,000, were given to Hod Stuart's
widow.

By that time, Frank had quit as captain of the McGill hockey
team, leaving the club with regrets "because the five men who
elected me captain after last season have, for one reason or an-

other, not been able to return to school, and it would mean building a whole new team. Also, we don't get the student support the football team gets, and it is very discouraging work."

He was due to get his B.A. degree in the spring, after which he was to rejoin the family in Nelson. The degree arrived on schedule, but Frank was late getting home. Playing shortstop for the McGill baseball team in an April game against a U.S. school, he broke a leg sliding into second base and didn't get to Nelson until September, after the limb healed.

It was a good thing that the leg had mended well, because he was barely unpacked before he was on his way into the woods. "I don't know whether my father thought I'd been hedging about coming home and going to work, but at any rate within twenty-four hours of my arrival in Nelson he ordered me into the woods to start work at the camps as a timer and begin learning the rudiments of the business.

"The system then was for a crew of about a dozen men to go into the woods in late summer and build camps to house the loggers for the winter and spring work. The plan was to build about four camps each about two miles apart and twelve to fifteen miles in from the little town of Slocan City. They were supposed to be working on the third camp when I arrived. The men were in the charge of a 'walking boss,' who was to run all four camps when they were finished. His name was Colby, a tough, wiry little man from Montana."

Colby didn't take too kindly to the arrival of the boss's son. Nor did the boss's son take too kindly to Colby. When he arrived at the third camp after a sixty-mile trip from Nelson by train and horseback, Frank found the site a mess. A crew had been there for nearly a month and practically nothing had been done. All that had been finished was the cookhouse, an extension of the bunkhouse. Frank found that Colby had spent more than $3,000 of the company's money over the past couple of weeks, a good deal of it in the saloons of Slocan City, the nearest watering hole.

The day after Frank's arrival, Colby rode in from a night on the town and was accosted as he dismounted from his horse.

"I'm Frank Patrick," said the boss's son.

"Go to hell," said Colby, and he shambled off to his tent for a nap.

Checking the payroll, Frank found that Colby had hired a cookhouse crew of seven to feed a crew of twenty men. "The head cook was a Bolshevik who spent all his time calling meetings and lecturing the loggers on the wonders of Socialism. So that he'd have time to study and prepare his lectures, he had bullied Colby into hiring two extra foremen, a second cook, a 'cookie,' a bull cook, and a stableman. At that time, I didn't know a cant hook from a peevee, but I did know that there was something rotten there."

With Colby off on another binge, Frank began his clean-up right at the top: with the cook, the man who was really running the show. The chap balked at the charge that he wasn't earning his money, and threatened to quit. Frank said not to worry about quitting, as he was fired. The cook stalked off in a rage and rode into Slocan City to find Colby. He was easily located, happily stoned in his favorite tavern.

The next day, Colby told Frank that he would quit if the cook was fired. Frank said that was okay with him, and that he was going to Nelson to explain the whole situation to the owner of the Patrick Lumber Company.

Back in Nelson, Joe Patrick at first gave Frank a very frosty reception, thinking that he had run out on the job, but then he listened to the tale of woe and agreed that Frank had handled the affair properly. He also offered an instant solution to the camp mess. He made Frank the "walking boss" to replace Colby. So there was the new boss, a twenty-one-year-old with just a few days' experience in the woods in charge of an eventual crew of more than two hundred men in a business about which he knew virtually nothing.

He really wasn't that much of a babe-in-the-woods, though. Frank could recall a time during his boyhood in Quebec when he had spent most of one summer in one of his father's logging camps. One day he fell into a river and was swept downstream. He was hauled out by a French-Canadian farmer and had stayed a few days in the farmhouse recuperating from the ordeal. To pass the time away he gave English lessons to the farmer's eight-year-old daughter, using the instructions on patent-medicine wrappers, which were the only text books available.

But there he was back in camp with the new cook that he had

picked up in Slocan City and with another problem on his hands. The old cook was still in camp, and when his replacement went to the cookhouse he was threatened with a meat cleaver.

"About that time," said Frank, "my Irish was aroused. 'Come on,' I yelled at the new man, 'we're going to throw that damned Bolshevik out of here.' Apart from being just plain mad, I knew I had to do something to establish myself with my crew, who just stood around watching and waiting." He grabbed a peevee, strode to the cookhouse and ordered the cook off the premises. There was no reply. The cook stood his ground, brandishing the meat cleaver.

"All right," called Frank, "I'm coming in there, and if you don't drop that cleaver I'll cut you to ribbons with it." Frank stalked in, the cook stood waiting with the meat cleaver, then wavered, dropped it, and left without a word. He rode out of camp and was never seen again.

Over the next year or so, Frank had some rough run-ins with lumberjacks who drank too much and with river drivers, blacksmiths, and filers who displayed some pretty mean streaks, but that cookhouse gambit was his most important test. From that time on, Joe Patrick had himself a pretty good walking boss.

And then there was Lester. In charge of the company books, with some help from young Ted, who had just finished high school, he had adjusted well to the rigors of the Nelson social life. He had spent a very pleasant summer in urban research, much of it concerning the female of the local species. There is no doubt that in those days both Frank and Lester were very big with the ladies, and vice versa.

"Womanizers," whatever that might really mean, is probably too strong a term, but ladies' men they certainly were, as naturally becomes two big, handsome youths who were hockey heroes by avocation. Although they generally practiced the good clean life as preached by their father, including abstinence from alcohol, they did more than just attend Sunday morning Bible classes in their travels across the country. Joe Patrick, no mean man himself with the ladies before he settled down with Grace and his general store back in Carmel Hill, must have been well aware of this, and being a practical as well as an earnest Methodist, probably would have had it no other way. The male Patricks with their families of

eight, nine, and ten children did not get to become prolific sires by
early training in the monastic way of life.

In Nelson, Lester had a head start, for in his first winter of
hockey with the local team he had greatly impressed the belles of
the area quite apart from the fans in general, who were ecstatic
over the team's first Kootenay League Championship. He had
made his official debut as the town's Most Eligible Bachelor at a
community social staged in the team's honor, and Lester had entertained the gathering with his stock recital of "Little Bateese,"
the light-hearted Quebec folk-poem delivered in the patois of the
woodsman. The poem had been Lester's *pièce de résistance* at
parties back in Montreal, and it was a smash hit in Nelson.

He had also displayed a very pleasant tenor voice during a
singsong featuring "Good-bye, Dolly, I Must Leave You" and
other such wildly romantic ballads of the day, and as a result was
invited to join the Nelson Light Opera Society. Lester graciously
declined the offer, but compromised by taking up for the summer
with one of the members, a pretty mezzo-soprano who had been at
the piano the night of the singsong.

Frank had plenty of time in town on week-ends from the logging camps, and apparently used it in a manner befitting a virile
twenty-one-year-old with a natural lust for life. There is one story
that Lester tells of his younger brother concerning Lake Street, the
dusty boulevard of "sensuous pleasures."

Shortly before Frank's arrival from the East, the ladies of the
street had attained certain notoriety in the pages of the Nelson
News because of a letter to the editor complaining of their "im-
proper public behavior." As the letter put it, the Sunday afternoon
habit of the Lake Street girls strolling the town in their best finery
and mingling with the other ladies of the community "both shocks
and embarrasses us, and something should be done about it."
Nothing of course was done about it, and as usual in such cases,
the publicity was worth its weight in full-page advertising.

It was against this recent background that Frank, dressed in his
own Sunday best, took his first evening stroll along Lake Street.
He was pleasantly absorbed in the scenic surroundings when he
was spied by his father, who was riding through town in his buggy.
The buggy pulled up abruptly at the intersection as Frank approached.

"Good evening," said Joe Patrick icily.

"Good evening, Father," Frank replied, with a smile.

"Get in," said Joe.

On the way home, Joe broke a stony silence with, "You know I don't like to see you on Lake Street."

Frank nodded gravely and said, "I know that, Father." Then, smiling engagingly, he added, "But look at it this way. I didn't stop to do any shopping."

There was a moment's silence and then Joe slapped his thigh and burst out laughing. It was a pleasant ride the rest of the way.

It was around this time in the early autumn of 1908 when Frank became enthralled by the story of the two Chinese prospectors who had spent several months working a dinky Kootenay River tributary called 40-Mile Creek with sluice-boxes, and had come out with more than a million dollars worth of gold. It was the kind of a gold-mine-in-the-sky story that gripped Frank's imagination, and one that would cost him—and his father—dearly in years to come.

For months after the two Chinese had left town with their riches and the first mad rush to locate the source of the gold had faded, Frank went off by himself on trips up to the head of the mountain creek, searching for the hidden vein. He never found it, and if one were to pick a capsule story of Frank Patrick's life this might be it.

Not so Lester, the practical man as opposed to the dreamer. By the end of September, he was to be frequently seen making rounds of the downtown saloons, hustling the patrons for handouts. This was an unlikely beat for a man whose taste in libations still hadn't gone beyond a double-sarsaparilla, but it was all in a good cause.

Having suffered through one winter of hockey in the town's ramshackle ice rink, he had decided that help was needed in providing a better one for the coming season. Joe Patrick had agreed to ante up the first $1,000, and with Frank in charge of the fund, Lester had been assigned to General Public Donations. By the start of the next hockey season, a new eight-hundred-seat rink with covered stands had been built on Cottonwood Creek, paid for in some substantial part by Lester's nightly forays through the swinging doors.

When the hockey season started, there were two Patricks in the local lineup, with Lester at rover and Frank on defense, at cover-point. That proved to be two too many Patricks for the rest of the Kootenay League.

The home opener was against Rossland, and the score was 14–1 for Nelson. Frank scored four goals and Lester got two, but the game itself was incidental to the occasion. Apart from the attraction of the Patrick brothers, who were the class of the league, there was the special enticement of the new rink, and local society was out in force. Their carriages filled the narrow road leading to the rink, creating Nelson's first traffic jam.

One of the vehicles was an automobile, a 1908 Franklin that sported the latest in fashionable accessories including fenders and a folding top. The magnificent machine was owned by a Mr. N. J. Cavanaugh, a local man who had created a stir the previous summer by bringing a gold brick weighing 465 ounces from his nearby Sheep Creek mine, where he was searching for zinc and silver deposits. The huge lump of gold was valued at $17,000, a small fortune in those days.

Unfortunately, the outing to the rink was too much for the Franklin. It had apparently overheated and stalled in the slow going, and as reported in the next week's social notes it was last seen sitting alone on the dirt road, with its revolutionary folding top collapsed like a shroud. It is not known whether Mr. Cavanaugh made it to the rink and saw the game, but there were a lot who didn't.

Arriving late, they found their seats occupied by a swarm of loggers who had taken over part of the reserved section and didn't care to be disturbed. Nor were they in any shape to be disturbed. Joe Patrick, who was there with Grace, was a little embarrassed, as he had passed out fifty rush-seat tickets up at the camps, and most of these were his boys. "Unfortunately," recorded the visiting Rossland reporter, "the opening ceremony featuring the Mayors of Nelson and Rossland was marred by the bawdy behavior of some of the local fans, who had arrived inebriated. Two of them got into a fist fight and fell out of the stands, delaying the start of the contest . . ."

True, there apparently was some "bawdy behavior" spiced with language that would make a maiden, not to mention Mr. and Mrs. Patrick, blush, but there were some cultural overtones that the reporter failed to mention. Such as, for instance, the sentimental rendition of various X-rated folk songs, only one of which can be recited here.

As he was the butt of the ballad's poetic message, Joe Patrick didn't laugh much then, but he did laugh many years later, in recollection, and even agreed that the lyrics of the little ditty called "The Loggers Camp Song" may have had a point. Here is the opening chorus of the song, judiciously laundered in a couple of places:

> I 'rived at the camp, and all I could see
> Was a lousy old cook, and a lousy cook-ee.
> The floors were all dirty, all covered with mud;
> The bed-quilts were lousy, and so was the grub . . .

All in all, the opening game in the new rink was a great success, as was the entire league season. In the second game, Nelson whipped Moyie 16–3. Lester had five goals, Frank four. In February the local heroes took on Moyie again and won 15–0 as the Patricks split nine goals to cap another unbeaten season.

Feeling their oats, the Nelson boys, champions of B.C., challenged Edmonton, champions of Western Canada, to a two-game series. This time they had bitten off more than they could chew, although they did push the powerful Edmonton team to the limit in the first game before losing by the score of 6–5. "It was," raved the Nelson *News,* "the best and fastest game ever seen in B.C." The Patricks were "outstanding," with two goals each.

Edmonton won the second game, 8–4, "despite the heroic play of the Patrick boys."

That was it for the hockey season, and apart from the pleasure of the game as the team breezed through the season, there was another development of special interest to Lester. It was at one of the games in the new rink on Cottonwood Creek that he met Grace Linn, the future Mrs. Lester Patrick. A very pretty and vivacious twenty-year-old from the town of Nanaimo, B.C., Grace, who was to be the second lady of that name in the family, was a visitor in town, staying at the home of a local doctor. After the chance meeting with Lester, the visit was extended indefinitely.

A faded theater program that has survived the years reveals the delights of one of the couple's first nights on the town. It reads:

EMPIRE THEATRE
Program—4 Reels
Kindness Repaid
Freedom for All
Mr. Softhead
Chorus Girl
SPECIAL ATTRACTION: Miss Violet
will sing "Any Old Time," and Prof.
A. Wilkinson will play a Violin Solo.

By the time spring of 1909 rolled around, the lumber business was booming, and in a newspaper interview Joe Patrick stated that "the prospects for the coming season were never better." The proprietor of the Patrick Lumber Company was not quite yet ready to challenge such giants as the Rockefellers and the McCormacks of International Harvester who had led a massive U.S. invasion of the B.C. timber country, but he was doing very well. So well that he gave two of his employees, Lester and Frank, a spring bonus of fifty dollars each.

Lester, never quite a dandy but always a smart dresser, went right down to Brown & Co. on Baker Street and blew himself to a new spring outfit. As a high-class hand-tailored all-wool tweed suit could be had for $14.95, and a stylish gray fedora for $1.50, Lester still had plenty left to spend on his courtship of Grace Linn.

Life in the Patrick household was centered around the Methodist Church, and Sunday morning and evening attendance was a ritual on which Joe Patrick insisted. Of the younger children, both Ted and Lucinda had graduated from high school, and Ted was now working in the company's Nelson office, with Lester. He had asked for a job at one of the camps with Frank, and when Joe gently explained that he'd be better off in town, Ted's moods became increasingly morose and rebellious. He spent more and more time away from the office.

During the previous December, with Ted now a strapping youth of nineteen, Joe had taken him on two trips to Vancouver to be fitted for a wooden leg to replace the peg that had for so long been a nagging visual reminder of his infirmity. When they returned from the second trip, Ted seemed delighted with his new appearance, despite the acute discomfort of the transition. The strain between father and son seemed to ease a little, and the family's Christmas dinner was the happiest in years. However, Frank later recalled his mother twice leaving the table and returning with eyes reddened "as if from weeping."

If Grace Patrick had a premonition that this would be the last time the whole family would sit down together at Christmas dinner, that premonition was correct.

That spring, the May 10 edition of the Nelson *News* carried the banner head: "I Think I Have Done My Duty." These were purportedly the gallant last words of King Edward VII, who had died two days before in Windsor Castle.

Although Nelson was a decently loyal outpost of the Empire and had, in fact, built a huge floral wreath across Baker Street with the words "The Queen Is Dead" at the end of Victoria's reign, the demise of the Profligate Prince caused little stir. The only gesture of mourning was the one-day closure of a few business houses, and one of these was the Patrick Lumber Company. The particular gesture was probably less the work of Joe Patrick than of Grace, who was always primly and staunchly proud of her English heritage.

Frank used the day off for another of his trips up 40-Mile Creek and got back a little late for supper. So did Lester, who had spent the day on the lake with Miss Linn. It was no special supper, and with Ted yet to show, it was kept warm a little longer. When the family finally sat down to eat, it was without Ted, and Frank recalled the youngest, Stan, then ten, saying, "Ted's gone away."

The next morning, Joe learned from the Great Northern stationmaster that Ted had bought a ticket and left on the morning train to Spokane. As usual in matters concerning the troubled third son, very little is known of this escapade by the surviving families other than that from Spokane, Ted rode the freight trains across the U.S. prairies and deep into the Southwest. He had very little money with him and there is no account of how he existed in the many weeks he was away. All that is known is that he was eventually located in the late summer through "friends of the family" living in Oklahoma, and was persuaded to return home. The identity of the "friends of the family" is not known, although present-day members of the Patrick clan believe they must have been people from Boston whom Ted had contacted when he needed help. Joe sent Ted money for the train fare, and he and Frank were there to meet the youth when he arrived in Spokane. This time, Ted was given a job as handyman at one of the camps, where he pretty well became Frank's personal charge.

It was while Ted was away wandering through the United States that the quarter-million-dollar log spill occurred, as previously chronicled here. That loss had been written off, and Joe now had more than two hundred men in the woods restocking the company's resources.

The long hot summer that was marred by both financial and domestic troubles was lightened a little by the visit to Nelson of Governor-General Earl Grey and his daughter, Sybil. The imperial party had detoured through the Kootenays en route to a visit to the Coast, and their arrival on the stern-wheeler *Nanooskin* was the social happening of the season.

Joe and Grace Patrick attended a civic reception and were accompanied, at Grey's special request, by Lester and Frank. The Governor-General, who had lost his topper to Moose Johnson during that memorable game between Ottawa and the Wanderers a couple of years before, had watched the Patrick boys during their brief but turbulent hockey days in the East, and had admired them both. At the reception, he said, "I've wanted to meet you, and I find it curious that I had to come so far to do so."

Lady Sybil, a pretty girl in her early twenties, was even more of a hockey fan, and was very impressed by her meeting with the Patrick brothers. She proudly informed them that she would be carrying a special memento with her on her return to England at the conclusion of her father's term in Ottawa: a hockey stick given to her by Frank's friend of brief acquaintance, Fred ("Cyclone") Taylor, who was now the biggest name in hockey.

Summer week-ends in Nelson were taken up with baseball, and with Frank moved to third base on the local ball club, this item appeared in the Nelson *News:*

> Lester Patrick, short-stop, singled home the winning run yesterday as Nelson defeated the University of North Dakota, 5–3. The single was Patrick's third hit of the game, and the University of North Da-

kota's Bill Hennesey, who once played for the Baltimore Orioles in the National League, said that the rangy Nelson short-stop was a fine professional prospect. He said he would so advise the Orioles, if Lester was interested . . .

Lester apparently wasn't interested, as nothing ever came of the offer.

As to the rest of that period in Nelson, it is adequately covered in Lester's own terse chronicle:

"The year 1909 was to bring new adventures. A depression on the Canadian prairies—our natural market for lumber—and an enthusiastic new hockey cycle in the East made it possible for me to get back into the eastern picture. There was a dearth of top talent in the eastern leagues, and every city and town seemed to want to get into the act with a team. I was besieged with telegrams asking my terms. With a relatively idle winter ahead in the lumber business because of the slumping market, I finally sold my father on the idea that professionalism was here to stay, and used various other arguments until I had his approval.

"After getting that approval, freely given once I fully explained the case, I studied the various propositions and made my decision as to where I should go. I decided to accept the offer from the new franchise in Renfrew, Ontario, a little town of about 3,500 population about seventy miles west of Ottawa. I had answered their wire merely as a matter of courtesy. I demanded—not asked, demanded—$3,000 plus all expenses for a twelve-game season. I believed this figure far beyond what could be obtained. In no other case had I gone beyond $1,800 in my salary request.

"You can imagine my surprise when Renfrew replied, okaying my proposition. No other club in the East wanted me at the figures I submitted to them.

"Frank was to join Renfrew also. I said he was available but would want $2,000. As Frank had not the experience I had had in the eastern leagues, I thought that this figure also was well beyond what they'd pay. But they agreed to the $2,000, and Frank came along too."

Lester was obviously unaware of a new affluence in eastern hockey as represented by a very ambitious and well-heeled patron of the arts named M. J. O'Brien. O'Brien was an elderly gentleman right out of an Old Country tintype, complete with elegantly tailored vest, massive gold watch chain, luxuriant but neatly trimmed beard, and a stern regal bearing inclined to portliness. He was also a shrewd mover and shaker whose latest enterprise was a silver mine in the northern Ontario town of Cobalt. Over the past few years, the mine had enriched O'Brien to the tune of several million dollars, and he could thus well afford to indulge himself in a hobby. Encouraged by his son, Ambrose, he had chosen hockey and bought himself a mini-league, a three-team circuit consisting of Cobalt, Pembroke, and Renfrew.

Financed by the old man, the little maverick organization was called the Upper Ottawa Valley League, otherwise wryly known as the O'Brien House League. M.J.'s favorite franchise was that in Renfrew, a dairy town situated just a ninety-minute train ride away from Ottawa, and his Renfrew Creamery Kings had won five straight league championships. This record had failed to excite the rest of the hockey world, which had more important challenges to try, but for the O'Briens this was just a beginning. It was just step one in their ultimate and plainly stated ambition: a Stanley Cup Championship.

Being an impatient man, and working on the reasonable theory that the building of such a championship team was both a long and a precarious proposition, he set out to buy one. His first notable step along that path had been the acquisition of that noted vagabond, Art Ross, who played part of the 1909 season with Cobalt and was reported to have been paid the then phenomenal sum of $1,000 for just one game.

However, the O'Briens' first real chance for recognition as a legitimate Cup challenge came following the 1909 season, when he applied for a Renfrew franchise in the newly formed Canadian Hockey Association. The new CHA was a peevish offshoot of the Eastern Canada League, which had been dissolved and realigned after a petty board-room squabble with the Wanderers over the division of the gate split at the Wanderers' home games. The Wanderers were ejected, and this little arrogance proved to be very bad timing on the part of the league executive. With the Wanderers on the loose and angry and M. J. O'Brien in need of a powerful ally in his rebel cause, the inevitable happened. The O'Briens and the Wanderers got together.

They added Cobalt, placed a new franchise in Renfrew, and presto: the National Hockey Association. The war was on.

Taking on a Renfrew gentleman named J. G. Barnett as a business partner, the O'Briens immediately went gunning for the game's top players, announcing that "money is no object." The signing of the Patrick brothers, with Lester held in particularly high regard through his two Stanley Cup Championship seasons, was their first coup. "That kind of money," raged Shamrocks' president W. P. Lunny, referring to the $3,000 and $2,000 pacts with the Patricks, "is lunacy. It is profligate spending, and if continued it will ruin hockey."

"Balderdash!" retorted the O'Briens, or words to that effect, as they proceeded to stock their roster.

A bigger and more expensive catch, Cyclone Taylor, was yet to come, and he would eventually be followed by Taylor's rambunctious and immensely talented adversary from the late-lamented International League, Newsy Lalonde.

No doubt about it, the O'Briens had started something. Whether or not they would finish it in the prescribed manner—as proprietors of the silver mug donated by Lord Stanley—was another matter, but that was no concern of the Patricks as they packed for Renfrew.

In referring to the bids for the brothers' services, Lester had understated the case. "In a period of two weeks," said Frank, "we received twenty-six wires from six different teams. They were mostly to Lester, as he was better known in the East. One wire was delivered to the house on a Sunday, and my father refused to accept it. But after church, Lester sneaked over to the telegraph office and obtained it. It was the original offer from the Renfrew people, which we later accepted after Lester had stated our terms."

In the December 15, 1909, edition of the Nelson *News* there was the headline: "Patricks Leaving for Renfrew," followed by a story mourning the loss of "the two greatest hockey players ever to play in British Columbia. With their departure, hopes for Nelson in coming season are dismal indeed . . ."

Said the top story in the next day's Spokane *Spokesman Review:* "There is gloom today in Nelson over the departure of the dashing Patrick brothers to their new jobs in eastern Canada . . ."

The headlines and stories were bigger in the East, where the hockey establishment had been rocked by the vulgar O'Brien challenge to their tight little island. The December 18 edition of the Ottawa *Evening Journal* carried a full-page story hailing the birth of the O'Brien's lovechild, the Renfrew Millionaires:

> All Renfrew is in a fever of excitement over the hockey situation, what with the sensational bidding and stupendous salaries to be paid for players representing the Creamery Town on the ice. It is small wonder that the people here talk of little else.
>
> Yet with all the enthusiasm and excitement, which it is safe to say will be at fever pitch all season, a remarkable fact is realized: that it is plainly impossible for the team to make money or so much as break even, no matter how it performs—and it is not expected by its backers to do so. The Renfrew rink holds only 2,000 spectators, and although the balcony will be extended for additional seating, the capacity will still be restricted to 2,500 at the very outside. Taking an average seat value of 75 cents, a very good figure, gate receipts at a single game would total no more than $1,800, and an outside limit of seven home games over the season would bring in just $12,000. The net figure would be considerably below that sum.
>
> The two Patricks themselves will draw half the net receipts, and as ten men will be carried as well as a trainer and a manager, the total salary bill will exceed $18,000.

The reporter was hardly playing fast and loose with cost figures, as the Renfrew payroll would turn out to be nearly double that sum.

> Although many other big names have been mentioned, only Lester and Frank Patrick are currently assured, and those names are on everybody's lips. Undoubtedly, in signing Lester Patrick, Renfrew has landed one of the biggest fish in the hockey pond, and he is expected to captain the team. Bert Lindsay, the fine young player from Edmonton who has opened a bowling alley and pool room in Renfrew is expected to take the goal position, and Larry Gilmour of last year's team is expected to travel as spare.
>
> Rumor has it that great players such as Marty Walsh, Bobby Rowe, the Quebec star Herb Jordan and even Fred Taylor, the Ottawa wonder, will come to Renfrew, and you can bet that Renfrew Manager, George Martel, is not in Ottawa this week for nothing. But even the millionaire backers of the team, Mr. M. J. O'Brien and his partner Mr. J. George Barnett, are said to know little of the

team's makeup. They have furnished the "wherewithal" and furnished it without stint, but they are generally credited with knowing as little of the doings of their agent, or for that matter of hockey, as the town's humblest shoe-shine boy.

It would take something of a strange crystal-gazer to see a man like O'Brien, who has built up his fortune by his own power of mind and limitless energy sinking many thousands into a wild gold-brick scheme, or Mr. Barnett either. It is therefore safe to assume that they know a lot more about the team than what they read in the papers, and that the team is one that is really going to put Renfrew on the map.

A whimsical aspect of this whole zany enterprise is the fact that its first two prize recruits were the brothers who would become known as two of the soundest, smartest operators in hockey history. And on the very day that the train bearing the Patricks huffed into the Renfrew station, Fred Taylor was in his Ottawa boardinghouse with George Martel, putting his name to the richest contract in the history of team sport.

Taylor had barely arrived from the International League to sign with the Ottawa Senators in the late winter of 1907 when M. J. O'Brien publicly labeled him as "my number one target." The Ottawa fans were still buzzing over the new man's spectacular home debut when the player now known as "Cyclone" became the central figure in a two-year chase that had all the ingredients of comic-opera spy thriller.

Three times, Taylor was whisked secretly out of Ottawa by Renfrew agents, and three times pursued and recaptured by Ottawa agents. For two wildly confused and melodramatic seasons, the wily Taylor, the new superstar who packed the arenas and hogged the headlines everywhere he appeared, played both ends against the middle in the highly publicized battle for his services.

When he finally succumbed to the blandishments of agent Martel, it was for the unheard-of sum of $5,250 for the twelve-game season, with the whole amount deposited in advance in Taylor's Ottawa bank. To put this figure into proper perspective, it should be noted that Ty Cobb, the new baseball sensation who had just won his second straight American League batting championship and was being hailed as the greatest player of the age, had just signed a two-year pact with the Detroit Tigers for $6,500 a season. The Cobb contract was for a 154-game schedule, as compared to Taylor's payoff for just a dozen games. That works out at around $45 per game for Cobb, and ten times that sum—$450 per game—for Taylor.

This comparison greatly impressed the New York writers who had seen Taylor play in their town, and would see him again in other years. Although they knew an extraordinary talent when they saw it, the Manhattan scribes found it difficult to understand how a player in a relatively obscure sport from a relatively obscure part of the world could command so much more money than their own gilded immortals.

The fact that Taylor was the highest-paid team player in sport also impressed Canadians, including the Patrick brothers. There, of course, had to be a reason for it, and the reason was that the man they called Cyclone generated a special kind of excitement that brought in the fans and meant money at the box office.

He was the precursor of the breed of player now known in the trade as "the franchise," and if that connotation meant nothing to the Patricks then, as Taylor headed down from Ottawa to join them in Renfrew, it soon would.

A long and historic partnership began on that afternoon before Christmas Day 1909, when the Patrick brothers welcomed the new lodger into their Renfrew boardinghouse.

Said Taylor nearly seventy years later, "I didn't know very much about either of them then, other than that they were pretty good hockey players. It didn't take me long to realize that they were much more than that."

3

THE BOARDING –
HOUSE BOYS

It was just two days before Christmas when the Patricks checked into the Renfrew boardinghouse that was to be their abode for the winter, and they were barely unpacked when a delivery boy arrived with a telegram. It was from Nelson, and it read: NUMBER ONE CAMP BURNED TO GROUND LAST NIGHT STOP AM INFORMING YOU SO YOU WOULD NOT HEAR SECOND-HAND STOP NOBODY HURT AND ALL WELL HERE HOPE LIKEWISE WITH YOU STOP JOE PATRICK.

For a God-fearing Christian who abided by the Good Book and attended church twice each Sunday, Joe was certainly getting his lumps from the fates. First a flood, now a fire.

This latest misfortune was not nearly as severe as the quarter-of-a-million-dollar loss from the Crescent Valley log spill, but it was severe enough. The destruction of the main camp meant the layoff of one of the woods crews, and it severely curtailed the winter's logging operations.

One of the men laid off was a crotchety old geezer remembered only as Gimpy Jack, who was known to drink a little. He was the camp night watchman, and he was blissfully asleep when the fire started. This was a little embarrassing to Frank when he heard about it because Gimpy Jack was his man; he had hired him over Joe's protestations, explaining that the poor chap was an old ex-hockey player down on his luck, and needed the job. For a long time after that, Joe had little use for ex-hockey players, other than those of his immediate family.

Although there would be no more floods to list in the family chronicle, the Patricks seemed to have an affinity for fiery disasters, as the Crescent Valley blaze was to be just the first, and the smallest, of three. There were two more yet to come, big enough to wipe out yet another family fortune. As Frank mused many years after the old hockey player went to sleep on the job, "There were times when we wondered just what we were doing wrong."

Meanwhile in Renfrew, the O'Briens prepared to host a belated Christmas dinner for their new hockey team, the roster of which was not completed until just before New Year's Day. When the Millionaires did sit down for their inaugural feast in M.J.'s luxurious Renfrew home, places were set for the Patricks, Cyclone Taylor, goalie Bert Lindsay, wingers Larry Gilmour and Bobby Rowe, and the center, Herb Jordan. Two other players, Fred Whitcroft and Hay Millar, were on the way, but it was for this original group of seven that M. J. O'Brien broke out a magnum—or two—of champagne for the launching of his unique enterprise.

It was at this gathering that Ambrose O'Brien, to keep the seers of the press honest, named Lester the team captain. It said something of Lester's leadership qualities that after being made captain of the Stanley Cup Champion Montreal Wanderers in his second year, he was named skipper of the Renfrew Millionaires in their first season, before the players had had even their first casual skate together.

Although M.J. liked to play Big Daddy to his boys at social functions, he left young Ambrose to watch over his investment while he, M.J., tended an industrial empire that was now expanding into railroad construction. He was also said to have had a hankering to expand his Ottawa Valley toyland, and had looked into the possibility of buying a piece of a major league baseball franchise, an item that could then be had for a mere $100,000 or so.

In spirit at least, M. J. O'Brien might be considered a sort of neanderthal precursor of Jack Kent Cooke, the expatriate Canadian tycoon who in 1979 sold his California sports holdings (the National Basketball Association Los Angeles Lakers, the National Hockey League Los Angeles Kings, and the Los Angeles Forum) for $60 million, while still retaining his majority ownership of the National Football League Washington Redskins.

O'Brien's interest in baseball stemmed from his fascination with baseball's most famous screwball, George Edward ("Rube") Waddell, a hard-drinking left-handed pitcher whose brilliance was matched only by his eccentricities. M.J. met Rube in the summer of 1907, during one of the mad-hat lefty's occasional disappearances from the fold, which at that time was Connie Mack's Philadelphia Athletics. Having run up a string of four seasons with the A's—in which he had compiled the remarkable total of 101 victories—Rube was big news on the U.S. baseball scene, and M.J. was greatly impressed when a team of New York reporters trailed the two of them to a fishing camp in the Muskoka Lakes country.

Rube went back to work but was hampered for the rest of the season by what was described in the papers as "a lame hand." He was traded to St. Louis in the off-season and went into gradual decline.

M.J., who had been briefly thrust into the colorful life and times of baseball's superflake, liked to express a sort of proprietary sense of remorse in that decline. He had been heard to more or less gravely theorize that the hand injury might well have been caused by Waddell's unorthodox wrist-action in casting for pickerel from a very relaxed reclining position in the bottom of the rowboat. It was during the Renfrew Millionaires' winter of 1910 that the once-great Waddell, after winning just three games for St. Louis, was sent down to the minors, his big league career finished.

If O'Brien did really entertain any idea of becoming a big league baseball entrepreneur, it was just a passing fancy. So, in the end, was his more persistent dream of winning a Stanley Cup Championship. One idea never got off the ground, and the other but briefly.

But meanwhile, there was his son Ambrose guarding the family stake as a member of the instant league's executive. One of his first actions was to support the admission of a fifth franchise, to be named Les Canadiens. And in a blatant but shrewd pitch for ethnic support at the gate, there was a special provision that the Canadiens would get first pick of Quebec's French-Canadian hockey talent.

The Canadiens' first two picks were the swift and cunning Didier Pietre and an even more talented *habitant,* Newsy Lalonde, the one-time scourge of the International League who was emerging as the hottest scorer in the game.

Ambrose O'Brien and the rest of that 1909–10 Canadian Hockey Association executives knew not what wonders they had wrought in creating Les Canadiens. In 1979, twenty-two Stanley Cup Championships later . . .

With the capture of the colorful Lalonde (who was hi-jacked from the All-Montreal club in the rival CHA), the NHA moved another step ahead of the CHA in the picky squabble of the initials.

The battle lasted just three games into the new season, at which time it became clear that the new league, stacked with the most of the game's best players, was getting the crowds while the old one was dying at the gate. Two of the troubled CHA clubs, Ottawa and the Shamrocks, jumped the sinking ship and boarded the NHA.

With the O'Briens' upstart establishment now indisputably the country's number one league, could the acquisition of their Holy Grail, the Stanley Cup, be far behind? If their costly flagship's eagerly awaited debut against the Wanderers was any indication, the answer was a shocking, sobering "yes."

In that historic unveiling, Captain Lester Patrick's Renfrew Millionaires charmed a derisive Montreal home-town mob of 4,000 by laying a large egg. They were bombed 7–2 as the Wanderers' big scoring machine, Ernie Russell, ripped four shots past Bert Lindsay, three of them in the game's opening minutes.

"Unfortunately," said Lester in a wry observation of that disaster, "the opening of the season interfered with our Renfrew social activities. We couldn't please the O'Briens in the drawing room and in the arena too." After a chat with the O'Briens, Captain Patrick informed his troops that henceforth there would be less extracurricular fun and games and more emphasis on hockey.

For Lester, this stern directive was one of those "it hurts me more than it does you" things. Always the life of the party, he was just that at the O'Brien soirées, and was held in particular esteem by M.J.'s pretty and vivacious daughter, Stella. The feeling appeared to be mutual, and there is little doubt that partying with

Stella O'Brien plus whatever socializing went on privately did a
good deal to help take the chill off the long Renfrew winter.

M.J. himself admired the engagingly handsome and articulate
twenty-six-year-old who seemed a cut or two above the average
itinerant pro-hockey player. He occasionally gave what looked
like a budding romance a nudge by lending Lester his best horse-
and-cutter for dates.

However, as teammate Cyclone Taylor, himself a romanticist
and like Lester with a "girl back home," put it, "It was just one of
those harmless flirtations that hockey players get into now and
then during the season."

It sounds like the age of innocence, and compared with today's
free-wheeling pro-hockey age of rich young swingers, dressing-
room hair-blowers, and hockey groupies, it probably was.

The platonic or otherwise relationship between Lester and
Stella notwithstanding, the Renfrew Millionaires got on track in
their second game with a 9–4 romp over the Canadiens, an affair
livened by a brawl between Frank Patrick and Lalonde. For some
reason, perhaps because of his deceptively quiet manner, the
younger of the Patrick brothers was always being "tested" by the
opposition, and Newsy was one of the best testers in the business.
On this particular occasion, it was Lalonde, frustrated at what he
felt to be Frank's overenthusiastic checking, clubbed him on the
side of his head with the butt of his stick, opening a gash behind
the ear. Staggered by the force of the blow, Frank had wheeled,
reeled, and while going down had expertly countered with an almost identical blow to the base of Lalonde's skull. Newsy also
went down, and out. It may—or may not, things being the way
they were in those days—have been the first time that both pro-
tagonists in a two-man brawl were carted off the ice together.

That incident occurred in the Renfrew rink, and of course the
natives were quite upset about it. The contest was halted for several minutes as Newsy's teammates fled to the comparative safety
of their dressing room. There was, however, no rancor between
Frank and Newsy, and in fact Frank brought his assailant back to
the boardinghouse for a late snack after the game, and they compared gashes over coffee. It may well have been during this clini-
cal discussion of emergency stitchwork that the groundwork was

laid for the deal that would bring Lalonde to Renfrew later in the season.

In Frank's recollection: "It was just after we'd lost a tough overtime battle in Ottawa when a Renfrew official came to me and asked what I thought about our chances of winning the league championship. I told him that we might have a chance if we could get that tough little Lalonde to play center for us. He was still a comparative unknown with the Canadiens, but that smart play of his the year before when he shot the puck the length of the ice into the open net during that funny Art Ross-Percy Leseur affair had stuck in my memory. We needed a smart, tough player like Newsy. And when he did join us at Renfrew, he certainly vindicated my judgment. Unfortunately, we got him a little too late."

Half the season was gone when Lalonde became a Millionaire, and the Renfrew team was already fated to finish third in a tough three-team race behind the Wanderers and the Ottawa Senators, in that order. With the league championship, in the absence of any strong challenges from elsewhere, went the Stanley Cup.

There were some pretty exciting and at times lurid high jinks along the way as the O'Briens got their comeuppance in their bid to buy the silver mug, and the Patricks learned a lot from the experience.

On the ice, the two brothers, even as every other player in the league including the redoubtable Lalonde, had to get used to the idea of playing second fiddle to Taylor, the master showman who hogged the headlines wherever he played. Off the ice, there was no doubt that the Patricks were out on their own as students of the game. Dinner talk at the boardinghouse was always about hockey, and it was at these sessions that the groundwork was laid for the rule changes and innovations that would be the brothers' special contribution to hockey history.

Invariably, it was Lester who dominated these dinnertime discussions, but while both brothers had a remarkable grasp of the science and techniques of the game, it was usually Frank, the quiet one, who distilled the knowledge into practical form. He was constantly searching for ways to improve the rules and would point out a flaw even when it might mean ruffling the feathers of his own teammates. As in the proposition involving Frederick Wellington Taylor, otherwise known as Cyclone.

The night following a game in which Taylor had again electrified the fans and mesmerized reporters with his dazzling end-to-
end rushes, Frank said, "Fred, you played a pretty good game last
night. In fact, you played a great game."

Taylor beamed. "Thank you, Frank," he said.

"But you got away with murder, as usual."

Taylor was puzzled. "What do you mean? I scored a couple
and set up a couple and we won, didn't we? What did I do
wrong?"

"You did what you do every time you think you need a
breather, and when the heat's on. You stopped play by flipping the
puck into the stands. Five times last night by my count."

Taylor bristled with indignation. "So? What's wrong with that?"

"Nothing, according to the rules. But it's wrong. It's cheating. It
cheats the player who's on your neck, and it cheats the fans because it spoils the fluidity of the game. Hockey is supposed to be
played with the puck on the ice, not in the stands."

"Frank," sighed Taylor piously, "you know I always play by
the rules."

"True. I think I'll propose one to stop that little trick of yours."

Noting the hurt look on Taylor's face, he grinned and added,
"But not this season, Cyc, not this season."

Another season, yes. Some years later, the Taylor Flip was
outlawed. A two-minute delay-of-game penalty was instituted.

"That," said Taylor, when he was deep into his nineties, "was
just a very minor example of the Patricks' genius for spotting ways
to improve hockey. They were always discussing new ideas, and
their grasp of the game was beyond that of us other players. We
mostly just sat around and listened, with the greatest respect.
None of us dreamed that their ideas would do so much to change
the game, but if anyone had suggested that this might happen, we
certainly would have believed it."

Of Taylor himself, Frank has written: "Taylor was the ultimate
hockey player. There'll never be another like him. He was blessed
with the complete skills, quite apart from a unique excitement he
generated every time he stepped onto the ice. I watched him very
closely, and some of our ideas, such as creating the two blue lines
to open up the center-ice area for passing, were inspired by his

marvelous style. But I used to needle him a lot, just so he wouldn't get too cocky."

As Frank noted, the game itself could at times be humbling enough, especially in the primitive outdoors conditions of those early days, when the temperature would sometimes plunge to cruel depths. "There was this one game in Haileybury—not really unusual in that northern Ontario mining country—when it was 25 below zero, with a bitter wind that made it seem much colder than that. We had to wear mittens to keep our hands from dropping off, and Art Ross, the Haileybury captain, wore a pair of fur gloves and a woolen toque rolled down over his face with peepholes cut out for the eyes. He looked like the very devil himself, and he played as mean as he looked.

"There was one funny incident when Art went after Lester with his stick, clubbed him on the jaw and Lester retaliated. Art—I think he was just looking for a good scrap just to keep from freezing to death—backed off, took off his gloves and tossed them onto the ice. He made a few gestures with his fists and then suddenly turned and scrambled to retrieve his gloves and get them back on again. Lester burst out laughing, and the fight was called off. Called on account of cold."

It wasn't all a laughing matter that cold day in Haileybury, though. Newspaper accounts recorded that three players in that game had to be treated for severe frostbite, and one, Haileybury's Fred Povey, was in danger of losing an ear. He didn't.

"The thing that always amazed me," continued Frank, "was how the fans stayed through games like this, or that they came in the first place, even though they were bundled in rugs and blankets. It struck me at times that the fans were a hardier breed than the players they watched. At least we could keep moving."

Those fans were served hot coffee at half time, brewed in steaming urns under the stands, and it should be noted too that the best imported scotch in those days cost one dollar a bottle. So, a fan, if he wished, could keep himself reasonably well-fortified against the elements through a form of anesthesia.

Many of them did just that, as Frank noted of this game in the frozen ides of February 1910. "It was a pretty wild crowd, and whenever Haileybury scored they sounded like a pack of wolves in on a kill. When a Renfrew player got a goal, the sound would turn to sort of an ugly rumble, and at one point, when Taylor got his third goal of the first period, he was showered with whiskey bottles, not all of them empty. His great speed and agility certainly paid off that day. Fred was a teetotaler and never liked to be seen close to whiskey anyway.

"There was one particular fan there that day in the howling mob pressed against the wire screen over the boards who was a particular pest. He had a very foul mouth and was on our necks all afternoon. Every time we skated by along the boards he jabbed a long stick through the screen, trying to gouge us. Then, at the height of the game, two of the Haileybury players hit Taylor from each side, and down he went. He hit his head a terrible crack on the ice, and lay unconscious. This pest came raving down the boards, rattled the screen just above Taylor and screamed, 'Get up, you yellow so-and-so . . . ! Get up! You're nothing but a chicken-livered, gutless coward . . . !'

"There was a lot more, all of it rotten, and I saw red. Taylor, as courageous a player as I've ever known, lay there perhaps very badly hurt, with this maniac baying obscenities at him. I skated to the screen, lifted my stick and let the pest have the butt-end right in the face. The blood gushed out of his nose and spurted over the boards, and the fellow just slid down out of view.

"Any remorse I may have felt at that moment was dispelled when Art Ross came over, pumped my hand, and shouted, 'Frank, that was a pip! That bum had it coming to him.'

"However, after the game while I was in the shower one of the boys came and told me that the local sheriff was waiting for me outside the dressing-room door, and I had immediate visions of spending the night in the cooler. I took plenty of time getting dressed, and delayed as much as I could, but my fears were unfounded.

"When I went outside, the sheriff rushed up to me and shook my hand in congratulation. He explained that Haileybury had been embarrassed by that pest all season, and he needed shutting up. I asked where the fellow was now. 'In hospital,' the sheriff said, grinning. 'Resting. Quietly.' "

The final score of that game was 15–8 for Renfrew. Taylor, a very tough nut, recovered nicely, got five goals, and Lester got four.

Two other games bear mention here as part of the early blooding of hockey players, in particular the Patrick brothers. One of these was a contest that was never finished, with the players this time more in danger of drowning than freezing to death. It was Renfrew versus the Shamrocks, in the latter team's Montreal rink. A classic account of this strange affair was penned by the Renfrew *Mercury* reporter who covered the game and, we can do no better than reproduce excerpts here. Noting that an unseasonably warm spell had turned the ice to mush, which had then turned to water, the *Mercury* reporter wrote:

> Throughout the game, attendants came constantly out and took up the water by the bucketfull. They scraped and rescraped the mushy surface to no purpose. The pools gathered again and skates stuck in the soft ice and the wearers went tumbling into the water. The dripping figures, putting on double strength when they got up, were a miserable sight as they tore through the slush. Yet they continued to play strong and capital hockey.
>
> Despite the horrible conditions, the eccentric Fred Taylor was there playing in all his glory . . . always he kept an opponent guessing. He loved to race ahead and then suddenly double back with the puck. This exasperated the enemy, but the coolness of it provoked thunderous cheers from the fans. This is not a play that scores as a rule, but it is a joy to watch, and every creature in the grandstand has this in mind.
>
> By the second half, the deteriorating conditions proved too much, and hockey gave way to pandemonium. It began when the Shamrocks' Barney Holden took a swipe at Taylor's head with his stick. Cyclone retaliated in kind, bloodying Barney's nose. The Renfrew rover, Lester Patrick, joined the fray and suddenly they all seemed to be going at it, slashing and swiping with the water flying and the puck stuck and immovable in great puddles of slush.
>
> It was then that the smoldering feud between Frank Patrick and the Shamrocks' Bad Joe Hall finally burst into flames.
>
> Through the contest, they had been exchanging pokes and chops, and already bloodied by a swipe from Patrick, Hall had had enough. After taking one more of these knocks, Joe went splashing up the ice after Frank, who hit him again. Hall stopped in his tracks and struck back with his stick, slicing Patrick's cheek. A lively scrap ensued during which Hall received yet another nasty gash, this time over the eye . . .
>
> The referee, Kennedy, tried to hold Hall back, but Joe, confused,

struck Kennedy in the face, for which he was banished from the game. But upon leaving the ice, Hall slipped and fell into the water and just lay there, refusing to be helped up, kicking his legs furiously and tearing at the referee's pants. Don Smith held Frank's brother, Lester, pinned against the boards as Hall, screaming epithets, was finally dragged to the dressing room.

The arena was a scene of wild confusion as the whistle blew signaling the end of regular time with the score tied 1–1. Overtime was in order, but when Kennedy went to the Renfrew dressing room to get them back onto the ice, the Millionaires refused to return unless Joe Hall was kicked out of the game. Kennedy, sporting a badly bruised eye, was inclined to sympathize with this stand, and called the game, allowing the 1–1 score to stand.

"Afterward," wrote the Renfrew scribe, "Joe Hall went to Mr. Kennedy, shook his hand, apologized for the swollen eye and explained that with blood in both of his [Joe's] eyes, he hadn't known whom he was hitting."

It is not known whether or not this curious plea of mistaken identity mollified Kennedy, but it is known that he handled the subsequent return match between the two teams and had no trouble with Bad Joe Hall. Joe, relatively speaking, was a model of good behavior. He never once slugged the referee as Renfrew won 10–2, with the Patrick brothers splitting six goals.

The other game of note was the last of the season, with the championship already conceded to the Wanderers. This one was between Renfrew and Cobalt, and the pre-destined star of the show was Newsy Lalonde. Little Newsy, who had been sensational since his mid-season switch to Renfrew, had scored twenty-five goals in his ten league games, but was still seven goals behind the Wanderers' Ernie Russell in the duel for the scoring title.

Many years later, in recounting that game at an Ottawa reunion dinner for the Renfrew team hosted by Prime Minister John Diefenbaker, Newsy said, "Before the game, I tell Lester it would be terrible if a great player like me don't win the scoring championship, and Lester, who was the captain, agreed. He asked me how many goals I need to win the title. Of course he knows how many I need, but I think it over anyway. I said I need eight goals to win, and Lester thinks it over, talks to the other guys and says okay, Newsy, we see that you get eight goals."

Newsy sighed and wagged his head morosely. "That showed me you just can't trust nobody. I got nine goals. But with a little help I could've had at least a dozen."

The Prime Minister got a kick out of that. And so, on that Saturday afternoon in March 1910, did the Renfrew fans. Against a Cobalt team weakened by the loss of two of its better players, the Millionaires had a field day as they set up Lalonde's nine goals with the classiest exhibition of hockey ever seen in the Renfrew rink, and maybe the whole Ottawa Valley. Taylor himself, declining chances to fatten his own scoring total, set up at least six of the Lalonde goals while getting two himself in the 15–4 romp. Both Patricks were in on numerous scoring combinations, and Lalonde was merely the trigger-man in a marvelous exhibition of teamwork by the entire Renfrew squad.

In those days, assists were not recorded, and it may well have been this game that gave the Patricks the idea that they should be. Later, when they had their own league, they were, and have been ever since.

In the season's scoring, Lalonde won the title with 38 goals in 11 games, followed by Russell with 31 in 12. Of the other Millionaires, Lester Patrick had 22 goals in 11 games; Bobby Rowe, 12 in 9; Taylor, 10 in 12; Frank, 8 in 11.

Today's fans might find Lalonde's torrid average of better than three goals per game, with defensemen such as Taylor and Frank Patrick going at nearly a goal-a-game clip a bit hard to understand, but it was the age of seven-man hockey, and the goaltender had an extra attacker to worry about. And as if that extra shooter wasn't challenge enough, the rules forbade the poor goalie to leave his feet to make a save. His stand-up stance made him a much easier mark than today's mobile net minders, who can use any acrobatics they like to keep down their goals-against-average.

That business of hobbling the goalie by restricting his movement was another bit of legislation that the Patricks would change —when they got their own league.

Still, in the early years, the fans who watched hockey and the men who wrote about it kept the high scoring in perspective. There was no great obsession with individual scoring statistics or, for that matter, with individual statistics period. The game stories reflected a better awareness and appreciation of the general skills and of the team play it took to produce a goal. The contests were reported accordingly.

Taylor, the man of immense skills who packed the arenas wherever he played, was the classic example of this. In a game where another player might get four, five, or six goals while he was being held to one or two or maybe none at all, it was invariably Taylor who got the headlines. It was then simply not yet the age of the big buildup, with goal scorers often exalted beyond their talents, and their contracts negotiated on the basis of how many goals they score over a season.

The statistic that did count that year, especially to the O'Briens, was the disappointing third-place finish of the Millionaires, with their total of eight wins, three losses, and a tie. The Ottawa Senators were nine-and-three, and the Wanderers were at the top with eleven-and-one, with their names inscribed for the fourth time on the Stanley Cup.

Despite dropping close to $20,000 on the season (actually recorded, improperly, as $12,000), the O'Briens would try again, but the word was out that you just can't go out and buy the Cup as you would a trinket from the local jewelry store. Fortunately for the Millionaires, who were as disappointed as the O'Briens over their failure to win the championship, there was an upbeat finish to the season, thanks to their resident genius, Cyclone Taylor.

In the early spring following the 1907–8 season, Taylor had accompanied his Ottawa teammates to New York City for a historic exhibition series in that town's St. Nicholas Arena. It was Gotham's first look at the Canadian game as played by the Canadian "professionals," and it was also its first look at Taylor. The New York fans loved the game, and they went wild over Taylor as they packed St. Nicks to watch him lead the Senators to two straight victories over the Cup Champion Wanderers.

The New York papers, especially the *Times,* raved over Taylor's play, and it was a *Times* reporter who dubbed him "The Ty Cobb of Hockey," in a flattering comparison to the Georgia youth who was well on his way to becoming the greatest player in the history of baseball. When the two teams returned to St. Nicks the next spring, the packed 7,000-seat arena was festooned with banners reading "Welcome Back Little Jeff," and hucksters up in the stands were doing a booming trade in "Little Jeff" lapel buttons.

This nickname came about from Taylor's facial resemblance to the U.S. boxing idol and ex-world heavyweight champion, Jim Jeffries. And in those pioneer visits to Manhattan that sowed the seeds of a future resident hockey dynasty called the Rangers, Taylor was no less an idol around the west-side hockey rink that boasted one of the world's three artificial ice surfaces.

As his appearance at St. Nicks was a guarantee of a full house, the New York promoters made it a condition of any future Canadian team visits that Taylor had to be part of the package. So it was that when the 1910 series was arranged, Renfrew was invited to New York to play a mixed team picked from the Wanderers and the Ottawa clubs.

Although hockey was still a curiosity to most New Yorkers, the impression made by the two previous series had earned this third visiting party a first-class reception, and a delegation was waiting when the train huffed into Penn Station after the run from Montreal. Hansom cabs were waiting outside, and the players were whisked in style down Thirty-fourth Street to their quarters in the Waldorf-Astoria, which stood on the site now occupied by the Empire State Building.

For newcomers, especially a band of hockey players used to the more or less exotic spas of Renfrew, Cobalt, and Haileybury, the Waldorf, with its daily average of 1,400 guests, was less a hotel than an exciting urban spectacle. With its grand lobby, lavish dining rooms, and spectacular Peacock Row where the elegant people celebrated the cocktail hour, the Waldorf symbolized the growing opulence of New York. Ambrose O'Brien would have been every bit as impressed as his traveling road show.

Saturday, March 10, the first sports page of the New York *Evening Telegram* bannered three feature stories. One was headed: "Cold Winds Hamper Highlanders in Early Practice in Georgia Hills." This yarn was out of Athens, Georgia, where manager George Stallings' baseball team was training for the start of its upcoming American League Season. (A smaller story lower down reported on developments from the training site of John McGraw's National League N.Y. Giants, down in Marlin Springs, Texas.)

The second top-of-the-page story carried the head: "Records Are with Jeffries for the Fight—Negro Has Never Met Any 'Mighty Men.'" This was an advance piece on the most talked-about sports event of the year: the upcoming fight in Reno, Nevada, where the one-time champ, Jim Jeffries, hoped to dethrone the current black champion, Jack Johnson.

The third story sported the two-column banner: "Famous Renfrews Play Hockey Here. Jeffries Taylor Among the Visiting Stars." The report, flanked by photos of the Renfrews' Bobby Rowe and Frank Patrick, read in part:

> The powerful Renfrew professionals play a picked team from the Ottawa and Stanley Cup Champion Wanderers tonight in St. Nicholas Arena, and the mixed team of stars are anxious to demonstrate their ability to beat the Millionaires team, comprising the highest salaried players in the Dominion . . .
>
> It will be the first time these famous Stanley Cup rivals have mixed their players to meet a common enemy in what promises to be a thrilling wind-up to the N.Y. hockey season. Among the Renfrew players will be Lester and Frank Patrick, hockey's two famous brothers, and "Jeffries" Taylor, the man who is paid more than $10 for every minute he is on the ice. Considering that he is paid $5,000 for playing just a dozen games, he is unquestionably the highest-paid player in team sport. His salary shames what is paid our star baseball players for a full 154-game season.
>
> Taylor played here last year with Ottawa, just after that team had won the coveted Stanley Cup, and his marvelous play on that occasion justified his reputation as the most exciting performer in hockey. His teammates on the Renfrew seven are noted for their exceptional skill, having been picked from the best professional teams in the Dominion.

It was a three-game series, with $1,500 going to the winner, and with St. Nicks jammed to the rafters for every game. The Millionaires took all three. Once again the rest of the players had to resign themselves to playing second fiddle to Taylor alias Little Jeff, the master scene-stealer, but nobody minded that much. It was a small price to pay for a free spring junket to the world's fastest-growing young metropolis, where excitement ran a bit higher than, say, in beautiful downtown Renfrew.

The Wanderers' big, fun-loving Moose Johnson, who had discovered a particularly friendly tavern off Times Square, just a

handy block away from Minsky's Burlesque, once confided to
Frank Patrick "that he was sure he had died and gone to heaven."
As a matter of fact, on the evening of the third game a search
party located him in heaven—where he was blissfully entertaining
one of Minsky's angels—and he was hustled off to the rink just in
time for the face-off. The Monday game reports showed that
Moose played a fine game, but then his contemporaries have
claimed that this skilled and honest tradesman never played a bad
one.

One of these contemporaries was his rival of nearly twenty
years, the all-but-indestructable Fred Taylor, who at the age of
ninety-four was the last surviving member of that 1910 troupe,
and thus the only one left to bring those New York memories
to life.

Of the Patricks' first fling in New York City, he said, "Make no
mistake, both Lester and Frank played hard and well in the series,
but they were by nature intensely curious and observant men, and
they got a lot more out of New York than just another hockey experience. In their off hours, they saw all they could of the city, and
we saw very little of them. They always gave the impression that
they were filing information away for future reference.

"Lester, like the rest of us, was taken with Broadway, and I
know that he did manage at least two shows in the short time we
were in town, with three nights spent at the rink. Some of the
Wanderers' boys, who had been in New York before and had
played against me there, told Lester to be sure and take in the
Ziegfeld Follies, and he did. Not once, but twice. I know because
he told me he was going back to see some new black comedian
they had there, and Lester thought he was the funniest man he
ever saw. [The new black comedian was Bert Williams, who
topped the Follies bill with another young star, a sensational new
Jewish comedienne named Fanny Brice.]

"A couple of the others who went along with Lester the first
time were more inclined to think that he had been even more
taken by the chorus girls, who were pretty good lookers. I know
we kidded him a lot about that, and he didn't say much to deny it.
Lester had a very good eye for the ladies.

"Frank seemed to spend most of his time just wandering
around seeing the sights. He said he just couldn't get over all the

languages he heard spoken during a walk along Sixth Avenue, which just teemed with people at lunchtime. I'd seen them before, but Frank couldn't get over the skyscrapers that were going up all over town, and especially the size of the big arena on Madison Avenue."

One of the skyscrapers then "going up" was Manhattan's latest man-made marvel, the Woolworth Tower, whose 60 stories would dwarf the 47-story Singer Building that then dominated the skyline.

The arena that so fascinated Frank was the original Madison Square Garden, pioneer predecessor to the one that would eventually rise on Eighth Avenue to house Lester Patrick and his New York Rangers. The one Frank saw was built primarily for circuses, horse shows, and occasional prize fights and other theatrical-type attractions. Taylor had visited that original Madison Square Garden on one of his previous visits, and had himself been suitably awed by what was then the world's largest indoor emporium, accommodating 10,000 people. It had no ice rink, but Frank must have seen something of interest in the structure, and in Taylor's phrase, might have been "filing for future reference. Frank even made sketches of the place, and maybe he had an idea in his mind that one day he'd build an arena just as big for himself—with an ice rink, of course. Which he did, in Vancouver, not many years later.

"Frank used to get a little mad at the way some of the boys 'wasted' their spare time hanging around the Times Square taverns instead of seeing what he thought were the real sights of New York. Frank, as well as Lester and myself—and Newsy—were teetotalers, so the taverns with their nickel beer and free lunches didn't interest us much.

"I remember one morning Frank waiting all dressed up down in the hotel lobby, collaring the boys as they came down for breakfast. He had three or four hacks waiting outside to take all those who wanted to go on a ride up Fifth Avenue and through Central Park, so he could explain the points of interest along the way. As I recall, he wasn't able to talk more than two or three into going, and I was one of them, although I'd already taken the tour myself. Poor Frank was stuck with all the hacks, and I guess it was the last time he tried exposing the boys to a little big-city culture.

"I don't think though that any of today's hockey teams that travel to New York have as much fun as we did on those trips. To us then, it was a whole new wonderful world."

The above comments are quoted here at length and with a certain sadness, as they were the last reminiscences of this marvelous old gentleman who was the last living link with hockey's pioneer age. This final firsthand look at a long-ago age came in a long conversation with this author on the afternoon of Wednesday, June 8, 1979, in a Vancouver nursing home. The words were spoken quietly, firmly, and with their usual deep affection for the past, and for the old friends who were part of that past. Four days later, the man who is acclaimed by many as hockey's greatest player and who in later years as an Immigration Commissioner was awarded the Order of the British Empire for special service to Canada, passed away quietly in his sleep. He was just twelve days short of his ninety-fifth birthday.

But during that week in New York City sixty-nine years before, hockey history was still in the making for the young Cyclone Taylor and the Patrick boys as the Renfrews coolly disposed of the Wanderers and pocketed their $1,500 prize money.

As he packed to leave, Lester had no idea that so much of his future would be here in the big town. Had anyone told him that he would return to spend twenty-one winters as one of the best known and most respected figures in New York, he would have laughed all the way on the train ride back to Montreal. Nor was he aware that a man who would play a big part in his New York future was in town that very week-end, booked into the same hotel. His name appeared in a *Times* item that ran alongside the newspaper's report of the final game of the St. Nicks series, headed "Rickard Here."

> Fight promoter Tex Rickard said yesterday that if Jim Jeffries defeats Jack Johnson in Reno July 4 to regain the championship he relinquished seven years ago, he will stage a rematch here.
>
> Rickard was in town to clean up details of his Reno promotion. He declined to speculate on the winner, except to say that Jeffries is remarkably fit after his long retirement, is training hard, and that the powerful black champion will have a very difficult battle on his hands.

The Reno promotion, which would end in the humiliation of

the aging Jeffries, was just another chapter in the meteoric career of Rickard, the brash adventurer and soldier-of-fortune who had dug for gold in the Yukon, run gambling saloons in the Klondike, hired out as an armed mercenary in South Africa and as a cattle-man in Paraguay. By the time Lester was ready to move to New York, Rickard would be waiting to open the doors to his office in the house that Tex built.

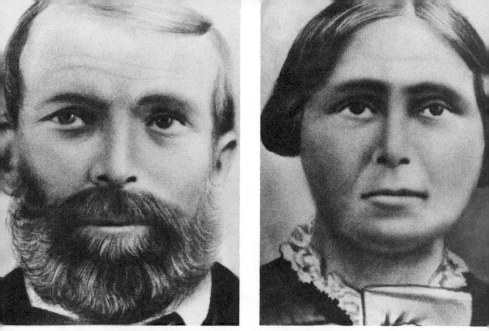

Thomas Patrick and wife, Lucinda, who emigrated from County Tyrone, Ireland, in 1848 to settle in Quebec.

The first family lumber mill, at Daveluyville, Quebec, 1893.

Joe and Grace Patrick on visit to the original South Durham homestead in 1902. Lester (*at left*) holds the horse's bridle.

The family home on Western Avenue in Montreal, 1903.

Joe Patrick with his youngest, sons Guy and Stanley, 1905 (*left*). Joe Patrick and third son, Ted, the boy with the peg leg, at the family home in Daveluyville, 1905 (*above*).

Joe Patrick and wife, Grace (*top left*), with (*left to right*) Guy, Stan, Myrtle, and Cynda at the family home, 1905.

Lester the cutup, always the life of the party, Nelson, British Columbia, 1909.

Lester (*left*) at Slocan camp in British Columbia, 1908.

Frank Patrick, camp foreman at Slocan
Valley, British Columbia, 1909. He is
wearing Montreal Victorias hockey-team
sweater (*above*). Frank at Slocan camp,
1909 (*right*).

Lester and Joe on logs, Slocan River, 1909.

Arthur H. Ross in uniform of the Montreal Wanderers. (Hockey Hall of Fame)

Fred ("Cyclone") Taylor as an Ottawa Senator, 1907–8 (*left*). Newsy Lalonde (*left*), Fred Taylor, and Frank Patrick in Renfrew, Ontario, 1910 (*right*).

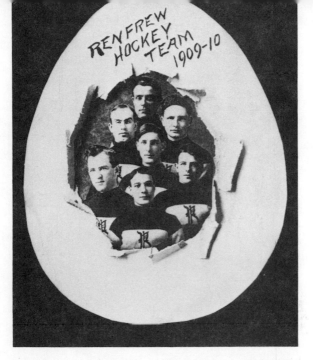

The Renfrew Millionaires of 1909–10. Top down: Bert Lindsay, Cyclone Taylor, Frank Patrick, Lester Patrick, Fred Whitcroft, Bobby Rowe, Newsy Lalonde.

Frank (*left*) and Lester (*second from right*) with members of the Renfrew team at Forty-second and Broadway, 1910.

Lester, with youngest brother, Guy, and wife, Grace, in the family Studebaker, Victoria, British Columbia, 1911.

At Cyndomyr, the family home in Victoria, 1911. Front row (*left to right*): Ted, Cynda, Myrtle, Guy. Back row: Lester, Dora, Stan, Grace, Joe, Frank.

THE REBEL
EMPIRE

Back in Renfrew, the New York victory was hailed as retribution for the Millionaires' failure to win the league championship, and preparations for a giant civic banquet were underway as the players headed home. The banquet, as the Renfrew *Journal* put it, was to be "a mark of appreciation for a magnificent aggregation of hockey players who upheld Renfrew's name in New York City, where the big purse was won and the winners acknowledged as the best team on the continent."

The pride in the New York venture was understandable, for until the name "Renfrew" appeared in the game program at St. Nicholas Arena, it is doubtful that anyone in Manhattan had ever heard of the Creamery Capital of the Ottawa Valley. As most of the Renfrew's citizens had heard of New York City, the matter was now considered squared.

Planned for Wednesday night, the homecoming party had been moved up to Tuesday when it was learned that some of the players would have to leave for their homes immediately after their arrival in Renfrew. The *Journal* reporter was right on the spot with the news of this quick switch:

> Upon hearing that some of the players would be in town just one night, Messrs. Cox and Ritza of the Municipal Council made hurried arrangements. Invitations to leading citizens were sent out and

Valentine's famous orchestra was secured from Ottawa, to be assisted by Mr. Charles Johnstone at the piano . . .

Of the banquet itself, little need be said other than that it was a smashing success, highlighted by a "grand closing dance," a gentleman's quadrille led by Captain Lester Patrick. This merry romp had followed congratulatory speeches by the mayor and aldermen, a promise from M. J. O'Brien to try again next season, and a Toast to the Ladies by Cyclone Taylor.

A week later, the Patrick brothers were back in Nelson. Lester returned to his job in the company office and Frank prepared a return to the woods to help rebuild the burned-out camp and get the others ready for the next timber harvest. "We were," in Frank's words, "pretty certain that we wouldn't be back East again to play hockey" as there was increasing pressure from Joe for them to tend the family lumber interests.

With some of the larger U.S. timber stands in places like Michigan and Minnesota deeply depleted and Oregon and Washington now the major sources, there was a growing fear of a worldwide timber shortage, and that meant a very prosperous summer for the British Columbia mills. It was a golden chance for the Patricks to recoup their flood-and-fire losses, and they went about the job of doing just that.

Outside Nelson, the general belief was that the Patricks' divorce from hockey was just a temporary enstrangement, and that they'd soon be back together again. With his flair for the dramatic, Lester had announced his retirement from the game in Montreal, on the way back home from New York, but apart from evoking headlines in the Montreal papers, the announcement was lightly treated, especially in the trade. "We'll see him back on the ice," said Moose Johnson. And of course they would. Frank too. At twenty-six and twenty-four respectively, they were barely in their prime as hockey players, and they could afford time out to help restock the family treasury.

Nothing much had changed in the house on Edgewood Avenue. Ted was still at home, but he was a loner of unpredictable moods, and was a continuing trial to Joe and Grace Patrick. The oldest sister, Cynda, now twenty-two, was being courted by a young minister from the nearby town of Moyie, a gentleman she would soon marry.

Grace Linn, Lester's lady-love, was still in town, and the romance picked up where it had left off a few months before.

In June, Frank was back as walking-boss of two hundred loggers, but only after surviving the challenge of a giant axeman who thought he should have the job. The axeman, popularly known as Big Jack, was the sole survivor of the twenty-two French-Canadian lumberjacks Joe Patrick had imported from Quebec as the nucleus of his B.C. woods crew. The others, homesick for La Belle Province and taunted for their tradition of early morning prayers and evening mass, had all returned to the East. Big Jack had stayed on as the company's best faller, and he expected to be rewarded.

When the big job he wanted went to the boss's son, his reaction was blunt and forthright. So was the brawl that took place outside the bunkhouse the night of Frank's arrival. The details are sparse, but the result was clear-cut. As Frank remembered it: "He just came right at me with his fists, which looked about the size of sledgehammers, and just as hard. He was a huge man and very strong, and he might have killed me but for the fact that he was drunk and I was sober. Bad whiskey can be a great leveler. I broke the poor fellow's nose, and that was enough for him. For me too, for that matter."

There was another and more light-hearted story of that stay in Nelson concerning Frank and the start of a friendship that would endure for many years, well into his future days as coach of the Boston Bruins. On his trips on the railway spur from Nelson to Slocan City en route to the camps, Frank became friendly with the train conductor, a fellow named Joe Bradshaw. An intelligent, literate man, Bradshaw was a great friend of Rex Beach, and supplied that famous author with a good deal of background for his stories about the western country. After one run to Slocan City, Frank invited Joe to visit the camps, and they made the twelve-mile trip into the woods by sleigh.

"The afternoon we arrived, we made a tour of our operations on horseback. It was a pretty rugged route through the snow, and I'll never forget poor Joe, who hated horses, limping around the bedroom back in Slocan City in his nightshirt clutching his backside. 'Frank,' he wailed, 'I'm terribly saddle sore. Haven't you got something that might help me? Some remedy?'

"I replied that yes, I certainly did have something. A fine, soothing salve called Capsolin. I told him he should be proud to endure his pain because he had ridden our famous 'wild horse,' Outlaw, that afternoon, and this was a feat to be envied because Outlaw had been the undoing of many experienced riders.

"That perked him up a little, but he soon began moaning again. Of course, I hadn't told him the truth—that this horse was one of our most ancient and docile nags. But I gave him the Capsolin and he applied it, on my advice, in generous gobs.

"In about two minutes he started to scream and jump around the room yelling, 'My God, Frank, I'm on fire! What is this damned stuff you gave me?'

" 'It's Capsolin,' I told him soothingly. 'Hot, isn't it?' Of course I knew it was pretty fiery stuff, especially when applied to very tender parts.

"I must say that his reply was unintelligible in all the yelping, and that was probably just as well. But the next morning I told him he should be thankful because the saddlesores seemed much better, even though he would be unable to sit down for a few days. He said no more about the incident, and I never heard the name of the soothing balm again until many years later when Joe phoned me in Boston. He just said, 'Hello, Frank, this is Capsolin,' and then broke up laughing. I took him to watch a game in the Boston Garden."

The brothers did get back into hockey that winter, but only for a couple of games with the Nelson team, in token appearances. With the camps closed for the winter, there was time for trips to the Coast, where Joe had timber connections. Lester made three trips to Victoria, a lovely slow-paced city on Vancouver Island, and was beguiled by the local scenery, which then included Grace Linn, who had moved there after Christmas.

As Frank had been similarly impressed by the urban charms of Vancouver, the fast-growing young metropolis on the Mainland thirty miles across the Straits of Georgia, the die seemed cast for the move West.

The matter came to a head following a major family transaction in January 1911, when documents were signed for the sale of the Patrick Lumber Company to an English syndicate. The sale price has been variously reported as anything between $400,000 and $1

million, but the actual sum was $440,000. Of that sum, $50,000
went to Joe's top hands, Lester and Frank, who were each given
$25,000. Although the entire sum was considered "family
money," the cash gifts were certainly windfalls to the two oldest
sons.

"In addition," wrote Frank in his Boston *Globe* series, "my father also helped me make a private timber transaction that netted
me another $35,000. There I was at twenty-five years of age with
$60,000 in my jeans. I was rich. I immediately bought a new car
and blew a good part of my new-found fortune racing around and
having a good time."

Frank's new hot rod was a snappy new Maxwell touring car. It
was a model made famous the year before by an American lady
named Mrs. John Ramsey. She became the first woman to drive
an auto coast-to-coast when she piloted her Maxwell from New
York to San Francisco in the dazzling time of fifty-three days.

There is no word on whether Lester was similarly well-heeled
through some extra enterprise backed by the old man, but the
odds are that he was. Joe was always careful not to play favorites.

Although it had been simmering for a long time, the idea of
opening up new hockey territory in the West was not actively considered until the Patrick Lumber Company was sold and the
money banked. In Lester's words:

"Frank and I had often discussed our isolation from hockey and
the exciting prospect of developing new ideas for the growth of
the game, and immediately after the sale my father, Frank, and I
sat down and discussed the family's future. It was at the first of
these discussions that the idea was firmly planted to move to the
West Coast, start a new hockey league, and pioneer Canada's first
artificial ice rinks. They would be of the type we had seen in New
York, at the St. Nicholas rink, which at the time was one of only
three in the world. I believe the others were in Pittsburgh and Detroit." (There were also others in Cleveland and Boston.)

It was Frank who first proposed the bold idea of building a new
hockey empire in virgin territory, complete with the family's own
teams and own arenas. The proposition was obviously a costly
one, but Joe Patrick's faith in his sons was such that he had no
compunction about risking the family fortune on what hockey's

eastern moguls would soon ridicule as a harebrained scheme that was foredoomed to failure.

But still, it must be a family decision, and it was put to vote. Curiously, considering Frank's reputation as the more conservative of the two brothers, Lester was the only one of the three who voted against the plan. Even many years later, in the knowledge that this decision made in the house on Edgewood Avenue in the winter of 1911 had changed the face of hockey and contributed much to the development of the present-day National Hockey League, Lester would rue the move—in at least its financial aspect.

"The decision to pioneer hockey in the West and introduce pro hockey to the Coast cities could be termed a major mistake in terms of money possibilities. I had just turned twenty-seven and Frank was twenty-five. We had much to learn as executives. We were just young hockey players with a lot of dreams. Our ideas of improving the game were never at fault, according to the records, but we were just too young to appreciate the fact that the population in the West—and therefore the drawing possibilities—were very limited. I'm convinced that had we gone eastward and developed our ideas in the larger centers of population, hockey history might have been different, and for us certainly more profitable."

But the decision was made to pack up and head for the Coast, lock, stock, and barrel. The family poke of just under a half-million dollars would be laid on the line, and once the decision was made, it was the Patricks against the world and hang the consequences.

Since then, a lot of entrepreneurs have invested many times a half-million-dollars in sports franchises and allied ventures, but there is no record of any one man or one family risking everything they owned on such a nebulous venture with such slim chance of reward. For a God-fearing Methodist who diligently shunned the vices and liked nothing better than to denounce them from the pulpit, old Joe was quite a gambler.

As was noted in the local paper, "the West Coast's gain is Nelson's loss . . ." Nobody agreed more than the players of the Nelson hockey club, which for a couple of seasons had basked in the reflected glory of two of the game's premier performers. It was, therefore, only fitting that the team should host the Patrick brothers at a farewell dinner in the Hume Hotel, from where the meeting subsequently adjourned to the Manhattan Saloon for a final toast or two.

It was probably the first time either of the brothers had passed through the swinging doors of saloon row since Lester had made the rounds during the cocktail hour a couple of years ago, soliciting funds for the construction of the new ice rink. This time, in the spirit of the occasion, both bellied up to the bar with the boys and had one or two. And inevitably, after what may have been his second sherry, Lester agreed to a request for one last Nelson rendition of his now famous habitant verses.

The performance so delighted the gathering that a well-known local character, a prospector known as Irish Mike, ordered drinks all around and then clambered onto the mahogany bar to deliver a very uncertain chorus of "Mother Machree" in honor of the Patricks. The incident, recalled in 1979 by Sid Desireau, the sole survivor of that hockey team party, is memorable only for the fact that right in the middle of ". . . Oh I love those dear fingers so toilworn for me . . ." the poor fellow fell off the bar and broke his leg.

Once the decision was made to go into the hockey business on the West Coast, events moved with stunning rapidity. Within a couple of weeks, even as the family packed for the train ride across British Columbia, the blueprints were drawn and territories assigned for a new major league. The family would settle in Victoria, and Lester would operate a franchise there. Frank would have Vancouver, and a third team would be located in the city of New Westminster, ten miles up the Fraser River. Calgary and Edmonton would be invited to join the league, under their own auspices. Frank was to mastermind a raid on the Eastern Canada and Manitoba leagues and sign the best players available. As an enticement, he would offer up to double their existing salaries, and more for the top players.

Opening up a whole new concept of operation that had hitherto been regarded as either too advanced or too daring, or perhaps not regarded at all, the Patrick plan called for outright ownership of not only their own franchises and players, but also their own arenas, which would be situated in Vancouver and Victoria. The one in Vancouver would be the largest indoor arena in the world.

As if this whole family enterprise were not audacious enough in its mere substance, there was an added stunner: the deadline for the opening of the new maverick league, complete with two arenas that had not yet even seen an architect or a drawing board was set for early January 1912, less than twelve months after the 2–1 vote to take the plunge.

The decision to construct two artificial ice rinks was not hard to make once the commitment to build a hockey league was made. The West Coast winters were too mild to produce natural ice except for occasional brief spells, so there was no other choice. The Patricks were taking hockey out of its natural habitat for the first time. There was a price to pay, and they were willing to pay it.

They were laying it all on the line in what surely would be the most daring, ambitious, and imaginative scheme of its kind in the history of sport. The fact that the venture's one-year deadline would be met in every respect only adds to the general incredibility of the plan.

Nearly five decades later, Lester said, "We didn't think of the scheme as a mad gamble, only that it was something we wanted to do, and we thought we could do it. It was a family adventure, and we were exhilarated by the challenge."

"My father," wrote Frank, "was the inspiration behind it all. It was his faith in our ideas and our ability that made it possible. There is no doubt that he was gambling just about everything he had on what the rest of the hockey world considered—with some justification—to be a crazy proposition, but the prospect of a heavy financial loss was never a consideration. I don't think there has ever been a finer sportsman or sports enthusiast, or a man with such wonderful ideals. My father was one of a kind."

The decision on the league franchise locations was the result of many trips to the Coast by Joe and his two sons over the year, but it is interesting to note how Frank came to inherit the prime franchise location in Vancouver, a fast-growing young metropolis of 101,000, nearly three times the population of Victoria.

As the population of New Westminster was barely 35,000, Vancouver offered the greatest gate potential, and with the projected construction of a mammoth 10,500-seat arena, it would be the Patricks' flagship operation. Frank had the big job, in the big town.

Bright and bustling Vancouver may have seemed better suited to Lester's flamboyant style than relatively staid Victoria, but then the younger brother had moved out from behind Lester's shadow and was emerging as the more forceful of the two. When the matter of locations came up at one of the Nelson confabs, Frank simply said that he'd like to have Vancouver, Lester nodded, Joe agreed, and that was it.

By February Joe and Lester were settled into the new family home in Victoria, and by month's end Frank had left for his bachelor quarters across the Straits in Vancouver. Within another couple of weeks, the twin cornerstones were laid for the physical establishment of the new hockey empire.

The site of the Victoria Arena was settled when six lots in suburban Oak Bay were purchased for what was then considered the madly inflated price of $10,000. In Vancouver, the location of the world's largest indoor emporium became official when Joe signed a check for $27,000 in payment for prime land on the picturesque ocean inlet called Coal Harbor, just a few minutes from the downtown district.

As the cost of the two arenas plus a fund for operating expenses would strain the family budget to the limit, it was decided that a public share issue would be offered so that others could invest in the enterprise. The offer was greeted with something less than wild enthusiasm. When only one fairly substantial investor came forward to support a scheme that the big eastern dailies were ridiculing as financial suicide, the offer was canceled. The $5,000 subscribed by the small group of believers was returned, and Joe took out a $100,000 mortgage to help finance the venture as it was originally intended: a pure family enterprise.

By this time, hopes of a five-team league had collapsed when the potential partners in Edmonton and Calgary withdrew, frightened off by the doomsayers in the East. However, the New Westminster operation was solid, backed by local money, and the group there had promised to have a home rink ready for the start of the league's second season. Meanwhile, it was agreed that the New Westminster team, which like the others was still non-existent, would play its home games in Vancouver.

There was still one snag in this grand plan, with the early January 1912 deadline now just ten months away. Nobody in Canada knew anything about the construction of artificial ice plants, and none of the few U.S. experts were available on such short notice.

The Patricks consulted their do-it-yourself kit, and Lester was put in charge of the problem.

So it was that on the afternoon of March 9, 1911, Lester stepped off the train in Boston accompanied by his new bride, the former Grace Linn of Nanaimo, Nelson, and Victoria. The marriage ceremony had taken place in Victoria on March 7, and one of the wedding gifts was a honeymoon trip for two to Boston and back. Frank had generously suggested that the tickets should include stops in Detroit, Cleveland, and Pittsburgh, a trio of more or less exotic honeymoon spas that also featured three of the world's five artificial ice rinks. That suggestion elicited the new bride's first family veto, but to no avail.

Lower berths being what they are, the jaunt to Boston may have been a little short on romance, but it turned out to be long on ice-plant data. Mrs. Patrick was along on the first of her husband's many busman's holidays.

By what was somewhat more than just marvelous coincidence, the newlyweds were in Boston in time for the arrival of the Stanley Cup Champion Ottawa Senators and their arch rivals, the Montreal Wanderers. The teams had just finished a three-game stand at New York's St. Nicks Arena, and they had now come to Boston to give the New Englanders their first look at professional hockey. The event, billed as a two-game total-goals challenge series, was lavishly hailed in front-page stories in the Boston papers.

It was like old-home week for Lester. He had played against most of this championship Ottawa team, which now included Bruce, the younger brother of his once great friend, the late Hod Stuart. With the Wanderers were his old teammates Ernie Russell, Walter Smaill, Riley Hearn, and Ernie Johnson, plus the tough and cocky old grad from the streets of Westmount, Art Ross. Ross, now a first-class defenseman, had taken over Lester's old job as captain of the Wanderers.

In town too was old friend Fred ("Cyclone") Taylor, who had come to Boston via New York straight from the last hurrah of the Renfrew Millionaires and the burial of the O'Briens' wistful dream of a Stanley Cup Championship, delivered C.O.D. After a third-place finish in league play following the disappointment of the previous year when the Patrick brothers were with Renfrew, the inevitable had happened. Taylor had said from the start that it couldn't last, that the little Creamery Town couldn't possibly support a high-priced professional hockey team, and of course he was right.

The Renfrew Millionaires had played their last game. The increasing financial losses were too much for even the O'Briens to bear, so they just decided to fold the franchise. They had failed with their impossible dream, and their golden toy was no more.

But what was Taylor, mercurial star of that short-lived Creamery Town dynasty, doing there in the city of Boston as a member of the Ottawa Senators? It was just part of the golden rule that had been established by the New York promoters of the annual St. Nicholas series that had begun in 1909. The first condition of the series was that Taylor, the Ty Cobb of hockey and the idol of St. Nicks fans, must be part of the package. He had thus been asked by the Ottawa management to join the Senators for the series, and, indeed, to make the series possible.

There was a reunion between Lester and Taylor in the team's Boston hotel, and as Lester laughingly recalled many years later, "Fred even paid for our dinner, although I think he was more charmed by my wife than by me. Fred always was a romantic, although rarely when it meant spending money." There is no record of Lester having approached Taylor about coming West to play in the new league, but the subject almost surely came up. Lester himself has written that "we had Taylor in mind for our league from the very beginning. He was our number one priority. It was just a matter of timing."

The Patricks knew Taylor to be a very willful, stubborn, and otherwise shrewd and complex character who liked to touch all the bases before being pinned down, and it was common news that every club in first-class hockey was slavering for his services. There in Boston it was a little too early to set the net for the superstar who would eventually become—in the modern jargon—Frank Patrick's "franchise" as a member of the Vancouver Millionaires.

Apart from such sentimental reunions and occasional loving attention to Mrs. Patrick, Lester had other things to do in Boston such as gathering technical data on the construction of artificial ice plants, with one of which the old Boston Arena was equipped.

Already there were rumblings of the need for a new and larger arena in Boston to accommodate a future professional hockey team, although nobody had yet suggested the name "Bruins." That would come thirteen years later.

The excitement generated by the first game of the Ottawa-Wanderers series did nothing to discourage the idea of a future for Boston in big league hockey. Press reaction was generally ecstatic, and the Boston *Globe* reporter wrote: "The first professional hockey game here was a great success. One would have to conclude from the enthusiastic response of the fans that the city will demand to see much more of the Canadian game."

As usual, it was Taylor who stole the show and got raves such as ". . . Taylor's cyclonic rushes electrified the audience . . ." And ". . . the player they so aptly call 'Cyclone' almost literally explodes with excitement. There is nothing quite like him in American sport . . ."

Both Taylor and Lester, the latter probably because he was known as one of the backers of an "outlaw" hockey empire, had caught the fancy of the Boston writers. They were asked to comment on an interesting rumor out of New York City.

A story in the New York *Times* claimed that a New York syndicate had plans to put a professional hockey league in the area next season, with three teams located in Manhattan and one in Brooklyn. It was further reported that some of the brightest stars of the Canadian pro leagues had already been signed, including Percy Leseur, Fred Lake, and Walter Smaill from Ottawa; Pud Glass and Moose Johnson from the Wanderers; and Cyclone Taylor, late of the Renfrew Millionaires.

"A pipe dream," said Taylor. "Nobody in New York has contacted me, nor, to my knowledge, any of the others."

"It isn't easy," said Lester wryly, "to get a new league together just like that."

He failed to mention that he and Frank were currently in the process of getting a new league together "just like that," and had little doubt that it could be done. Nor did he mention that four of those players named in the *Times*—Smaill, Leseur, Johnson, and Taylor, would be part of the Patricks' enterprise that was taking shape several thousand miles west of the Manhattan "pipe dream."

Lester was not only good copy for the Boston papers, but his presence was also a godsend for the promoters, who were having trouble finding officials competent enough to handle their two-game series. When the transient bridegroom was asked to work as the referee, he gladly agreed. Lester's fee was $50 a game, a record payment for any local official in any sport, and, as it turned out, it was dirt cheap at the price. It was Referee Patrick's smart thinking in the first game that saved that contest and the series from a very awkward situation.

In a late move that scandalized the Boston press, Wanderers' manager Sam Lichtenhein had threatened to pull his team out of the series and leave town. Sam, one of the powers of hockey back in eastern Canada, was in a rage over a matter of eligibility, and was venting his wrath in cavalier fashion, threatening concellation of the historic event. The innocent villain of the piece was Taylor, the little firebrand who seemed to spark controversy every time he so much as blew his nose.

When it became clear that the Renfrew Millionaires were about to close shop, there was a mad rush to sign the players who would be thrust on the open market. The prime target was Taylor, the game's biggest gate attraction.

At the suggestion of Lichtenhein, a humanitarian who didn't want anybody to get hurt in the rush, the league called a hurried meeting and declared the Renfrew players league property. They would be put into a common draft pool and their names would be drawn out of a hat.

By intriguing coincidence, the Wanderers drew Taylor's name, whereupon Lichtenhein claimed his services and made him "a very generous offer" to sign. To Sam's indignation, Taylor bluntly rejected the claim and refused to join the Wanderers. He said he preferred to play in Ottawa, where he had his job with the Civil Service, also the girl he intended to marry. "I am a free agent," said Taylor, adding in a rare burst of profanity, "and I'll go where I damn well please."

Thus was born pro hockey's first holdout and first claim to free agent status, with the then unheard-of rebellious plaint that was to be echoed many times a half century later by players and/or their agents.

However, Lichtenhein had no sense of history, and by the time he got to Boston he was ready to blow off steam over Taylor's

traitorous stance. His mood hadn't been helped any during the
New York series, as it was the rebel's spectacular performance
that had set up the Ottawa victory in Manhattan.

So, on the eve of the first Boston game, Sam dropped his bomb-
shell. He filed an official protest claiming that Taylor was his
property and was with the Ottawa club illegally. He announced
that unless Taylor was removed from the Ottawa lineup, the Wanderers would refuse to play. Rejecting all entreaties to forgive and
forget for just a couple of days, Lichtenhein told Captain Ross
that if the matter was not resolved by game time, the team was not
to leave the dressing room.

The next evening, with a packed house of 6,000 on hand, the
promoters were in a state of panic, particularly as many of the
fans had come to see the man who was hailed as the Ty Cobb of
hockey. A couple of minutes before the game's scheduled starting
time, the announcer took to the ice with his megaphone to an-
nounce the starting lineups. First came ". . . the World Champion Ottawa Senators . . . winners of hockey's greatest prize, the
Stanley Cup . . ."

Moments later, the crowd roared as the name of Cyclone Taylor came bellowing through the megaphone, announced as the Ottawa cover-point. Seated in the stands, Lichtenhein leaped up and
raced off to find the promoter to have the game canceled. In the
Montreal dressing room, with the door ajar, the Wanderers heard
the lineup announcement, and after a moment's hesitation Captain
Ross said, "Okay, boys. Let's go."

The opposing centers had skated out to center ice when the
enraged Lichtenhein came racing along the boards, obviously intent on stopping the face-off. At this juncture, referee Lester Patrick, always a fast thinker in times of crisis, quickly called the
centers together and dropped the puck before poor Sam could get
there to stop the procedure.

Once begun, the game was finished to everyone's satisfaction,
except Lichtenhein's. Even the Wanderers, whipped 7–5 by Taylor's three goals, seemed quite content, and Captain Ross himself
left the ice with a sly grin on his face. Accosted by Lichtenhein,
who demanded an explanation for his defiance in bringing the
Wanderers onto the ice despite his order not to, Art said, "I'm very

sorry, Sam, but when we heard Taylor's name announced we just figured that the problem had been settled."

The baffled manager turned and left to ponder the sweet innocence of this statement, but he must have had his suspicions.

A notoriously fierce competitor with an abundant love of the game but somewhat less for the men who ruled it, Ross would have needed more than just a manager's pique to keep him off the ice that night. He never ever admitted it in as many words, but the long odds are that having come to town to play hockey, he had simply disregarded his boss's provisional order not to. One might well call the act an early down payment on the many years of distinguished service he would eventually give to Massachusetts fans as the builder and boss of the new NHL Boston Bruins dynasty.

With Lichtenhein having withdrawn his complaint, the second game went on without incident, other than the elements of a rousing 6–6 tie that gave Ottawa a 13–11 total-goals victory on the series.

The next day, the teams headed back north, and with them on the Montreal-bound train were Referee Patrick and his bride, bound for the Pacific Coast and the continuing saga of one man's family.

At home, blueprints were being drawn for the two arenas, and with Lester's data on the artificial ice plants now on hand, the plans were completed and the contracts let. The 4,000-seat emporium in Victoria was to cost $110,000, and the 10,500-seat structure in Vancouver would cost just short of double that sum: $210,000. The ground for both buildings was broken in late April, and the buildings were to be completed and ready for the first game by the end of December.

There had been one change in the family's homestead in Victoria. Ted had left home, this time for good. The restless twenty-one-year-old, whose infirmity had made him odd-man-out in his talented older brothers' scheme of things, simply told his father that he was leaving to go it on his own. Declining a $500 going-away gift from Joe, he took the boat to Seattle to start a new life there. He would henceforth return to the family home only for brief visits. Frank had come over from Vancouver to take Ted to the boat. Of all the children, he was still the closest one to the boy with whom he had shared the tragedy of that unhappy accident in the Quebec woods seventeen years before.

But Frank, as the brains of the brash family venture, had enough problems of his own to handle. Here he was along with Lester with two rinks under construction, vague plans for a new league to open in January, and no players signed. Apart, that is, from the two brothers themselves. They were already slated to be league officials, owners, managers, coaches, and players. Also rule-makers. This represented a two-man consortium that would be viewed with horror and brusquely dismantled in this age of anti-trust and monopoly legislation. Even then, the conflict-of-interest aspects of the situation was causing a little cynical head-wagging, especially in eastern Canada.

It was up to the two self-assigned benevolent dictators to prove that the citizens of their fiefdom would get a fair shake in every legal and moral sense of the word. The challenge didn't bother the Patricks, who never regarded it as a challenge at all. Their integrity had never been questioned, and it would not be questioned then as they set out to stock their rosters. Rarely was a written contract offered, or requested. Even though branded as maverick operators by the National Hockey Association and thus not to be trusted, the brothers had little trouble getting the players they wanted. With Frank masterminding the raid on the NHA's best talent, the contract was invariably just a handshake. This would be the way of business throughout the fifteen-year tenure of the Coast League.

In these days of twenty-man NHL rosters with many more bodies stashed away and ready for instant call from the minor-league affiliates, it is interesting to note that the new league's entire three-team roster totaled just twenty-three players.

That was for seven-man teams, for although the East had now gone to six-man hockey, the Patricks had spurned this change. They charged that it was a cheapskate move that had been made merely to save money. They would later change their minds about that—one of the few times they would adopt someone else's innovation—but for the present their league would play seven a side.

Of the twenty-three players they had signed and distributed among the three new Coast clubs, sixteen had been recruited from the National Hockey Associaton, which tried, with scant success, not to notice. Four of the sixteen, Ernie Johnson, Jimmy Gardner, Harry Highland, and Walter Smaill, came from Sam Lichtenhein's Wanderers. Other top-line players lured from the NHA included Newsy Lalonde, Tom Phillips—the man regarded as the game's finest winger—Tom Dunderdale, Bobby Rowe, Fred Harris, and two of hockey's best goalies, Bert Lindsay and Hughie Lehman. The others, including Si Griffis, the one-time superlative forward of the Kenora Thistles who was brought out of retirement, came from the Ontario Professional League and the prairie circuits.

The one big one the Patricks had not landed was Cyclone Taylor, the stormy petrel who was still involved in a highly publicized squabble over his playing rights. In defiance of the Wanderers' claim to his services, he had refused to report to Montreal and had gone back to live and work in Ottawa. At Lichtenhein's angry insistence, he was suspended by the league and thus prevented from making his own deal with the Senators, who wanted him badly.

Lichtenhein never dreamed that Taylor would be so mule-stubborn as to sit out an entire season rather than report to the Wanderers, but he was prepared to do just that. But even there, the testy little rebel had struck a shrewd bargain, and one that made him unavailable to the Patricks at least for a season. The Senators agreed to pay Taylor $1,200, nearly twice their average salary, just to hang around Ottawa so that they would have first crack at his services when the one-year suspension was lifted. Taylor had thus become the first hockey player ever to be paid not to play hockey.

Meanwhile, a raid of that size and involving that caliber of talent with or without Taylor had to hurt, and it hurt nobody more than Lichtenhein, who commenced to squeal like the proverbial stuck pig. He appealed to the press, blasting the Patricks as bloodthirsty pirates and all but demanding arrest and capital punishment.

"I had not yet met Sam," recalled Frank, "but he began bombarding me with acrimonious letters that almost literally smoked. He was furious and demanded that we cancel the contracts of his four players. I politely pointed out that the acquisitions were quite legal, which they were, and that the players had come to us of their own free choice. However, that didn't seem to pacify him.

"I must say that I never read more than the first and last pages of his very long letters, but could always answer them without his being the wiser. He got so mad that without any legal grounds at all he sued Ernie Johnson for breach of contract. It didn't bother Moose much. Nor me. I finally met Sam personally a year later, and we became the best of friends. We had a bad start, though."

Remarkably, with all this going on, the new Coast League was not yet even born, at least not officially. This oversight was rectified on December 11, 1911, when the first organizational meeting was called to order in the Hotel Vancouver. A Mr. W. P. Irving was elected the first president of the new hockey organization, and the two Patricks were named to the four-man board of directors. There was no doubt as to who was running the show. Frank was instructed to draft the league constitution, and Lester formally announced that franchises in the new Pacific Coast Hockey Association had been granted to Vancouver, Victoria, and New Westminster.

Everything was now official. The arenas were nearing completion, the players were either on hand or en route, but the eastern moguls still doubted the sanity of it all. Harrumphed the Montreal *Star:* "The old man and his two kids must be suffering from a very high fever."

Fever or no fever, the old man and his two kids were there with the rest of the Patrick clan on a gloriously sunny Christmas Day 1911 for the grand opening of the Victoria Arena. With them in the gondola hung high from the rafters was the Lieutenant-Governor of British Columbia and other distinguished guests, all with a bird's-eye view of the West Coast's first skating party. Down below, more than eight hundred people jammed Canada's first artificial ice rink to capacity, frolicking to the waltz strains of a brass band from the Canadian Navy Base in nearby Esquimalt. People had flocked to the grand opening by streetcar, horse carriage, and on foot, most of them to probe the mysteries of what was to them a foreign exercise. The great majority of those attending had never even worn skates, a fact that caused a record run on the city's sporting goods shops and, later, the household medicine cabinets.

The big crowd watching from the seats probably had more fun than those down on the ice, where the skaters engaged in a hilarious melee, with bodies all over the ice and strewn around in piles. Some of the smarter ones wobbled their uncertain way around the ice-surface clutching the boards while the band played on. As a local newspaperman described the scene: "You could tell who the Easterners were. They were the ones standing up."

The scheduling of the opening had been a rare concession by Joe Patrick, who remained the power behind the scenes as his two rambunctious sons raced along with their dazzling new venture. Already a valued member of his new Victoria church, Joe was unswervingly set against any kind of public entertainment activity on Sunday. Throughout the life of his sons' new league, he would steadfastly oppose Sunday game dates, even though at one time such dates seemed critical to the survival of one of the new franchises. There was never any argument. However, for this unveiling of the family's first physical monument to hockey, Joe, after some personal anguish, was able to find a fine religious holiday distinction between a Sunday and a Christmas Day that fell on Tuesday.

Nine days later, the night of January 3, 1912, Mr. and Mrs. Joe Patrick were again up in their special box, presiding over another bit of history: the first professional hockey game ever played west of Ontario or Michigan. It was the opening of the Pacific Coast Hockey Association schedule, with owner-coach-captain-player Lester Patrick's Victoria Senators hosting the New Westminster Royals, coached by Jimmy Gardner.

The Senators, a name that would be changed to "Aristocrats" the following season, sported colors of red and white with blue bars. The Royals wore black and orange. Bert Lindsay, later to become father of Terrible Ted, the redoubtable Detroit Red Wings star of a subsequent era, was in the Victoria goal with Lester Patrick and old friend Walter Smaill on defense, Tommy Dunderdale at rover, Don Smith at center, and Skinny Poulin and Bobby Rowe on the wings. The Royals had Hughie Lehman in goal, Archie ("Sue") McLean, and Moose Johnson on defense. Harry Highland was the rover with Ken Mallen at center, and Jimmy Gardner and Ran McDonald the wingers. That, with Lieutenant-Governor Patterson making the ceremonial drop of the puck, was the cast of featured players in this historic scenario that made hockey a coast-to-coast pastime.

A supporting cast of 2,300 sat in the stands, little more than half filling the arena in what for the Patricks had to be a disappointing turnout. Still, the fans, many of them seeing their first hockey game, gave their team a standing ovation as it came out on the ice, and thundered their approval as none other than owner-coach-captain-player Lester Patrick slipped in to score the first goal on a pass from Dunderdale. After that, it was all New Westminster. The Royals took over as Ernie Johnson went on a rampage, leveling everyone in sight while scoring two goals in their runaway 8–3 triumph.

What that New Westminster win did, apart from shocking the first-night audience, was prove the impartiality of the player distribution process. Lester, who with Frank was obviously in a position to do so, had plainly not dealt himself a pat hand. As a matter of fact, the balance produced by the carefully managed distribution was so fine that it would eventually and perversely lead to charges of skulduggery.

In Victoria, press reaction to the new game in town was a curious mixture of enthusiasm and bemusement, tinged with a quaint touch of parliamentary prose. The latter was a spillover from the press gallery over in the Parliament Buildings, the elegant edifice that dominated Victoria's waterfront as well as city life in general. One reporter, probably on loan to the sports department from the press gallery, mysteriously referred to the contest as "a lesson in political dynamics," whatever that might mean. But the fellow was certainly an enthusiast and an instant "homer," the first of the new Victoria breed.

Said he, in his Victoria *Times* report:

> Buck up now, Victoria forwards! Get together! You are among friends.
> This is a day of mergers and combinations. The tariff has nothing to do with team combination. Never mind politics, Victoria. Combine, combine, combine!

Other press comments were just as enthusiastic if, like the following, somewhat less esoteric: "For genuine thrills, hockey has every other game faded to a shadow. It is the swiftest exhibition of skill in the sporting world, bar an aeroplane race." As aeroplane races at that time were producing giddy speeds of up to fifty miles per hour, this was a considerable compliment.

Another reviewer, no doubt a stalwart of Victoria's very large English quarter, had a different idea: "With all due deference to hockey, I think that cricket is a trifle faster."

Nonetheless, the new game was here, and it was apparently here to stay.

Now it was Frank Patrick's turn to consolidate the arrival on the Mainland, over in Vancouver. The January 5 Vancouver inaugural again co-starred the New Westminster Royals, who were this time matched against the Millionaires, with another Patrick juggling four hats on defense. Curiously, as in the Victoria opener, the score was 8–3, but this time the Royals were on the losing end.

The big story of that opening night was not of the game but of the arena, an imposing building that was about as close as the local citizens could get to civic proprietorship of what they might regard as the eighth wonder of the world. A massive, homely rectangular monster of brick-faced concrete walls supporting a trussed roof that rose 110 feet above the center-ice surface and housed 10,500 seats, it was exactly as advertised: "The globe's largest indoor sports emporium." The marvel was not so much the size, but rather the fact that the building could comfortably accommodate more than 10 per cent of the urban population it was built to serve. Applying this pro-rata ratio, New York City would have then needed a 400,000-seat arena to match it for spaciousness.

The ice rink itself was not only the second (by just three days) artificial ice surface in Canada but, with its 90′ x 220′ dimensions, it was the largest artificial ice surface anywhere. Below the rink was an underground area that contained the world's largest refrigeration plant and ice-making machine. There were also provisions for a giant swimming pool or "natatorium," and four sheets of ice for curling. Here, in Frank Patrick's fertile mind, was not just a hockey arena but a multi-purpose building for hockey, public swimming, and curling. Plus, to help with the overhead, the manufacture of ice for commercial sale.

Unfortunately, several things transpired to rule out the lower area complex as practical developments. For one thing, the estimated arena cost of $220,000 had ballooned to $275,000 and rising, and for another there just wasn't the time for Frank, with his many other obligations, to supervise it all.

There was one other opening-night point of interest in this historic edifice: the expression of public disinterest where it mattered most, at the box office. Despite the fact that the Millionaires were unveiling a star-studded lineup that had Si Griffis paired with Frank on defense, Tom Phillips and Fred Harris on the wings, Sibby Nichols at center, and the inimitable Newsy Lalonde at rover, less than 5,000 fans showed up.

Attendance picked up a little as the season wore on, but Frank was resigned to the fact that he wouldn't fill his building until he had the game's greatest gate attraction, Cyclone Taylor. A letter written to Taylor in late January said simply:

> Dear Fred:
> Having a wonderful time. Wish you were here.
> > > > Frank.

It was later in January 1912, the night of the twenty-third, that Frank turned in one of the greatest games ever played by a defenseman as Vancouver beat New Westminster, 10–4. He scored twice in the first period, three times in the second, and once in the third for a total of six goals. That is a scoring record for defenseman that still stands.

It wasn't until a half hour before game time that Frank had decided to play. He had sustained a deep cut under the eye five days before in a 10–7 loss in Victoria, and although the stitches had been removed, the eye was still badly swollen. Against New Westminster, the cut was reopened in the third period and began streaming blood, but he stayed on the ice for the full game and beat Hughie Lehman for his sixth goal just before the final whistle.

Ten days later over in Victoria, Mr. and Mrs. Lester Patrick celebrated yet another kind of a family milestone: the birth of their first son, Lynn.

That victory over New Westminster drew Vancouver level with the Royals in what had developed into a very close three-way fight for the league championship, with the issue in doubt until the final game. Such a tight race with all three teams exchanging leads along the way produced the inevitable: a charge that the Patricks were operating "syndicate hockey" and that the games were fixed to keep the race close and thereby swell the gates. The public charge came in a letter to the editor of the Vancouver *Province,* and the Patricks' response ranged from incredulity to outrage.

Said Frank, years later, "Little did we dream when we took over this very difficult and costly venture at the sacrifice of much of our family's timber profits, that this sort of prejudice would arise to taunt and accuse us. To that point, the honesty of the game and our operation of it had never been publicly questioned, nor questioned at all except for the inevitable cranks, and we decided to silence the charge right then and there. We posted a notice of reward in both of the rinks, offering $1,000 cash for any information concerning the league operation that might even remotely question its honesty.

"Nobody ever came forward to claim the reward, and not a speck of evidence was offered to substantiate even the weakest charge of dishonesty or connivance of any kind. I personally thought that the accusation originated in the East, but if so it backfired. From that time on and until the league was liquidated in 1926, hockey in the West was held in highest esteem and was preeminent over that in eastern Canada."

Moose Johnson, the New Westminster defenseman, had a shorter, blunter answer to the charge of "fix." Said he, "I wish that idiot, whoever he is, would count the bruises on my body and then tell me that the games are fixed."

The league race finished with the Royals on top with a 9–6 record, Vancouver was second with 7–8, and Victoria third in the unbalanced schedule with 7–9. The scoring battle was just as tight, with Lalonde getting 27 goals, the Royals' Harry Highland 26, and Victoria's Tom Dunderdale 24. And the Patricks lost only $9,000. If, that is, you care to overlook their capital investment in the two arenas, which now totaled more than $400,000.

To help recoup some of their loss as well as legitimize their teams as logical challengers for the Stanley Cup, the Patricks led a move to promote an East-West All-Star challenge series to take place right after the close of the 1912 season. The idea was for a team of National Hockey Association All-Stars to come West for a three-game series against the PCHA All-Stars for a world series of hockey. A Stanley Cup challenge, theorized the Patricks, could be next, perhaps the following season.

Everyone considered this to be an excellent idea. Everyone that is except the directors of the National Hockey Association. And especially Sam Lichtenhein. Sam was still stinging from the loss of his four players and was not about to play footsie with those robber barons out West. So, the NHA bluntly rejected the proposal, calling it completely unworkable. Unhappily for Lichtenhein, his team captain, Art Ross, thought otherwise.

Having already fought a bitter battle with the league directors and owners over the matter of low salaries being paid to the players, Ross was not about to pass up a chance for those players, including himself, to make a few extra dollars in the Patricks' so-called World Series. He wired Frank that he himself would pick an All-Star team and have it on the first train West. Frank wired back that he was delighted and told Art to go ahead and pick his team. He did, but it did not include the All-Star the Patricks wanted most to see on the Coast: Cyclone Taylor.

Frank wired his objections to the omission, pointing out that Taylor would be of great value as a gate attraction. Art hedged by saying that Taylor had sat out the season and was out of condition. Frank wired back that he wasn't concerned with Taylor's condition, only with his presence. It was Taylor as part of the package, or no deal. Ross, who had engaged in more than one testy feud with Taylor on the ice and was said to be just a bit aggravated by the immense publicity the man reaped the year-round, grudgingly added Taylor to his team.

With the series now set, the NHA people jumped in and ordered Ross to abandon the project on threat of suspension or worse. Ross responded by suggesting they go fly a kite up the Ottawa Valley, or blunter words to that effect. Nothing more was heard of the matter.

The three-game series was a huge success, even though the East All-Stars were overmatched and were butchered 10–4 and 5–1 in the first two games. More than 7,000 watched the first game in Vancouver and 4,000 were at the Victoria game, despite the fact that Taylor, who had arrived with an enormous buildup, got very little ice time. Just before leaving the East, he had refereed a benefit game, had been caught in a collision on the boards and suffered a badly gashed left hand. As he could barely hold the stick, he was asked to play just a few minutes of the first game and none of the second. But, after all the buildup, the pressure was on for more of Taylor in the final game back in Vancouver, and Frank was all for it.

There seemed little doubt that Taylor would be with Frank's Millionaires the following season, although both parties denied that a tacit agreement had already been reached. And with the so-called World Series already lost, Art Ross was not averse to obliging Patrick and throwing his man to the wolves. So, with 8,000 fans in the house, the score tied 3–3 midway through the final period and the East All-Stars visibly sagging, out came Taylor, gimpy hand and all.

The story of the game is more fully told in my earlier book, *Cyclone Taylor: A Hockey Legend,* so suffice it to say here that Taylor came out just like his nickname and all but blew the West All-Stars off the ice with his blinding speed and hell-for-leather aggressiveness. The arena was in an uproar as he broke up a rush, stole the puck, and then split the defense before slipping a silk-slick pass to Art Ross for the go-ahead goal. The fans were on their feet again minutes later when Taylor repeated the maneuver, this time setting up Jack Darragh for the score. He got a two-minute ovation for that little gambit.

Frank Patrick, who had been beaten badly in the second rush, must have had mixed emotions. As a dogged competitor first and foremost, he had to have been a little chagrined, but as an operator looking ahead to next season, he could hardly have suppressed a feeling of elation.

The first season of the Patricks' little hockey empire was now history, and the brief spring respite that followed came none too soon for the two brothers. With so much already behind them, Lester was still just twenty-eight and Frank twenty-six, but their multiple duties and responsibilities had taxed every bit of their remarkable exuberance and vitality. The season had taken its physical toll, and in what had been precious close to a cruel stroke of irony they both suffered serious injuries in a late-season game between Vancouver and Victoria, in the big arena.

This excerpt from the game report tells the story:

Victoria put a damper on Vancouver's championship aspirations last night as the visitors defeated a badly crippled home team by the score of 7–3 to give New Westminster a clear edge in the league race.

The Patrick brothers, rival managers, suffered through a gruelling and painful session that they will both long remember. Both were badly cut during the game, both suffered concussions and had to retire for repairs several times. Each time, they insisted on returning to the ice, despite doctor's orders to the contrary.

Lester was felled first, suffering a bad cut on the forehead from the stick of Newsy Lalonde, who was endeavoring to check him. That happened just a minute before the end of the first period, and Lester was back on the ice again at the start of the second. After ten minutes of play, he met Frank in a violent head-on collision at mid-ice that sent them sprawling to the ice, both momentarily stunned and both still very groggy when play was resumed.

Five minutes later, in a melee behind the Vancouver goal, a stick swung by one of his own teammates opened a gash under Frank's right eye. He was taken off for medical attention, and Lester, still dazed by the earlier collision, was ordered off with him. Again, against the advice of the attendant physician, both players returned after a few minutes, Frank with his eye heavily bandaged and completely obscured. He made a game but fruitless attempt to rally his team and pull the game out of the fire.

At the end of the game, both brothers were taken to the hospital for examination and treatment. It was doubtful this morning whether either of the brothers would play again this season.

It was just four days later that Frank scored his record six goals against the New Westminster Royals, and three days after that when Lester scored the only goal in his team's 1–5 loss to the Royals, over in Victoria.

The end of the first season, with its trials, tribulations, thrills, and a $9,000 loss was celebrated at dinner in the family home in Victoria. A large, solid but unpretentious manor, the house on Michigan Avenue with its great bay windows and fine mahogany paneling had been named "Cyndomyr," after the three daughters, Cynda, Dora, and Myrtle. Lester and his wife were now living in a small California-style bungalow nearby. It was there, apart from the various rented abodes they would occupy in New York during the Rangers years, that they would spend the rest of their lives and raise their two sons, Lynn and Murray.

The whole clan turned up for the family dinner, a function that was always a command performance. Ted arrived from Seattle, where he was working as a salesman, and Frank took the overnight boat from Vancouver, his valise stuffed with, among other things, plans for the next hockey season. Those plans included what had been inevitable ever since the row with Sam Lichtenhein: an all-out raid on the eastern Canada player market, which meant all-out war with the National Hockey Association.

But at the moment peace prevailed, it was springtime in Victoria, the cherry trees were in blossom, and all was well with Joe Patrick's world.

Now fifty-six, Joe had gone into semi-retirement. He was spending his time tending the garden, admiring the magnificence of the Parliament Buildings and the town's other imposing waterfront landmark, the opulent 540-room Empress Hotel, dabbling in civic, club, and church affairs, and investments.

Not all of Joe's money had gone into his sons' hockey business. What he had left was shrewdly invested, and there was no rancor over the dropping of a mere $9,000 on the hockey operation. "My father," said Lester, "had a marvelous capacity for brushing off adversity. He was rarely rattled by anything."

Although still practically a newcomer in town, he was already on his way to becoming a pillar of the church community, a leader in civic affairs, and a firebrand of the Rotary Club.

Although he rarely if ever got rattled himself, he didn't mind rattling others when they bucked what he thought was the right cause.

In a tribute that appeared in the Victoria *Rotary Club* magazine, the writer said:

> Why is it that anyone with the name "Joe" should take it upon himself to be the stormy petrel of any meeting in which he might take part? That is Joe Patrick. But although possessed of a ready and a biting wit, he never takes unfair advantage of it to rake an opponent. With great Christian forebearance, he takes everything aimed in his direction and says nothing. His fortitude in this respect has earned him the admiration of all.
>
> When he has something to say, he comes to the point quickly and lucidly, so that there can be no misapprehension or misunderstanding. He is a man of full, honest, and forthright conviction.

His two oldest sons were equally admiring and appreciative of his qualities. As a token of their esteem, which was costing the old man a dollar or two, Lester and Frank made a special presentation at the family dinner: a brand new Victor & Berliner, the absolute latest thing in the stylish new line óf Gram-O-Phones, complete with a set of recordings by Joe's favorite singer, Enrico Caruso. Joe became especially fond of Verdi's *La Forza del Destino,* and for years insisted on playing it for anyone who walked into the house.

Before loading the guns for the war on the East, Frank made a trip to Montreal in an attempt to avert hostilities through some mutually agreeable player exchange arrangement. He got a cold reception. The NHA still preferred to believe that the Coast League did not exist, and bluntly rejected the peace offering. Frank was not terribly disturbed by the rejection, feeling that a showdown was inevitable anyway, and he and the fiery Sam Lichtenhein got along quite well together despite their differences.

The same applied to Sam's powerful friend and ally, George Kennedy, owner of the Montreal Canadiens. Frank became particularly fond of Kennedy, but the tale of one of the otherwise astute fellow's promotional gaffes became one of his favorite stories.

"Kennedy was a very smart promoter and businessman. In addition to owning the Canadiens, he operated a professional lacrosse team, several billiard halls and bowling alleys, and a very popular Montreal bar. A quick-witted man with a fine sense of humor, he sent his listeners, including me, into gales of laughter when he told us about his famous—or infamous—bullfight promotion.

"He had seen the sport in Mexico and was sure that it would go over big in French-Canada. He contacted a bullfighter in Mexico City and sent men scouring the Quebec countryside in search of an appropriate bull. They brought back the wildest-looking beast they could find and proceeded to starve the poor animal for three days before the event, so that he'd be mean and ready.

"The bullfighter arrived in Montreal, Kennedy had hired a park, sold tickets at a dollar each, and to his delight more than 10,000 people showed up for the great event.

"Finally, the big moment arrived. They gingerly opened the gate and the bull came snorting out, pawing the ground. He eyed the bullfighter who stood waiting with his cape in the center of the arena, advanced a few paces and then suddenly stopped and began eating the grass. Ignored by the animal, the Spaniard stalked off in a huff as the mob hooted and hollered and demanded their money back.

"Someone had forgotten to tell Kennedy that fighting bulls are a very special breed developed for the sole purpose of death in a bullring. And also that they are well-fed for days before they are brought out to fight.

"The only paid patrons there that day who got any fun out of the debacle were the small boys who raced out onto the field to play bullfighter as they twisted the poor bovine's tail. Because the ticket staff had all departed, there was no way of refunding the money, and Kennedy was getting it in the neck from Montrealers for months afterward.

"The week I was in Montreal, a young fellow walked into Kennedy's bar, ordered a very fancy cocktail priced at sixty-five cents, drank it, and when the bartender asked for the money, the customer said, 'That's on Kennedy and his bull,' and walked out.

"That," Frank added, "taught me a valuable lesson in promoting. Forget bullfights and stick with hockey. You can always tell a mean hockey player when you see one."

The free lesson did nothing to cool the player war that began in early November when the Patricks opened up with an offer to sign the entire Quebec team of the NHA. Three players accepted, and the ones that remained demanded and received raises for doing so. Seven other NHA players left their teams to come West, but no defection was as hard to take as that of Cyclone Taylor.

Taylor had been finally declared a free agent and had been offered a fat contract by Ottawa, but when Frank Patrick was seen going into Fred's boardinghouse one day in early November, the Senators knew the jig was up. When Frank emerged, he had Taylor's promise to report to the Millionaires in time for the opening game on December 10. His pact called for a salary of $1,800, which was then tops in hockey and $500 more than Patrick had paid Newsy Lalonde for the inaugural Coast League season. But Newsy, pining for his friends in Quebec, had gone back East to join the Canadiens, and Taylor was his replacement in the Vancouver lineup.

Frank and Lester were delighted with the exchange, for their league now had hockey's number one prestige player, and he was cheap at the price.

For the opening game in Vancouver, even though Taylor had been stricken with appendicitis just two days before and had left his hospital bed to play in defiance of his doctor's orders, 7,400 fans were in the Arena. Taylor scored only once in the 7–2 win over New Westminster, but there was no doubt that the Vancouver fans had a new idol, the league had a bright new star, and that Frank Patrick had his "franchise." Despite his weak condition, Taylor put on a dazzling display that had the fans out of their seats most of the night, roaring in appreciation. And after his night's work, Taylor went right back to his hospital bed.

For the next home game, against Lester's Victoria Aristocrats, the building was packed to the rafters. It was the Arena's first complete sellout, and the crowd of 10,500 was the largest ever to watch a hockey game, anywhere. For the Patricks, after that first uneasy season, it was confirmation that their Coast empire had taken root. It was also a good start in office for the new league president, Frank Patrick, who would occupy that post for the next dozen years.

5

THE CHANGING
GAME

MAMMOTH SPORTS PALACE FOR
SAN FRANCISCO EXPOSITION

That was the headline that greeted the citizens of the Bay Area
when they opened their edition of the San Francisco *Chronicle*
one day in early June 1913. Beneath was a long and lavish account of a scheme that read like something out of *Alice in Wonderland*. It was, in fact, a wild and wondrous project right out of
the fertile mind of Frank Patrick. Here is the *Chronicle* yarn, in
very small part:

> Foreign ingenuity will contribute to the coming Panama Exposi-
> tion in San Francisco with a feature that will unquestionably prove
> to be a major attraction. This will be a vast $25,000 ice hippodrome
> with a crystal palace, toboggan chutes, sleighing course, arena, and
> roof gardens. The structure is complete in plan and has been per-
> fected in every detail by the Messrs. Frank and Lester Patrick of
> Vancouver, B.C.
>
> The architectural drawings, plans and elevations of this stupen-
> dous structure have been submitted to and approved by the directors
> of the Exposition, and an attractive location has been allotted on the
> Exposition grounds. Mr. Frank Patrick has made several visits to
> San Francisco to talk to the directors and inspect the location. The

process of the manufacture of ice in a hot climate has been perfected by Mr. Patrick and protected by his patents . . .

Lester was credited as a partner in the plan, but it was Frank's brainchild. A person can only wonder how men, already so heavily involved in hockey, could find time for this trip into Fantasia.

The roof covering the area will rise 80 feet above ground level and will be supported by a series of gracefully arched trusses that will span the huge surface in a single clear sweep. The building forms a gracefully massed design on classical lines of the Corinthian style of architecture, with a massive central pavilion flanked by arched colonnades and surmounted by a stately Quadriga and pedestal statuary. The colonnades terminate in lesser pavilions, which are enlivened by ornamental pennant supports and parapet cornices.

Above the colonnades is the roof garden, taking in the entire 176 feet of frontage and extending 139 feet to the back of the arena wall. Along the facade extends an ornamental parapet surmounted by a pergola. The open beams of the pergola are to be overgrown with vines and flowering plants, where, shaded from the sun, you will be served with refreshments including a Canadian specialty of heated maple sugar on platters heaped with pure snow. A small model of the Ice Hippodrome will be served as a souvenir, molded in crystal maple syrup, a speciality invented by Frank Patrick.

After the refreshing snow-syrup, you will be ready to visit the toboggan chutes, which are a quarter of a mile in length, with steep dips and curves.

Next in order will be a visit to the Gothic Ice Palace, which will be a beautifully designed structure of solid ice etched with a delicate lacework. The ice is maintained in its frozen form by a system of gravity and brine circulation also perfected and patented by Mr. Frank A. Patrick.

The interior and exterior walls of this palace will be of solid blocks of ice, with colored lights frozen into the mass, and with specimens of Canadian fish and game. From the rainbow-arched ceilings will hang rainbow-hued stalactites, and through the mullioned windows the colored lights will produce a fairyland effect of novelty and beauty . . .

There was a good deal more, including a lyrical description of "a moonlight droshky ride through a quarter-mile tunnel over real snow, and drawn by reindeer or huskies through the land of the Aurora Borealis and snow igloos." And of "the great arena itself, on whose giant surface will be presented four shows daily, comprising fancy skating, hockey games, clowns, skaters on stilts and made up as animals such as elephants, giraffes, horses, and dragons and other beasts of every description . . ."

It was enough to boggle the mind of even P. T. Barnum, but unhappily, San Franciscans never did get to test the accuracy of this ecstatic preview, or to taste Frank Patrick's Famous Refreshing Snow-Syrup on a romp through that winter wonderland. With the outbreak of war on March 11, 1914, plans for the Exposition were severely curtailed, and the ice palace project was one of the first to go.

Still, it had been an interesting journey for the rough sketch that Frank had stuffed into his valise for the trip to Victoria and the family dinner in Victoria the previous springtime.

Long after, recalling his first glimpse of the drawing of the wonderland that never was, Joe said, "I didn't quite understand it, but I figured that if it was Frank's idea, it must be a good one." That was Joe. My sons, right or wrong.

In the season of 1913–14, the Patricks won two battles but lost a city. First, the directors of the National Hockey Association reluctantly announced that the Coast League could now officially challenge for the Stanley Cup, and ground rules were laid for a best-of-five series with a $2,500 guarantee to the winning team. This tacit recognition of the renegade PCHA was inevitable in the wake of the West's demolition of the East in the World Series competition, and it represented a major victory for the Patricks.

The other victory concerned the always hectic affairs of Fred Taylor, who had been trapped in a bitter tug of war as the Ottawa Senators fought for the return of the one man who could restore at least some of the NHA's tarnished prestige. Living and working in Ottawa between hockey seasons, Taylor was threatened with the loss of his government job if he returned to the Coast. "Evil forces," Frank Patrick told the Montreal *Star,* "are at work in the Federal Government to blackmail Taylor into jumping back to the NHA."

As to whether heavy lobbying by influential MP friends of the Ottawa management could be rightly described as the work of "evil forces" was a moot point, but Frank was ready to fight fire with fire. With a little help from Joe, who was becoming a well-known figure over in Victoria, he formed his own lobby and appealed to the B.C. Premier, Sir Richard McBride. He asked Sir Richard to intervene directly with the Prime Minister of Canada, Sir Richard Borden. It helped that both of these distinguished gentlemen (including Taylor) were staunch Conservatives, with no great burning affection for the Liberal Members of the Loyal Opposition.

The outcome of this mismatch was that arrangements were made to have Taylor moved to a desk in the Immigration Building on the Vancouver waterfront, where he would work until his retirement as B.C. Commissioner nearly four decades later.

Despite Taylor's permanent return to the fold, Frank's Millionaires finished last in a league race dominated by Lester's Aristocrats, but it was the New Westminster Royals who were the big losers. Their new arena had never materialized, and with their home games still booked into the Vancouver building, they dropped $10,000 on the year, and decided to fold. The PCHL was down to two members and was practically a non-league.

Meanwhile, Victoria hosted Toronto in the last unofficial East-West Stanley Cup series and lost a three-game sweep. It was the tail-end Millionaires who picked up the Grand Prize, for as they had Taylor in the fold they were the ones who got the invitation for what had become the annual glamor junket to New York and Boston.

Plans had been made for a stopover in Ottawa for a two-game exhibition series with the Senators, also for a wedding ceremony co-starring the Vancouver Millionaires' rover and a local society girl. Among the large supporting cast at this happy affair were Frank Patrick, who was the best man, plus the entire Vancouver hockey team and assorted other guests.

As noted in the Ottawa *Free Press:*

> Fred Taylor will be playing his last game as a bachelor tomorrow, for on Wednesday he will be wedded to Miss Thirza Cook. Taylor's bride-to-be worked with him in the Department of the Interior when he first came to play for Ottawa in 1907.

Another important social event that week in Ottawa was the surprise visit of His Royal Highness, the Duke of Gloucester. On a tour of the Eastern provinces, he had written to say that he had changed his itinerary so that he could be in Ottawa to watch "that western hockey team of which I have heard such splendid reports . . ." The Duke attended both games, but respectfully declined an invitation from Frank to visit the Vancouver dressing room. That was probably just as well, as there is nothing quite so disenchanting as a hockey fan's first look at his heroes stripped to their long johns right after a hard night in the rink. Especially as it was the general custom to wear the same fragrant apparel throughout the entire season.

After the marriage ceremony, the newlyweds boarded the train bound for New York via Montreal, accompanied by both the Vancouver and Ottawa hockey teams. If the honeymoon special seemed a little too crowded for comfort or at least for privacy, this was because the Ottawa team had been invited to take part in the three-team series in New York, with the winners of the knockout competition there moving to Boston.

This was Taylor's fifth trip to Manhattan to play hockey, and it would be his last. It would also be the last for this colorful annual series that had given New York its first hockey idol. Put aside for the duration of the war, the series was never resumed.

Oh yes, there was one modest peace gesture there in the spring of that fateful year. It had surfaced in Ottawa in the form of a telegram from Montreal. It was addressed to the Taylors, and it read: ALL PLAYERS AS WELL AS I WISH YOU AND YOUR BRIDE ALL POSSIBLE HAPPINESS AND PROSPERITY IN YOUR WEDDED LIFE STOP SAM LICHTENHEIN.

It was a nice thought, but Sam could have saved himself the cost of the telegram since he was there in New York with his Wanderers when the party from Ottawa arrived.

Sam wasn't in the lobby of the Waldorf-Astoria to greet the newlyweds as they checked in, but his captain, Art Ross, was. For the Patricks' old neighborhood chum, it was like a reprise of Lester's honeymoon trip exactly three years before, when there was no such thing as a Coast League, and the only Millionaires were those on Wall Street and the ones who had just gone down the drain up in Renfrew.

Apart from the fact that Taylor's spectacular play was again the talk of Manhattan as the Senators were eliminated in the knockout round, the New York swan song was an uneventful one. In Boston, where the Millionaires' illustrious player-coach-manager and his even more illustrious rover were pictured side-by-side in a full-page-length Boston *Globe* photo, it was the Wanderers who won the $2,500 winners' share of the purse as they took the two-game total-points series, 11–9.

It had been an unusually rough affair for an exhibition series, marked by three near riots during which Taylor was twice decked by the Wanderers' Sprague Cleghorn and Frank had found himself up in the seats after a crushing check by Ross. When Frank climbed back over the boards, the other Cleghorn, Odie, came at him but was blindsided by Taylor who had come flying to the rescue. In the ensuing melee, Cleghorn, Taylor, and Hughie Lehman were all banished from the game.

As Hughie was the Vancouver goalie, the Millionaires were in a bad fix, but none other than Arthur Howie Ross came to their aid. He informed the referee that he would agree to waive the penalty against Lehman. Frank, bleeding heavily from the nose and looking definitely glassy-eyed, at first refused this generous gesture, suspecting some kind of a trap. However, he did accept it, Lehman went back into the net, and the game resumed.

Later, when queried about his sporting act, Ross snarled: "Sporting, hell. If Vancouver had won I would have protested the game and demanded a forfeit. Once a player is ruled off the ice, the referee can't change his decision."

It was a thinker like this that the Boston fans would eventually need (and get) for their NHL Bruins.

A week later, the travelers were back on the Coast. With the outbreak of war, Victoria, with its very large first-and-second generation English population, was very sensitive to the plight of the Old Country, and the link was almost as strong in Vancouver. Joe Patrick himself, although his family ties were Irish, was a British Loyalist, and he approved when his two oldest sons decided to volunteer for service. In the spring of 1915, there was a Montreal *Herald* story headlined: "Frank Patrick, Hockey Leader, Enlists for War."

> Frank Patrick, president of the Pacific Coast League and former star of the National Hockey Association, has enlisted with the Irish Fusiliers of Vancouver. He will go to the front with the second contingent, according to his father, Joe Patrick, who is visiting the

city. It will be several weeks before the second contingent is mobilized, and in the meanwhile the head of hockey affairs on the West Coast is getting league affairs in shape for the coming season, which will be played without him.

The story was a little premature. Frank had gone to Vancouver army headquarters and applied for enlistment, offering to form a Sportsmen's Battalion along the lines of one then being raised in Toronto. Two weeks later, a letter arrived from Ottawa noting that since both Vancouver and Victoria were key ports and shipyard and naval-base communities, entertainment such as the Patricks provided was considered vital to home-front morale. The two brothers were told to stay put.

A year later, right after his seventeenth birthday, the fourth brother, Guy, enlisted and went almost immediately overseas to serve at the front with a Red Cross unit, as a stretcher-bearer.

While Joe had approved his two oldest sons' efforts to enlist, he was dismayed by Guy's decision.

"He is too young," said Joe.

"They are all too young," said Grace Patrick. "But Guy will come back."

Three years later, he did.

Although six thousand miles from the battlefields of Europe, Victorians suffered occasional attacks of war nerves. The city was alarmed in the late autumn of 1914 when a German battle squadron under the command of Admiral Graf Spee was reported steaming northward from the tip of South America. There was no explanation as to why a battle squadron known to be eight thousand miles away should now be headed on a collision course with downtown Victoria, but just to be on the safe side Premier McBride decided to upstage the British Admiralty and raise his own emergency defense force.

Through some peculiar maneuvering that nobody ever quite understood, the Premier extracted $1,150,000 from the Provincial treasury for the purchase of two U.S. submarines from the Navy base near Seattle. They were to provide a line of defense for Victoria and Vancouver, although their effectiveness in such a cause may have been somewhat in question. When the subs arrived in Victoria they were found to be woefully obsolete, without torpedoes or any other means of defense for themselves, let alone the Canadian West Coast. Their arrival as the flagships of McBride's Navy did, however, cause some excitement. Sighted cruising north just below the Victoria naval base at Esquimalt, they were nearly sunk by gunfire from the alert shore battery at The Rock.

As there was nobody aboard the subs skilled enough to submerge the relics, if indeed they could be submerged, the Canadian sailors sent to bring them up from Seattle almost became Canada's first home-front war casualties. Fortunately, the aim of the shore battery was poor, and both subs and sailors survived. The sailors presumably went on to serve a useful purpose, but once berthed at the Esquimalt dock the submarines never left port again.

A few weeks after that little panic, the German cruiser *Leipzig* was reported seen steaming up the Coast, and the ancient Canadian Navy destroyer *Rainbow* was ordered out to protect the shipping lanes. A chronic mismatch was avoided when this too turned out to be just another case of war jitters.

Joe Patrick served throughout this shaky period as a volunteer Coast lookout, but sighted nothing more menacing than a couple of ugly-tempered sailors weaving their way back to barracks after a night on the town.

As far as the hockey front was concerned, the Patricks had dug in for another season and faced their first salvage job. It was the first of several that would nag them throughout the league's future, plagued as it was by the sparsity of the Coast population.

The league roster went back to three teams when the players of the defunct New Westminster franchise were relocated in Portland, where they became known as the Portland Rosebuds, coached by Pete Muldoon. Portland thus became the first U.S. city to join a Canadian-based major hockey league, and with Victoria's Moose Johnson added to their lineup the Rosebuds made their debut with a respectable 9–9 season record in a league race dominated all the way by Vancouver.

The Millionaires' sensational rookie center, Mickey Mackay, had 34 goals in seventeen games to win the scoring title, followed by Taylor, the playmaker non pareil, with 26. Frank was now easing out as a player, but after playing just four games of the regular schedule he came back to be a vital force on defense in the Stanley Cup series that brought the Cup to the West for the first time.

The Millionaires' opponents in this milestone event were the eastern champion Ottawa Senators, who were simply no match for what has to be rated one of the finest hockey teams ever assembled. The Ottawas were humbled in a three-game sweep by scores of 6–2, 8–3, and 12–2. Every player on that victorious 1915 Vancouver team was eventually ushered into the Hockey Hall of Fame. The names of that elite band were Hughie Lehman, goalie; Frank Patrick and Si Griffis, defense; Fred Taylor, rover; Mickey Mackay, center; Frank Nighbor and Barney Stanley, wings.

Fans had jammed the Arena to witness proof of the fact that after just four years of "outlaw" existence, the West Coast brand of hockey was now established as the best in the land. Twenty-three years later, after savoring his first Stanley Cup victory as coach of the New York Rangers, Lester Patrick looked back for the Manhattan press and updated what he had said of his brother's Millionaires way back in 1915: "That, in my view, was the best hockey team that ever stepped onto the ice."

By this time, hockey was feeling the impact of the Patricks' constant search for ways and means of improving the game. Many of their new rules were already in use, with others on the way. True, as they were the two most powerful men in PCHA, they had virtually their own proving ground. When it came to proposing a new rules change, Frank or Lester merely had to make the suggestion and the change was instituted, or at least tested. It was a classic case of a benevolent dictatorship in action.

Said Frank, "In all new suggestions for bettering the game, I always consulted Lester and had his invaluable support, and vice versa. We'd argue about every suggestion from all angles, and if we then thought it might be good for hockey we tried it out."

The first innovation was the numbering of players, with the numbers keyed to the game program. That was done in the 1911–12 season, in the opening game in Victoria between the Aristocrats and the New Westminster Royals. It was perhaps poetic justice that the Patrick who sparked this idea was Joe, whose generosity and consummate faith in his boys had made everything possible.

During a family discussion on ways and means of better servicing the paying customers, Joe produced a photograph in the popular *London Illustrated* depicting an English harrier (cross-country) race. The harriers were identified by numbers pinned to the backs of their shirts, and on the following Saturday at the PCHA inaugural, the hockey players were similarly marked. The idea was a hit with the fans and was immediately adopted throughout the league. Three seasons later, the numbering of players was standard throughout hockey.

As with all the Patrick innovations, universal acceptance, grudging at first, inevitably followed. Sometimes, as in this matter of numbering the players, the Patrick ideas were adopted by many other team sports, to their great profit.

In that same fledgling season of 1912, Lester expressed distaste over the hobbling of goalies, who under the existing rules were not allowed to leave their feet in an attempt to block a shot. "It doesn't make sense," said Lester. "A goalkeeper should be allowed to make any move he wants, just like the rest of us. He should be allowed to make the most of his physical abilities."

The rule was changed to allow a goalie to "stop a shot in any way he chooses, except by throwing his stick, but must not hold the puck nor pass it forward with his hands . . ." With that stroke of emancipation the goalie's acrobatics became one of the most thrilling parts of hockey, and the defensive style of the game was changed immensely.

Another point of concern to the Patricks in their search for the perfect game was the constant stoppage of play for offside calls as players broke ahead of the play to receive the puck. Seated in the stands to check this situation during a 1913 World Series game between Victoria and Quebec, Lester counted fifteen stoppages in the first five minutes of the first game. The whistle-blower was Art Ross, who had come West to referee the series, and was just adhering to the offside rules.

After that game, Lester and Frank got together to devise a rule to cut down on those dreary stoppages. The result was the installation of the blue lines that divide the rink into three equal parts, with unrestricted passing allowed in the center zone. That change, which proved so popular that forward passes were eventually also allowed on both sides (but not across) the blue lines, blew the game of hockey wide open. The blue lines, which quickly became standard throughout hockey, may have been the most significant of all the Patrick hockey innovations.

In 1918, with the Seattle Metropolitans (replacing the temporarily defunct Victoria Aristocrats) running away with the league race, Frank Patrick felt compelled to come up with an idea to help the flagging attendance. He thought he had one, and on the night boat from Vancouver to Seattle for a game with the Metropolitans, he called Fred Taylor and Si Griffis into his cabin to discuss it.

"What we need," he said, "is a second chance for teams that for whatever reason have fallen too far behind to make a race of it. It's not right, for instance, that a team strong enough to make a challenge should be ruled out of early-season contention by injuries." His cure for the dilemma: A post-schedule play-off series between the first- and second-place teams, with the winner moving into the inter-league championship competition.

"It won't work," said Taylor. "The fans won't like it."

"We'll try it," said Frank. He ordered up hot cocoa all around. They drank to the idea, and went to bed.

The idea was tried, and the fans liked it. They've been liking it ever since, while providing a multimillion-dollar bonanza for sport in North America. The brainwave has made untold millions for owners and players and concessionaires in pro football, basketball, and baseball, as well as hockey. Said New York *Times* columnist Arthur Daley in a 1967 column eulogizing the Patrick family:

> They [Lester and Frank] should have a monument raised in their memory for that one idea alone. A mere one-tenth of one percent of what the NFL alone has earned from it would provide a life-size sculpture of purest marble, with enough left over to stock a franchise.

It was in 1921, when he and his wife, Catharine, took a trip to the Old Country with Joe and Grace Patrick that Frank got the idea for what he called his most exciting rules innovation. "While we were in London, we traveled out to Chiswick to see a polo match. We paid the equivalent of $15 each to watch the match, as did about 10,000 others. Early in the contest, the referee called for a penalty shot, something I had never seen before. The shot produced the winning goal, and I got a terrific kick out of it. So did the other thousands in the stands. The way I saw it, if a rule like that could excite this very conservative English crowd, it would go great with hockey fans."

It did. Although not often seen, the penalty shot can produce a rare bit of one-on-one drama.

Sensitive to the fact that some of the game's great playmakers received little credit in the statistics, the Patricks introduced the awarding of points for assists. Tired of play stoppages caused when the puck was kicked, they rewrote the rule to allow kicking, except in the scoring of goals. They initiated the idea of standardized nights for home dates and the double-referee system. They pioneered the strategy of making line substitutions as play went on.

In 1925, in the Stanley Cup series between the Canadiens and Victoria, complete line changes were tried for the first time in a highly successful experiment that not only won the Cup for Victoria, but also changed the whole tempo and offensive strategy of hockey.

But now, with the East-West player war still hot, the Patricks tossed the fat on the fire at the start of the 1916 season by luring away almost the entire Toronto NHA roster to stock a new Coast League franchise in Seattle. The big heist included the outstanding goalie, Hap Holmes, and two forwards who were headed for the Hockey Hall of Fame, Frank Foyston and Jack Walker.

To solidify the Americanization of the once All-Canadian Patricks League, the Portland Rosebuds had the audacity to win the league championship. They lost to Newsy Lalonde's Canadiens in the Cup finals, but the U.S. incursion had made its mark. So had the roistering Moose Johnson, who during one game hurtled right through the boards and brought down a whole section of the stands. Another bulwark of the Rosebuds that season was Dick Irvin, the brilliant young center who was destined to be one of the great coaches of NHL history, as the mentor of the Montreal Canadiens.

Another item of note that year was the birth of two more Patricks: Frederick Murray, second son of Lester and Grace Patrick, and Joe, Jr., first child of Frank and Catharine Patrick. That completed Lester's family. Frank would have two more children, both daughters.

The birth of Murray, later better known as Muzz, coincided with a less happy event: the eviction of Lester's Victoria Aristocrats. The Canadian government commandeered the Victoria Arena for military purposes, and the Aristocrats, who were doing badly at the gate anyway, headed south. Lester took them to Spokane, where they became known as the Canaries.

That move left Vancouver as the only Canadian city in the league, and the Seattle Metropolitans emphasized the new foreign look by winning the league championship and then whipping the Canadiens—Lalonde, Georges Vezina, and all—in the Stanley Cup finals. The name of a U.S. city was inscribed on the mug that now traveled abroad for the first time.

However, not enough people there or in Spokane cared, and within a year their teams had gone back up across the border. The Canaries, their feathers badly ruffled, flew back home to Victoria, and the Rosebuds were distributed among the other three teams.

It was in 1917 that Frank Patrick decided to quit as a player, although he was still just thirty-two. He reckoned that he had enough to do as coach, owner, and league president.

That year also marked a change in the life and times of the Patricks' old adversary Sam Lichtenhein.

On January 2, 1918, the Montreal Arena, home of Sam's Wanderers, was destroyed by fire. Already depressed by the war situation that had cut deeply into attendance, Sam decided to fold his operation and the Wanderers were disbanded. A proud era that had begun in 1904 and had been shared by the Redbands' one-time captain, Lester Patrick, was over.

Although Lichtenhein claimed to have lost more than $30,000 on his hockey operation, he was not exactly in dire financial straits. He was a director of twenty-two companies, owned Montreal's International League baseball club as well as the Wanderers, and was said to be worth several million dollars. Still there was a sentimental side to Sam's surrender, and the touch of pathos was not lost on the Patrick brothers, both of whom had known the Wanderers in their great days. When word of Lichtenhein's decision to quit hockey arrived on the Coast, Frank called a meeting of the PCHA directors and moved that the league should make some special recognition of Sam's long service to hockey, even though part of that service was as the league's arch enemy.

It was decided that the league should send him a suitably inscribed silver loving cup.

A handsome trophy was procured, inscribed, and shipped to Montreal. The Canadian press duly reported this generous act and noted that the trophy was en route to its recipient. Weeks went by and no trophy. Frank was puzzled, and then embarrassed when a Montreal *Star* story expressed doubts that the trophy existed. "We queried the railway express company," he explained, "and the people there said that its records showed that the cup had definitely arrived in Montreal, but had disappeared. We wired Lichtenhein apologizing for the fact that the cup was apparently lost, and Sam offered a $100 reward for its recovery.

"The reward put every Montreal fan on the lookout for the trophy, but it wasn't until the spring that it was found. A charwoman on her way to work at the railway offices spied a crate lying in a snowbank at the side of the road. The cup was in the crate, which had apparently fallen from the railway express wagon and had lain there for months, buried in the snow.

"Sam paid the $100 reward and the cup was put on display in the window of Riley Hearn's store on Peel Street. Thousands flocked there to see it, and we got a very nice letter from Sam thanking us for the gesture. We, in turn, wrote back apologizing for the slow delivery."

In Victoria, Lester was back at the old stand with his Aristocrats and Joe Patrick was stirring things up at City Hall. Now an alderman, Joe was off on one of his pet crusades: the preservation of the Sabbath as a day of rest. He was trying to push through a bylaw to prohibit streetcars running on Sundays, but received opposition from an unlikely source: his oldest son.

For the first time, Lester felt compelled to buck the old man. "I'm sorry, Father," he said, "but I think you're going a little too far. After all, some people have to work on Sunday to keep things going."

As Joe harrumphed and muttered, Lester led him gently by the arm to the kitchen. It was Sunday. The lady of the household, Mrs. Joe Patrick, was at the sink, preparing dinner. Later, in accepting the overwhelming rejection of his bylaw proposal, Joe was quite gracious.

On Saturday, July 6, 1918, the Patricks picked up their morning paper to see a big black headline mourning the death of Art Ross. Ross, pronounced as one of hockey's greatest players, was reported killed in a road accident near Boston. The story contained a lengthy tribute and chronicled the deceased's long-time friendship with "the famous Pacific Coast magnates," Lester and Frank Patrick. Both Lester and Frank were contacted, and both expressed their deep shock over the loss of a lifetime friend. A telegram of condolence was sent to Ross's relatives. A similar telegram was received the same day from Newsy Lalonde, who was in Quebec City.

The next day there was another headline. It read: "Art Ross Arrives in Montreal. He Is Alive and Well."

That story reported that "Mr. Ross, who had been presumed dead, had arrived home in Montreal with the remains of his nephew, Hugh Ross, for burial on Monday. Hugh Ross died of a fractured skull in a motorcycle accident on a New England road . . . each had been riding his own bike, and Hugh had swerved to avoid a lumber rig, causing him to crash into an embankment."

Art had also tumbled, but suffered only slight injuries. He said later that his greatest shock, apart from the death of his nephew, was his receipt of the Patrick wire lamenting his death.

Otherwise in that early autumn of 1918, the future looked increasingly grim for the Coast hockey enterprise that still lay deep in the shadow of the war, but then came the signing of the Armistice.

"We were just about ready to give up," wrote Frank, "but now with players returning from the Armed Forces and a feeling of optimism abroad, we went to work with renewed hope and vigor. With Portland out and our three-team league now consisting of Vancouver, Victoria, and Seattle, we were ready to embark on what were five of our finest years."

As league president, Frank had one difficult and depressing duty to perform in the spring of 1919, when the Seattle Metropolitans hosted the Canadiens in another series for the Stanley Cup Championship. After five games of a series that had all of Seattle in an uproar, the two teams were dead even with two wins and a tie each. The Seattle Arena was jammed to the exits for the sixth and deciding game, but several players were reported ill with the flu. A world-wide influenza epidemic that had begun in Europe had spread to the Coast.

In the fifth game that had ended in a bitterly fought 3–3 tie, three of the Canadiens and one of the Seattle players, Joe Hall, just barely made it to the finish, looking desperately weak in the final minutes. Bad Joe Hall, the old war horse who had survived more than a dozen campaigns dating back before the playing days of the Patricks, was near collapse. He had to be carried to the dressing room and was then taken to the hospital. He was soon joined there by the Canadiens' Newsy Lalonde, Didier Pitre, Jack McDonald, and then their manager, George Kennedy.

Frank Patrick was in charge of the series, and had to make a decision. He went to visit Kennedy at the hospital, and on hearing that the Arena had been sold out for the sixth game, Kennedy insisted that it should be played. Frank disagreed. "I announced to the press that the game was canceled and that the series would be called a draw. The Cup would be retained by the current holders, the Toronto Arenas. I phoned the Seattle Arena and ordered the ticket money refunded. The Seattle club backed Kennedy and objected strongly to my decision, but it stuck. I discovered later that at least half of the Seattle team were suffering from the flu."

Ten days later, Joe Hall died.

Kennedy's own flu attack was the start of a spell of ill-health that was ended a little more than two years later by his death at his home in Montreal.

The next season was a lackluster one for the Patricks as Vancouver and Victoria languished behind Seattle in the three-team league race, and the Metropolitans went on to lose to Ottawa in the Stanley Cup final. Attendance had again dropped off, and Lester in particular was in dire need of an exciting new attraction for his club, which was now called the Cougars. He got his man when he landed Frank Fredrickson, a twenty-six-year-old forward from Winnipeg.

Throughout the years, Lester and Frank had brought some brilliant rookies out to begin their pro careers on the Coast, but Fredrickson was considered the cream of the crop.

Said Lester of his first season, "For natural talent and all-round skills I can compare him only to Fred Taylor and Mickey Mackay."

Even Taylor, the game's designated number one star who was then in the twilight of his career and always defensive about his own great reputation, chimed in with his view, "Fredrickson is as fine a player as I've seen. He is fast, shifty, and smart, and has a wonderfully quick shot."

Having signed perhaps the best-looking rookie ever to come into the league at a time when its finest veteran, Taylor, was about to bow out, Lester proceeded to make the most of the situation. The first confrontation between the new star and the fading meteor was set for New Year's Day 1921, and it was billed as a battle between the World's Greatest Professional and the World's Greatest Amateur. That lavish billing was part of the bait used to lure Fredrickson away from Winnipeg and out of the clutching grasp of the East's newly named National Hockey League.

Apart from being a hockey player of outstanding talent, Fredrickson was also an adventurer, and Lester liked that. They had something in common there, although Fredrickson's exploits had been well beyond the range of Lester's travels. An Icelander by birth, Fredrickson had come to Winnipeg as a small boy, had grown up to captain the University of Manitoba hockey team, then left after his second year to go overseas with the Canadian Army's 196th Battalion.

On his arrival in England he was transferred to the Royal Flying Corps and won his wings at a training unit in Egypt. While returning for active service in France, Fredrickson's ship, the *Leasowe Castle,* was torpedoed by a German submarine and the passengers and crew took to the lifeboats. They were picked up twelve hours later in the Indian Ocean by a Japanese destroyer.

In 1919, after a year's flying service in France, Fredrickson returned to Winnipeg, recruited a rag-tag team called the Falcons, was refused entry into the Manitoba Amateur League, organized his own independent three-team loop, and then hammered the Manitoba League champions in a challenge game. Fredrickson himself was sensational. Two weeks later, his Falcons drubbed Toronto Varsity to win the prized Allan Cup, emblematic of the Canadian Amateur Championship. The Falcons then left to represent Canada at the 1920 Winter Olympics in Antwerp and won in a breeze over the U.S. team. All but one of that team, Allan ("Huck") Woodman, were first- or second-generation Icelanders.

With that background, Fredrickson was a prime target for Lester Patrick, who not only knew a good hockey player when he saw one but also knew the value of good newspaper copy. When Fredrickson arrived back from Antwerp there was a letter from Lester, offering a job in Victoria "at what I'm sure you will agree is an excellent figure."

But Fredrickson was no sooner back in Winnipeg than he was gone again, to Iceland. There, he signed a five-year contract with the Icelandic Aero Company to study the feasibility of air transport in that remote region, especially in the area of development of flight for fishing exploration and postal services. Lack of funds forced cancellation of this contract after just six months, but not before the star of the Winnipeg Falcons had proved that air surveillance could be a great aid in locating schools of fish, and had staked out several suitable airport sites for a national transport system. The idea of sighting fish from the air eventually became a common practice, and three of the airport sites he surveyed became part of Iceland's air routes.

Fredrickson again went back to Winnipeg and found yet another letter from Lester, who was becoming as stubborn as he was impatient. Fredrickson read the letter, and then joined the Canadian Air Force.

Lester accepted the challenge. He went to Winnipeg to talk to Fredrickson personally. The pitch and the charm didn't work, and Lester returned to Victoria without his man. Four months later, Lester was in Winnipeg again, and this time Fredrickson succumbed.

The surrender took place in an unlikely setting: the grand ballroom of Winnipeg's Fort Garry Hotel, where on his nights off from his Air-Force duties, Fredrickson played the violin in the hotel's five-piece orchestra. Lester had reserved a table up front near the band, had dinner, and then stayed on to listen as Frank fiddled happily away at such soulful ballads as "Ma, He's Making Eyes at Me," "K-K-K-Katy," and "The Sheik of Araby."

After each solo, Lester applauded discreetly but generously, and during a break between dance sets he invited the violinist over to his table.

"Frank," he said admiringly, "I never knew you had so much talent. I wonder if you'd do me a favor?"

Fredrickson was beaming.

"Certainly, Mr. Patrick."

"Call me Lester."

"Okay, Lester. What's the favor?"

"I wonder if you could play me my favorite song. It's called 'Good-bye, Dolly, I Must Leave You.' Do you happen to know it?"

"Well," said Frank, "I don't know if the boys remember that one. But what about something else, like, say, 'Ain't We Got Fun.' It's new and it's a beaut."

"My second favorite," beamed Lester. "That's a great song."

Frank not only played a couple of choruses of "Ain't We Got Fun," but also sang a chorus in a croaky baritone that barely reached beyond the table where Lester sat with a paternal smile, gently fingering the contract he had tucked away in his vest pocket. The contract wasn't needed. Later that evening, Frank Fredrickson, pilot, adventurer, world-traveler, violinist and crooner, shook hands on a $2,700-a-year pact to play for Lester in Victoria. Hockey, of course, not the violin.

Having resigned from the Canadian Air Force, Fredrickson was in Victoria in good time for the highly ballyhooed showdown with the old guy, Cyclone Taylor, on New Year's Day 1921. The World's Greatest Amateur scored two goals while the World's Greatest Professional was shut out as the Victoria Cougars defeated Vancouver 5–3. Although he had played brilliantly in that night's losing cause, it was the beginning of the end for Taylor. This was to be his last season after seventeen years in pro hockey as the game's most exciting performer.

There is no doubt that the flamboyant Icelander had made a great hit with the Victoria fans, but their sentimental favorite was still the man Lester had brought out a decade ago from the ranks of Sam Lichtenhein's Wanderers.

Moose Johnson was now thirty-five, a battle-scarred veteran of eighteen campaigns and nearing the end of his career. After four seasons in Portland, he had returned to the Victoria fold, and on the evening of March 4, 1921, he was the designated star of Moose Johnson Night at the Victoria Arena. The building that

had made hockey history ten years before as the cornerstone of
the Patricks' hockey empire was jammed to capacity for the rare
testimonial to the West's most durable player.

A rugged, completely honest tradesman who always gave his
last ounce and then dug down for a little more, Moose was regarded as something special. By players, coaches, and owners, as
well as the fans. Nobody held him in higher esteem than did
Lester, who had admired him as a player and a person ever since
they took to the ice together in Montreal thirteen years before. It
was Lester who had arranged to stage his friend's Night at the Victoria Arena.

Using a stick that was noted as the longest in hockey, Moose
was the game's most tenacious poke-checker—the most tenacious
checker, period. Taking him on, as dozens of opponents had discovered, was like taking on a piece of The Rock. The fans had
seen him sustain a broken jaw, put on an improvised mask that
offered scant protection, and come right back out onto the ice.
They had seen him almost blinded by a flying puck, retire to be
bandaged, and return within minutes to resume play. Right in that
Victoria Arena, he had suffered a broken nose (twice), a broken
cheekbone, broken arm, plus countless cuts and gashes that had
required more than sixty stitches. (Lester himself, a tough player
in his own right, had fifty-five stitches etched into his hide.)

Once asked to explain the art of hockey as he saw it, Johnson
scratched his head and said, "Well, there's the puck, and there's
the net. The idea is to get the puck into the net." Also to stop it
from getting into the net, which was his specialty.

Johnson was immensely touched by the tribute that had his
name up on the arena marquee. He himself bought five hundred
$.50 tickets for Victoria youngsters who were to attend the game
as his guests. When a huge crowd of kids arrived at the arena to
claim their tickets, Moose, who was never known as loquacious,
felt compelled to say something to them.

Asking them to gather round, he said, "Boys, I just want to say
a few words while you're quiet, because when I start giving out
these things there's going to be a real holler. You boys are all
young and getting to the age where you'll be involved in athletics.
Now, when you jump into a game, don't forget that above all
things you must go into it prepared to win. Don't ever figure that

you're beaten before you start, because if you do you'll get an awful trimming. Give the best that's in you. Don't be too reckless, but don't be afraid to take chances. And play clean. Don't come out with the deliberate intention of getting somebody. Play clean, play hard, and play to win."

As speeches go, it wasn't a classic, but it was vintage Moose Johnson: no frills, forthright, and from the heart.

And then a few hours later he went out onto the ice to provide his five hundred kids with a demonstration of his philosophy. The game itself was a regularly scheduled contest against Seattle. First, there was a ceremony at center ice at which Johnson was presented with a cup inscribed with the words: "Presented to Ernie "Moose" Johnson, by his pals, the kids of Victoria, B.C." Skating out with the cup to make the presentation was one of those kids, five-year-old Murray Patrick. Then a fan jumped over the boards and handed Moose a set of diamond cuff links with a card that read: "From your fans in Victoria." Referee Mickey Ion skated over to the Victoria bench and returned with another cup, inscribed with thanks from the league. The ladies in the crowd added a huge Kewpie doll and a birthday cake. The Victoria Police Commissioner presented a bouquet for "Mrs. Moose."

After sixty minutes of tough, rousing play, the score was tied at 4–4. Three twenty-minute overtime periods later, the score was still tied. When the gong sounded at the end of the third overtime, it was past midnight and Johnson's five hundred boys were still in their seats. The game had already established an all-time record for length, but this bit of history had taken its toll on the players.

This, remember, was still the day of seven-man hockey played by a nine-man squad. The players of both teams were stretched out on the benches and floors of their dressing rooms, completely exhausted. Lester looked around his own dressing room and then went to the Seattle room to talk to goalie Hap Holmes, who, in the absence of coach Pete Muldoon, was in charge of the team.

Both men agreed that it would be inhuman to ask the players to go out for another overtime.

"Hap," said Lester, "I think we should pack it up."

"You'd better ask Moose," said Holmes. "It's his night."

"I did," Patrick answered, with a smile. "He says it's fine with him. And when the Moose has had enough, it's enough."

An announcement was made stating that the game was called, and if the tie result were to have any effect on the league standings, it would be replayed. The fans, themselves exhausted after one of the most exciting games ever seen in the West, filed quietly out. Nobody asked for a refund and nobody complained. Least of all Moose Johnson's five hundred kids, who probably hadn't been up that late before in their lives.

Nine days later, in the same arena, Cyclone Taylor played his last game. He went out that night as he had come in twenty-five years before as a thirteen-year-old junior playing his first game in organized hockey: with a hat trick. With that three-goal swan song against the Cougars, Taylor had wrapped a seventeen-year pro career during which he had played in five leagues and had been selected to the all-star team in every league, every year. It was a record hardly likely to be equalled.

After that game, Taylor and the two Patricks had a quiet dinner together at the Empress Hotel, and the next day Taylor put away his skates and went to work at his desk in the immigration building on the Vancouver waterfront.

That PCHA season also marked the end of another playing career of note: that of Lester Patrick, who quietly announced his retirement. At thirty-eight, a year older than Taylor, he was in fine physical condition, but was too involved to face up to the grueling demands of another season in uniform. Unlike Taylor, Lester would be back to answer a few emergency calls, one of which would lead to a dramatic episode that has become part of the folklore of sport.

The next season, yet another of the old guard stepped down when Moose Johnson told Lester he was through. The end had been hastened by a shuddering body check during a game in Seattle. Getting up off the ice, he had caught a stick over the eye and he was taken to the bench, bleeding heavily. Lester had to have him held and his skates removed to prevent him from going back out again. A week later, Johnson played his last game.

As the old boys moved out, the new ones moved in, and that year a new one, Jack Adams, serving his third season with the Millionaires, won the league scoring title. Adams was another example of the fertility of the Coast League as a proving ground not just for great players but also for great coaches and executives. A quarter of a century later, when he was well into his more than two decades of service as general manager and guiding genius of the Detroit Red Wings, he told a Detroit reporter, "Managing a hockey club is easy, if you've been properly educated. I had the best teacher in the world: Frank Patrick."

The next season, Adams was joined in Vancouver by another outstanding player who also learned a thing or two from Frank about managing before testing his skill in the new NHL: Frank Boucher. Ironically, it was Frank's 1923 recruit who would one day take over as manager of the New York Rangers as Lester Patrick moved grudgingly aside and into the vice-president's office. Long before that, though, and before Boucher entered the Coast League scene, Lester got his first emergency call to arms in a game against Vancouver. The date was January 9, 1922.

In the second period, the Victoria goalie was banished for ten minutes for fighting with Mickey Mackay, whereupon Lester donned the pads and went into the net. Almost immediately he was forced to face a penalty shot by Jack Adams. Adams roared in, blistered one toward the top corner, but Lester snared it with his glove while sprawled on the ice. For the next several minutes he was bombarded with shots from the Vancouver forwards but went to his knees time and again to smother the shots or pluck them out of the air. Just before he was relieved by Fowler, he was beaten by Adams, but he got an ovation when he left the ice.

The Millionaires got their 4–0 shutout, and for his ten-minute emergency stint with so much of the time spent on his knees, Lester was dubbed "The Praying Colonel."

There was another new name in the league the following year when the Vancouver Millionaires became the Maroons. In a more substantive change, the Patricks finally followed the eastern Canada example and went to six-man hockey, eliminating the rover.

The player of the year was Fredrickson, who came of age as a full-fledged star with 41 goals over the 30-game schedule. A source of pride and joy to Lester while he was on the ice, Fredrickson was at times what Lester called "a pain in the neck" elsewhere. The trouble with Fredrickson, who was a very likable, intelligent, witty, and literate chap, was that he was also garrulous.

To quote Lester again, "That man could talk the hind leg off a moose. In mating season."

One day, Lester called Frank into his office, gestured for him to sit down, and said, "Okay, Frank. From now on we have an arrangement. You like to talk to me about various things, so you can do that. You can come in here once every day and I'll give you exactly thirty minutes, during which time you can say anything you like. Okay, Frank, you can start right now. You've got thirty minutes."

That seemed to work, although after a week of this Lester was heard to complain that although Fredrickson never talked past his thirty-minute limit, he managed to get in at least forty-five-minutes' worth.

All was forgiven when Fredrickson checked in with his bag of 41 goals, but then he aggravated Lester by turning right around and marching to the beat of another drummer, his new bride, Bea. Bea, a pretty Winnipeg girl, was homesick, so after the season ended, Frank helped her pack and off they went, back to Winnipeg. They rented business premises at the corner of Maryland and Sargent, Frank splurged his salary savings on stock, and they became the proprietors of "Frank Fredrickson's Melody Shop."

The senior partner then wrote to Lester telling him the news and informing him that he was considering retirement from hockey in order to devote himself to the musical arts. Lester took the next train to Winnipeg and visited the Fredricksons in their new establishment. He found his hockey star behind the counter, while Bea, an accomplished classical pianist with a Toronto Conservatory Degree, was out front playing sheet music for the patrons. "Actually," Lester admitted to Bea some years later, "you were very good."

"I was versatile," replied Bea modestly. "I remember the two most asked for new numbers were 'Cut Yourself a Piece of Cake and Make Yourself at Home,' and 'Yes, We Have No Bananas.' I played them quite well."

However, at the time, it was all sour notes to Lester, who seemed about to lose his star attraction.

"Frank," he said, "you're crazy to give up hockey and stay here. I'll bet you $100 this business won't last a year."

To quote from Frank's reminiscences: "He was wrong. A year later, we were still in business and I won the $100. Unfortunately, we'd lost $2,400 on the store."

But by that time, Fredrickson, who was crazy like a fox, was back playing hockey in Victoria, finishing one goal back of Mickey Mackay in the next season's scoring race.

That scoring duel was a prelude to the Patricks' last hurrah in a league that was now on its last legs. The handwriting was on the wall when the Seattle Metropolitans failed to show for the start of the 1924–25 season. The landlords of the Seattle rink announced that the site was needed for the construction of a garage, and that the lease, which had one more year to run, would not be renewed. The league was given the option of staying on for one more season or taking a $10,000 cash settlement and getting out now.

Noting that the Seattle attendance was terrible anyway, president Frank Patrick advised taking the $10,000 and getting out.

A couple of swings of the wrecking ball and down tumbled the walls of the building that had housed the first Stanley Cup Championship ever won by a U.S. city.

With the Seattle franchise down the drain and just Vancouver and Victoria left, the PCHA closed the books on its turbulent twelve-year history and merged its tattered remains with the four-team Western Canada League, a struggling organization that was heading into its fourth season.

The new WCHL lineup now consisted of Calgary, Regina, Saskatoon, Edmonton, Vancouver, and Victoria, but it was just a case of drawing the wagons together for the last stand. With the East's revitalized National Hockey League going international on a big scale, major league hockey in the West was clearly doomed. New franchises had been granted for a second team in Montreal to be called the Maroons, and for one in Boston, hailing the birth of the Bruins. Another franchise had been set aside for a New York bootlegger king named Bill Dwyer, pending the completion of the new Madison Square Garden, and still other U.S. cities were lining up to get in on the new hockey boom.

Grocery-chain tycoon Charles Weston Adams was the owner of the new Boston franchise, and for his coach and manager he hired Art Ross, who thus became the first grad of the old Westmount street gang to move into a position of power in the new NHL. Stuck with a motley first-year roster, Ross was already on the prowl for quality players. As he well knew, many of these were out in the Western Canada League, so what better than to contact his old chums, the Patrick brothers.

He wrote to Frank to say that he was in the market for some good hockey players and would appreciate anything Frank might do along that line. Frank wrote back a nice polite letter that said, in effect: Not yet. Ross did not push the proposition, but did suggest that they get together in maybe a year or two to talk things over. That was fine with the Patricks, who were already plotting survival with honor, plus a few dollars cash.

Meanwhile, there was this first season in the WCHL, which as far as the caliber of the players was concerned was certainly no rinky-dink operation. The Saskatoon Sheiks were led by the eternal Newsy Lalonde, a historic landmark who was just off an amazing league-leading 29-goal season. The Sheiks also had a promising goalie named George Hainsworth and a winger named Bill Cook. Regina had Dick Irvin and a raw but rambunctious rookie defenseman named Eddie Shore. The Edmonton lineup boasted Barney Stanley, Duke Keats, and Bullet-Joe Simpson. Calgary had Merv Dutton and Harry Oliver.

All these names had one thing in common: they would all be eventually inscribed on the wall of the Hockey Hall of Fame. Two, Shore and Cook, would be numbered among the very best in history at their positions. Add the Patricks' own crop of future Hall of Famers in the persons of Mickey Mackay, Frank Boucher, Jack Walker, Frank Foyston, and Frank Fredrickson, and it was easy to understand why the WCHL would soon become the NHL's happy hunting ground.

In that first WCHL season, Victoria finished third behind Calgary and Saskatoon, with Vancouver two notches back behind Edmonton. However, the big story of that 1924–25 season was not the early domination of the prairie clubs but the stirring comeback staged by Lester's Cougars to earn a berth in the Stanley Cup finals and then whip the Montreal Canadiens for the championship.

That ultimate victory was especially sweet to the Patricks because it served to accent the superiority of the rules code they had developed and installed in their Coast League. The Cougars would not have had their chance against the Canadiens had it not been for the play-off formula Frank had dreamed up five years before on the night boat from Vancouver to Seattle.

After finishing third in the league race they had clawed their way through two frenetic play-off rounds to earn the showdown with the eastern champions. It was the first classic example, oft repeated since, of a team dogged for whatever reason by early failure cashing in on a second chance to prove itself. Then in the Cup confrontation with the Canadiens, it was the shrewd deployment of two other pieces of Patrick legislation that did the visiting easterners in. Game one of the best-of-five championship series was the perfect example.

With the eastern and western codes to be alternated throughout the series, the host Cougars chose to open with the western rules. The only glaring difference was in the West's use of the forward pass in the attacking zone, plus the use of multiple substitution with the game in progress.

With a powerful attack built on the searing speed of his new young star Howie Morenz and a rugged defense led by the aging but redoubtable Sprague Cleghorn, Canadiens' manager, Leo Dandurand, professed to be little concerned over the rules differences. Leo's apparent bland indifference was fine with Lester Patrick, who for a full week had drilled his club in perfecting the use of the forward pass over the enemy blue line. He had also worked hard on the substitution of lines on the fly.

In the first game, to quote a stunned Montreal reporter: "The westerners simply skated the Canadiens dizzy . . . the blazing speed of Morenz was negated, and they just couldn't handle the Cougars' non-stop attack . . ."

At game's end, Morenz and his speedy linemates Aurel Joliat and Billy Boucher were gasping like gaffed salmon from trying to keep pace with the fresh lines that kept flooding out over the boards. The exhausted Canadiens goalie, Georges Vezina, who would confirm his own prodigious stamina by siring twenty-three children before his tragic death from tuberculosis at the age of thirty-nine, said that he had never seen so many flying forwards, nor so many flying pucks. That 5–2 rout by the Cougars was considerably more one-sided than the score indicates.

The second game was played in Vancouver, where more than 11,000 fans stormed into the 10,500-seat arena to see the Cana-

diens lose again, this time by a score of 3–1, while playing under
their own rules. Morenz, headed for what was to be one of
hockey's most memorable careers, managed to salvage some ves-
tige of pride for the outclassed easterners. Back again in Victoria,
the aptly named Stratford Streak who had stepped into the flying
boots of Cyclone Taylor defied the western rules code with a hat
trick that gave his club a 4–2 decision in game three, but the damage had been done. Worn to a frazzle, the Canadiens surrendered
the Cup when they were demolished 6–1 in the deciding contest.

The Cougars were now the hockey champions of the world, but
to the Patricks the honor had a special and very personal meaning. Frank's Millionaires had won the Cup in 1915 in the first vin-
dication of their bold and much maligned venture, and now, in the
twilight of their little Coast empire, Lester's Cougars had completed the family sweep.

At the final whistle, Lester climbed over the boards to stand
with Frank and his father and mother as the Cougars made their
victory skate around the rink with the silver mug held aloft. "It
was the first time," Lester had said, "that I ever saw my father
give in to his emotions. He was a very warm and sentimental man,
but he always kept himself under control. There were tears in his
eyes. Of course, he turned away."

Joe Patrick was now sixty-eight, still strong, straight and robust,
still a crusty pillar of the church, the Rotary Club, and a regular
playing member of a volleyball league down at the Victoria
YMCA. He had served three terms as alderman, had been defeated in a bid to become mayor, and was now content with his
role as patriarch of his burgeoning brood. All of his children were
now married, including Ted, who had wed a widow in Seattle.

Joe remained a crusty martinet and a puritan, especially when
it came to the demon rum, but he had retained his genius for
finding the exception to prove the virtue.

The exception in this case was the family's second Stanley Cup
Championship, and when the case of French champagne he had
ordered from the wine cellars of the Empress Hotel arrived at the
Cougars' dressing room for the victory party, a visibly impressed
Frank Fredrickson murmured, "Good God, Lester. This must
have set the old man back at least sixty bucks!" A few minutes
later Joe himself sat on a dressing-room bench smiling happily as

corks popped and magnums of Piper Heidsieck sprayed the premises.

There was just one more season to play before what an eastern journal had once derisively called "Joe and the kids" closed shop on the Coast, but with big things brewing in the East it would be a hectic one.

It was plain now that the power pendulum had swung back East. The NHL now had Bill Dwyer's New York Americans ensconced in the new Madison Square Garden rink on Eighth Avenue, and the Maroons and Canadiens were co-tenants in their own new beauty, the 11,000-seat Forum in Montreal. In addition, another U.S. city, Pittsburgh, had joined the league, which now had seven teams.

The Patricks got some hint as to the clout wielded by American money when Dwyer moved the entire roster of the 1925 NHL Hamilton Tigers to New York to stock his franchise, which was under the managership of Tommy Gorman. The Hamilton players had been suspended by the league at the end of the 1924–25 season when they refused to withdraw demands for an extra $200 each in play-off money, and the franchise had folded. The players were still under league suspension when they were heisted by Dwyer and stuffed into the gaudy, star-spangled uniforms of his Americans.

The transfer was illegal, but no matter. The deal was quietly approved. The total cost to Dwyer was $75,000, little more than that of a truckload or two of the Canadian whiskey he imported on a more regular basis. But of course he had to smuggle the whiskey.

The power merchants were in, and the Patricks and their ilk were out, and nobody knew this better than the family that had a dollar or two at stake in this dilemma. Frank was already working on a salvage plan even as the patchwork Western Canada League embarked on its final season.

Lester was also working on a plan. Leaving the more complex challenge of survival to his brother, he had his sights set on a second Stanley Cup Championship as a final glorious swan song for their fading empire. The bid would be a brave one and it would feature yet another comeback story starring the venerable figure of Lester himself.

Now forty-two, with streaks of gray flecking the thick shock of hair that would soon beget him the nickname of The Silver Fox, Lester hadn't skated in anger for three seasons. True, he had turned up in that dramatic ten-minute emergency stint in the Victoria net the previous season, but that was as the Praying Colonel, a role played within the tiny confines of the goal crease. But here in early December 1925 with the Cougars down to just one defenseman because of injuries, Lester shrugged, laced up his boots, grabbed a stick and went out to help.

After a shaky start in his first game in Calgary, the old boy got his legs back and set up Frank Fredrickson for the winning goal. A week later against the powerful Edmonton lineup he had two assists in a 4–2 victory, plus a direct hit on Eddie Shore, the young hard-rock who was already being hailed as the toughest, meanest defenseman in hockey. Eddie, who had come to Edmonton in a roundabout deal with Portland, figured to no more than toy with the forty-two-year-old from Victoria before, if necessary, dispatching him to the infirmary. But it didn't work out that way. Instead, the old crock caught Shore with a crackling body check that sent the cocky youth, eighteen years Lester's junior, off the ice on a stretcher.

Portland, back in hockey for this one season, was next. There, Lester tied the game with an unassisted goal and then set up Fredrickson again for the winner. Then before a hostile but admiring crowd in Saskatoon, he stick-handled through the entire Saskatoon team and beat goalie George Hainsworth with the winning shot in overtime.

Several games later, it was the Cougars' ageless defenseman who assured his team of a play-off berth when he again netted the winning goal, against Vancouver. That victory gave the Cougars a streak of six straight, and during that spell Lester had scored five of the club's twenty-six goals. Paired with Clem Loughlin, he was the bulwark of a defense that had allowed just seven goals in return.

The boss was still out there for the first game of the play-offs against Saskatoon, and he received a thunderous ovation as he skated out to his post. The Cougars came from behind to salvage a 3–3 tie in that game, but they lost their ace defenseman in the process. Lester had to leave the ice midway through the second period when a stick swung by the Sheiks' Cy Denenny broke his thumb. The Cougars now had another defenseman ready to play, so Lester, his thumb in a cast, put away his skates and resumed his place behind the Victoria bench. "The amazing old gaffer," chronicled a Saskatoon bard, "has at long last played his last shift."

Well, not quite. But those twenty-one games played in relief by a forty-two-year-old following a three-year layoff must surely represent one of the more amazing comebacks in the history of sport, and name your pastime.

Now, having personally shown the way into the play-offs, Lester settled back to watch his team win the league title and the right to travel to Montreal for the Stanley Cup round against the NHL champions.

It wasn't until the Cougars were halfway across the continent, rolling West in their Pullman, that they learned the result of the NHL play-off battle between Ottawa and the Maroons. As a Cup series in the new 11,000-seat Montreal Forum would just about double their cut, the Cougars were pulling for the Maroons to win. They did. Frank Patrick brought the word from the station telegrapher during a brief stop in Winnipeg.

Frank was along with the party on a special mission that was known only to Lester. The players had no inkling of the carefully laid plan that would soon make them chattels in the biggest mass sale of players in sports history.

6

TALES
OF MANHATTAN

The best-of-five Montreal series went just four games and the Maroons scored shutouts in three of them. A cat-quick goalie named Clint Benedict and a fearsome young defenseman named Nels Stewart were well-nigh impregnable as the book was closed on the Victoria Cougars and the fifteen-year chronicle of the Patrick brothers and their rebel empire in the West.

If Lester had harbored any doubts as to the wisdom of closing shop, they were dispelled during this series. "Frank," he said back at the hotel, "these easterners are out of our league. Some of these Maroons are making close to $10,000 a year, and the owners are throwing their money around like confetti. I dropped into the Maroons' dressing room tonight and there was Stewart standing with a wad of bills big enough to choke a horse. Somebody had walked in and slipped him $1,000 as a bonus for his play in tonight's game. My goodness, Frank, it's immoral. We can't compete with nonsense like that."

Frank agreed. That was why he was in Montreal.

His own account of his mission, written nearly two decades later, tells the story about as well as it can be told.

"With our top salary range of about $4,000 we were already squeezing our population draw to its limits, and there was no way we could keep good hockey players in the West beyond maybe one more season.

"I'd been wrestling with this dilemma for months, and I knew we had only two options. We could ease our inevitable losses by selling our better players—we had already been offered as much as $15,000 for some of them—but I was firmly set against this course. It would reduce our league to minor status, and we still wouldn't have enough money to stay afloat. It was going to be sell all or none.

"I told this to the other WCHL owners, and before going East I got five of the six clubs to entrust their players to me, to do with what I thought best. As Saskatoon had already given an option on its players to the Montreal Maroons director, Tom Duggan, for $60,000, they were not part of the arrangement. My plan was to merge the remaining five rosters into three strong teams and then sell the teams intact for $100,000 each."

The three teams were to be the bulk of the Portland Rosebuds and the Victoria Cougars, plus the pick of the best players from Vancouver, Calgary, and Edmonton. It was a bold plan, with what in those days was considered a pretty large price tag, but the timing seemed excellent.

Frank knew that a New Yorker named Colonel John Hammond was about to acquire a franchise to share the Madison Square Garden premises with Bill Dwyer's Americans; and that Detroit and Chicago were both after franchises. They would all be looking for quality players, as would Boston's Art Ross, who had C. F. Adams' grocery-chain millions behind him in Boston.

The prospects for a fast sale looked good, although by Frank's own admission, he was in a "very delicate" position.

"Our league contracts had no reserve clause, so we had no option on our players' services in any subsequent year. We may have had some kind of protection under an inter-league agreement, but I'm glad we were never put to a test."

He was thus peddling property that nobody owned. Any one of the players could have made his own deal as a free agent, but there was an obvious reluctance to make a case of it. Fortunately for Frank and his Western League colleagues there was as yet no such thing as a player's agent. Just one Alan Eagleson could have queered the whole deal.

In Montreal, the Patricks checked into the plush Windsor Hotel along with other visiting owners and directors, and it was there that Frank, who was playing his hand very close to the chest, got his first nibble. They were in their suite with Victoria *Times* reporter Archie Wills when Art Ross walked in, struck up a friendly conversation and then casually inquired about the health of a few Western League players. He seemed particularly solicitous about the well-being of Eddie Shore, Duke Keats, and Frank Fredrickson.

He expressed a special admiration for Fredrickson.

"No deal," Frank said, smiling.

"I haven't suggested any," Ross replied. "But I will."

No deal was made at that time, but the wheels had begun turning and Frank had an important ally. Ross listened to the sale plan, agreed that there might be some benefit there for his Bruins, and said he would help swing the $300,000 deal. He seemed quite confident that it could be done.

"Let me say right now," Frank explained, "that without Ross's support from there on in, we never would have succeeded."

Ross seemed quite sure that with Hammond building his franchise from scratch, New York would be happy to ante up a mere $100,000 for a team of proven players. But the Colonel was as mean and stubborn as a drill sergeant, and would prove to be a very tough nut to crack. This stubborn streak was compounded when Hammond engaged Conn Smythe, to put his team together. Smythe, a young, hockey-smart battler from Toronto, was as tough as he was intractable.

Frank never got to talk to Hammond in Montreal, but he and Lester did get to spend an evening with another New Yorker of some influence. His name was on the message left at the hotel desk, addressed to the Patricks and announcing that a Mr. Tex Rickard would like the pleasure of their company over a drink in his suite. The Patricks accepted the invitation, and although there is no record of that little tête-à-tête, there seems no doubt that it got them a friend in high places. And as far as the U.S. sporting set was concerned in those days, nobody walked in higher places than did George Lewis ("Tex") Rickard.

Born in Kansas but raised in the Lone Star State, Rickard was part carnie barker, part adventurer, part hustler, but all promoter.

As one of the sights of New York City in the era known as the Roaring Twenties, he liked to sport a jaunty straw hat and black bow tie and was rarely seen without a well-stuffed cigar-holder clenched in his teeth. As a youth, he had operated saloons in the gold-boom towns of Nevada and the Yukon and then used his $30,000 stake to get into the fight-promoting business. He staged the 1906 world lightweight title fight between Joe Gans and Battling Nelson in Goldfield, Nevada, and then the Jack Johnson-Jim Jeffries world heavyweight title brawl in Reno.

With his original stake more than doubled, he proceeded to blow it all on an ill-fated cattle-raising venture in Paraguay. By 1911 he was in New York running boxing at the old Madison Square Garden. He was put out of business when prizefighting was temporarily outlawed in New York State, but he turned up again in 1918 with a beetle-browed young heavyweight named Jack Dempsey under his wing.

The partnership of Tex and the Manassa Mauler is of another legend, but suffice it to say that with Dempsey on his arm, Rickard became sport's premier promoter. In the so-called Golden Age of Sport dominated by the likes of Dempsey, Babe Ruth, Bill Tilden, Bobby Jones, and Walter Hagen, Rickard's name was as big as any. It was Rickard's promotional guile that had built the new Madison Square Garden that would house the New York Americans and the New York Rangers, a team that would first be known as "Tex's Rangers."

The Patricks knew all about this background when they adjourned to Rickard's suite in Montreal's Windsor Hotel, and they were properly impressed.

The only reference on record concerning that meeting was in an observation made long after by Lester, in a chat with a New York reporter, "It was my first meeting with Mr. Rickard, and what impressed me most about the man was his style. The man certainly had style."

So, in a different fashion, did Lester, and it was natural that the two of them should hit it off at first sight, even though Rickard blandly admitted that he didn't know "a damned thing" about ice hockey. Nor did he then, or even later, particularly care for the game, other than as a means of making money. It was the latter qualification that got an ice rink into the new Madison Square

Garden and thus made the Americans and the Rangers possible, not to mention Lester's eventual reign as boss of the Broadway Blues.

An ice rink was not in the original plans for the new Garden, and this was a studied oversight entirely due to Rickard's disinterest in the foreign game. His view was important, as he was the man who recruited a consortium of millionaires to finance the $5-million project. Among Tex's angels were the circus tycoon, John Ringling North; the auto magnate, Walter P. Chrysler; and the wealthy financier, Kermit Roosevelt. They too had little aesthetic interest in the Canadian pastime as part of their new emporium's bill of fare.

Had it not been for the wiles of Frank Duggan, the Montreal Maroons director who was said to be a partner in Dwyer's thriving bootlegging business, there might never have been a Madison Square Garden ice rink.

In the late winter of 1925, with construction already started on the new arena, Duggan cajoled Rickard into coming North with Dwyer to watch a game in the Forum between the Canadiens and Ottawa. Rickard grudgingly consented to make the trip, and brought along a bright young Manhattan scribe named Bob Considine. As Rickard liked a drink just as well as Duggan and Dwyer, a pre-game cocktail party was arranged. By the time Rickard arrived at the Forum, he was in great good spirits.

He was in even greater good spirits a little later, after getting a look at the Canadiens' Howie Morenz in action. The mercurial Howie was having one of his better nights, meaning that he was positively dazzling, and Rickard was thrilled right out of his pearl-gray spats. He couldn't keep his eyes off the fellow.

After a while, Duggan said, "Well, Tex, what do you think of the game?"

Tex bit into his cigar-holder, looked at Morenz, surveyed the packed house, looked at Morenz again and replied, "Okay, Duggan. I'll put in an ice plant and we'll have a team in the Garden if you'll guarantee to have this guy Morenz there for the opener."

The bargain was struck. The new rink was assured and Dwyer could now activate the franchise he had in his pocket.

In the remarkably short space of just eight months later, the Garden was finished, the ice was in, and on December 15, 1925, the Montreal Canadiens and the New York Americans skated out for the building's official grand opening.

A throng of 17,000 was there, Rickard was there, Morenz was there, and so was New York's dapper Mayor-Elect, Jimmy Walker, who coolly upstaged incumbent Mayor Hyland by standing and doffing his hat during the opening ceremonies. It was all very grand and elegant, with the Governor-General's Footguard from Ottawa and the West Point Band leading the teams into an arena that glittered with New York high society, resplendent in evening dress.

An artistic smash, the evening was one of what *Variety* would call boffo entertainment as the Canadiens belted the fledgling Americans 3–1 in a real bruiser. Morenz put the icing on the cake with a brilliant solo goal to close off the scoring, and hockey had begun an indefinite run on Broadway.

The crowd on that gay evening didn't really care much who won or lost or even who played the game. That was probably the briefest spell of naïveté and good fellowship in the history of sport.

In a sense, the man who invited the Patricks to his suite that evening in the early spring of 1926 was the key figure in their $300,000 sales pitch, as New York was and still is the NHL's U.S. flagship city. But as Rickard headed back to Manhattan and Lester took his Cougars back to Victoria for their last rites, there was still a lot to do.

Frank himself followed Rickard to New York to meet again with Art Ross and, hopefully, with Hammond. They got the meeting with the Colonel, but he flatly refused to pay $100,000 for the fourteen players Patrick offered. By that time, Hammond had sent his manager, Conn Smythe, to Minneapolis to sign Taffy Abel and Ching Johnson, a strapping pair of defensemen from the Canadian prairies who were playing in Minnesota. The signing had defied an inter-league agreement that gave the Western Canada League first right to players from the Canadian Midwest, and Frank made a sly point of this bit of piracy at the meeting by addressing Hammond as "Captain Kidd." That so infuriated the Colonel that he stalked out of the meeting.

To Frank Patrick the incident was comical only in retrospect. "Come to think of it, Hammond did look a little like a pirate as he

strode around the room, angrily shaking his fist as though brandishing a cutlass. But he was certainly stubborn, and had me in a
corner. The next day, Art and I went to see a couple of banker
friends of Hammond's down on Wall Street to explain the Colonel's mistake in not taking fourteen good hockey players for
$100,000, but Hammond had already been on the phone, instruct-
ing the bankers not to listen to me.

However, as Frank liked to put it, the recalcitrant Colonel
"soon had to eat a little crow."

"With the exception of Abel and Johnson, the players that he
and Smythe had gathered at that time were a mediocre lot, and
when he realized the quality of players we were offering to the
other two new franchises in Detroit and Chicago, he panicked. He
took the elastic off the bankroll, made a deal with the Maroons,
and bought six of the Saskatoon players they controlled. He paid
$30,000 for the Cook brothers, Bill and Bun, $15,000 for Frank
Boucher, and $20,000 for goalie Lorne Chabot. They were all fine
players, but they cost him $65,000 whereas he could have had
fourteen good ones from me for just $35,000 more."

Hammond's refusal to deal was a severe setback, but Art Ross
was not perturbed. He left New York for Boston on the 5 P.M.
train, and was on the phone to Frank the next morning. He reported that he had contacted his boss, C. F. Adams, at his vaca-
tion home in Bermuda, explained the dilemma, and Adams had
agreed to underwrite the whole $300,000 deal. Frank was to go
ahead with his efforts to sell players to Chicago and Detroit, but if
those cities didn't want them for their new franchises, then Boston
would take the whole lot.

Within a week, Adams had talked the Chicago entrepreneur
"Tack" Hardwick into buying players from Patrick, and Charles
Hughes, who along with Jim Norris represented the Detroit syndi-
cate, seemed sure to follow. A few weeks later, with a nudge from
Frank, he did. Chicago agreed to buy the Portland Rosebuds, and
Detroit took the Victoria squad. Both groups were strengthened
by the addition of players from other WCHL rosters, including a
few from Frank's Vancouver Millionaires.

Just as everything looked great, financial problems surfaced in
Chicago. The NHL directors dispatched president Frank Calder
to investigate a disturbing rumor that the promised new arena

would not be ready for the opening of the 1926–27 season. He was met in Chicago by Frank, who was concerned that the franchise might be revoked if the arena commitment was not met. The Chicago people admitted they had a problem, and with the whole deal heading for the rocks, Frank went to work setting up meetings with the Chicago attorneys in an attempt to save the situation.

On his arrival in Chicago, Frank had received a wire offering to finance the Chicago project on the condition that he would take on an executive position in the organization. Frank identified the Canadian "angel" only as "a wealthy sportsman who wished to remain anonymous until, if and when, a deal was made." It never was.

Frank expressed himself as "very dubious about the immediate outlook in Chicago," and told Calder privately that in his opinion it would take several years before a franchise there would start to make money. That was a shrewd reckoning as the club would lose more than a quarter of a million dollars before the upward turn began, years after the Black Hawks had moved into their new 18,000-seat Chicago Stadium. Meanwhile, Frank had managed to extract a guarantee for an early start on the arena, so the franchise was back on track again.

With the Portland players headed for Chicago, the gang from Victoria headed for Detroit, and the pick of the Prairie-Vancouver crop, including Eddie Shore, ticketed for Boston, everything once again looked rosy. Still, as Frank knew, all three sales yet had to be approved at the NHL Annual Meeting, where they would have to run the gamut of a covy of lawyers who were by nature wary of fast, big-money deals made by a one-man corporation operating out of his valise.

Armed with his verbal agreements plus $50,000 in cash advanced by C. F. Adams, Frank arrived at the June meeting in Montreal and stated his case to the directors and their attorneys. Everything was going along just fine until it came time to sign the sale papers, at which time the one-man corporation ran into trouble.

"There was a whole slew of lawyers in the room, and the gentlemen from Detroit asked for my documents authorizing me as the agent for the sale of the hockey players. I told them I didn't have any such documents. In fact, I hadn't so much as a single scrap of paper to show my authority as an agent of the players or the WCHL owners. I told them that all I had was my word, and that should be good enough.

"The lawyers expressed utter astonishment at the idea of such a big-money transaction taking place without what they considered proper contracts, and they advised their clients to have nothing to do with the proposition. The Chicago and Detroit representatives were on the verge of accepting this advice and pulling out when I rose to my feet and said, 'Gentlemen, I have no papers. All I have is my word, and, hopefully, your good will. Now. If you hope to have hockey in Detroit and Chicago next season, you will accept these intangibles as contracts and pay me the money. If not, I will forget the whole arrangement and withdraw my players.' "

A half hour later, Frank walked out of that meeting with a quarter of a million dollars in his pocket. That tidy fortune was made up of $100,000 each from Detroit and Chicago, and the $50,000 from Boston. There was no concern over the other $50,000 that was still due from Boston.

Over the next few weeks, a few individual sales brought another $17,000, bringing the total sale figure to $317,000. As Saskatoon had already collected $60,000 for its players, the total price of West-East player transaction was $377,000.

The $317,000 payment to Patrick was split among the five other WCHL cities. The only extra money received by the Patricks for their fifteen-year stake in the proposition plus the consummation of the deal itself was Frank's travel-expense money.

Now, with the big sale completed and the expanded NHL stocked with quality players, Frank Patrick, salesman *extraordinaire*, headed back to the Coast to ponder his own future.

When he arrived home and took the boat to Victoria to talk things over with Lester, he found a curious footnote to his eastern venture.

Upon his own return, Lester had received a letter from D'Alton Coleman, vice-president of the Canadian Pacific Railway, expressing concern over reports that big league hockey in the West was about to go under. He offered to subsidize the Patricks in an attempt to keep it afloat.

The gesture from this powerful industrialist was not all sentimental. As a top executive of the transcontinental railway system, Coleman was all for the preservation and development of any substantial East-West link, and he didn't like to see this one severed. However, by the time the offer arrived in Victoria, the end was already a *fait accompli.*

Both now unemployed apart from their jobs as operators of two arenas that had been stripped of their main tenants, Lester and Frank spent the summer tending their growing families. Lester's boys, Lynn and Muzz, were fourteen and ten respectively, and Frank's son, Joe, was also now ten years old. With two daughters, Gloria and Frances, added to the family, Frank now had three children.

It was mid-October in that autumn of 1926 when the telegram arrived offering Lester the job in New York. It read: WOULD LIKE TO HAVE YOU AS COACH OF THE RANGERS STOP IF INTERESTED PLEASE WIRE ACCORDINGLY AND I WILL ARRANGE IMMEDIATE TRANSPORTATION TO NEW YORK FOR FULL DISCUSSION STOP JOHN HAMMOND

The next day, Hammond was on the phone to personally confirm the offer. Lester had already made up his mind to accept and had told his family that he would be leaving for New York within the next few days.

Long after he and Lynn joined their father there to begin their own eventful NHL careers, Murray, or Muzz as he would be better known, recalled that sudden break in the tightly knit family. "I'd just turned ten and I felt both sad and a little confused about my father leaving to live in New York. I was told that it would just be for the winter and spring, but that seemed like a pretty long time. To me, and I'm sure to Lynn too, it was not just a matter of losing the companionship of a father, but of a good friend.

"We were all very close, and had a lot of good times together. We had lots of family picnics, and I remember the rides home from the hockey rink in our Studebaker touring car, with me or maybe Lynn clutching the night's gate receipts in our laps. We'd come home and count the money on the kitchen table. Lester—we always called him that in the later years—would always make sure the blinds were drawn. He was always afraid of being robbed.

"There were times too, after an official had had a bad night at the rink, when he would be bundled into the car for a fast getaway. I remember the time I got into the car and blurted out, 'Gee, Dad, that ref was really awful tonight . . .' He gave me a little cuff on the ear and pushed me down into the seat as he drove off. I didn't know that the poor ref, a fellow named Ivan Donovan, was crouched down in the back.

"I thought all those good times were gone forever, but of course they weren't. Lester always came home between seasons, and we had our mother, a shy but wonderfully warm person, and Aunt Veni, her sister, who lived with us. And then there was Grandpa. He was something special. He liked to put on a gruff front, but he was soft as putty inside. He thought his grandchildren were the greatest kids in the world. We were very fond of Uncle Frank, too, but he was always pretty busy over in Vancouver, and we didn't see a lot of him through the years."

But what about Uncle Frank, now that Lester had been called up to the big leagues? What about the younger brother who had been left behind, overlooked despite his brilliant hockey mind and his preeminent role in the fifteen pioneer years on the Coast? Lynn, who at fifteen was old enough to sense the family mood at the time of Lester's departure, remembered no sign of envy or disappointment on Frank's part.

"He was always involved in more things than Lester. He was more the executive type, and I don't think he was too interested in coaching as a career. I believe he was quite content to wait until, if and when, there was an NHL offer that suited him. And he still had the big arena in Vancouver to operate. No, he wasn't too concerned about a job in the NHL. Not yet, anyway."

The sudden summons from Hammond was Lester's first indication of the break between the Colonel and his manager-coach, Conn Smythe, although the rift, which had been simmering for weeks, was hardly unexpected. The two men, both stubborn, willful, and opinionated, were just too much alike to last as partners.

There is no doubt, especially in retrospect, that Smythe had done a masterful job of assembling a team at short notice. His line of Bill and Bun Cook, centered by Frank Boucher, would prove to be one of the finest units in NHL history, and his choice of the two amateur defensemen, Ching Johnson and Taffy Abel, was but little less inspired. His goalie, Lorne Chabot, was also first-rate. But Hammond was not satisfied or at least claimed not to be satisfied with Smythe's recruiting job. He said nothing as the Rangers opened their first training camp in the little Ravina rink in Toronto, but he showed up midway through the first week in a bad mood.

After watching a morning workout, he called Smythe over and said, "Conn, we can't start the season with a bunch of rank amateurs like this."

"The hell we can't," snorted Smythe, or more vulgar words to that effect. Conn turned and went back to the workout. He was steaming. A few hours later, he was also fired.

When deep in his seventies, Murray Murdoch, who would become known as the Iron Man through eleven great seasons with the Rangers, was out on the ice that day, and remembered it well. "We had heard a rumor that Lester Patrick had come up from New York with John Hammond and was checked into a Toronto hotel. I'm sure Conn had heard the rumor too, and it could mean only one thing: He was out. It seemed a rank injustice at the time because Smythe had collected the nucleus of a pretty good team, but Hammond had apparently come to the rink with his mind made up."

What Murdoch and Smythe didn't know was that just prior to leaving New York Hammond had visited Tex Rickard in Rickard's office. As president of the Madison Square Garden Corporation, Rickard always knew what was going on, and why. And what was going on was the ratification of Lester's contract, calling for $18,000 a year, by far the biggest salary in hockey at that time.

Hammond never admitted that it was Rickard who suggested that Patrick be hired to replace Smythe, but it is not likely that Lester would have been Hammond's choice. Because of his recent feud with Frank Patrick over the players' sale, when Frank had as much as called him a pirate, he was known to be not particularly enamored of the Patrick family.

As for Rickard—the man who didn't "know a damned thing" about hockey—he knew a lot about people, especially the kind of people he wanted to front his Garden attractions. With his new emporium the "in" place for the New York sporting society as well as the peasantry, he wanted people with, as he liked to call it, "class." Smythe, in Rickard's view, didn't fit.

The man he had met a few months before in Montreal did.

Murdoch agreed. "Conn and Lester were totally different per-sonalities. There were a couple of incidents that I think illustrate the difference between them.

"When Smythe got the New York job, I was one of the first players he contacted. I was just out of the University of Manitoba and had gotten married in Winnipeg when I received a wire from Smythe in Duluth, where he had signed Abel and Johnson. The wire said: MEET ME HERE IN DULUTH STOP ALL EXPENSES PAID

"I wired back: IF YOU WANT TO SEE ME COME TO WINNIPEG

"Well, he came to Winnipeg, we talked, and he offered me a $1,500 signing bonus and a $5,000 salary. I remember sitting in the lobby of the Fort Garry Hotel, thinking it over, and I was just about to say no when Conn leaned over a coffee table and slowly counted out $1,500 in $100 bills. That clinched it. For a young guy just married and with a summer job selling insurance, that looked like an awful lot of money.

"Lester never dealt that way. He just made his proposition, and you knew his word was his bond.

"Then when I reported to the Ravina rink training camp I had a little problem with Conn over my skates. I was one of the last holdouts against the tubular skates, as I still preferred the solid racing blade, open at both ends. Conn took one look at my skates and said, 'You can't play hockey in those damned things. Get rid of them and get a decent pair of skates.' I switched to tubes, and I couldn't play worth a damn.

"When Lester took over, he came over to me during the first workout and said, 'Murray, what's the matter with you? You look terrible out here.' I explained about the skates and he said, 'Mur-ray, if you like the other skates better, put them on.' I did, and I was O.K. again.

"Lester took over from Conn quietly, without any fuss, and after a couple of days he called a team meeting. 'Gentlemen,' he said, 'when we start playing in the National Hockey League you're going to win some games and you're going to lose some. I just want to stress this: If you lose more than you win, you won't be around.'"

The boys liked Lester, and they didn't grieve for the departed Smythe. They knew Conn was a tough little street fighter who would have no problem surviving. And how right they were. He took his $2,500 cash settlement from Hammond, bet the whole bundle on the University of Toronto to beat Queen's in an inter-collegiate football game, switched to hockey and bet his win-nings on Toronto St. Pats over the Ottawa Senators. He won again, and with $10,000 plus some help from mining tycoon J. B. Pickell, he showed his gratitude by buying the St. Pats franchise.

That was the start of Smythe's trek to his own millions as builder, owner, and resident curmudgeon of Maple Leaf Gardens, and sole proprietor of the Maple Leafs, his very own money ma-chine. Colonel Hammond had done a splendid job of kicking his employee upstairs via the express escalator.

The irascible Smythe replacement at the helm of the Rangers took the team straight from Toronto to New York and checked into a room in the Lincoln Hotel at the corner of Forty-eighth and Eighth Avenue, just a five-minute walk from Madison Square Gar-den. That modest abode, rented for the sum of twenty-two dollars a week, would be his home during the first winter in Manhattan.

It was early November 1926, and New York, a metropolis of 6 million souls, was a far and raucous cry from the sleepy suburbia of the old homestead back in Victoria. It was the era of the flapper and the sheik, the Charleston, jazz bands, and of prohibi-tion, which was the Great American Joke. In Manhattan, the cul-tural capital of the Roaring Twenties, a citizen could quench his thirst at any of an estimated 100,000 speakeasies and a thousand nightclubs. The liquid fare ranged from homemade nickel beer at your friendly neighborhood blind-pig up to $35-a-bottle "im-ported" champagne, liberally diluted and served up by the "Hello Sucker" girl, Texas Guinan, at the gaudy El Fay. Forty-fifth Street, which was just an innocent three-minute stroll from Lester's hotel, was proudly known as the "wettest street in the USA."

Another brassy blonde, Mae West, was currently holding New Yorkers in thrall at her obscenity trial, coyly defending a lively performance that had closed down her Broadway hit show *Sex*. And between court appearances, Miss West passed the time doing a shimmy in a skintight gold dress in another kiddies show called *Virgin Man,* bankrolled by dear friend and mobster Ownie Mad-den, who was out on parole from Sing Sing.

Society folks went slumming in Harlem, where they jammed the Cotton Club and Connie's Inn to listen to the music of the great black bands—Cab Calloway, Jimmy Lunceford, McKinney's Cottonpickers, and Duke Ellington. The marquees of Broadway glittered with a record crop of hit shows, mostly frothy, madcap musicals such as *Oh, Kay!*—a Gershwin concoction that had just opened, starring the girl from England, Gertrude Lawrence.

Had he wished to take the short walk from his hotel, Lester could have whiled away his first night in town eyeing a comely bevy of naked chorus girls soaring out over the audience on beribboned swings to open the second act of *George White's Scandals*. Or he could have just stood and watched the elegantly attired figure of the handsome and debonair James J. Walker as New York's new playboy mayor made his nightly rounds on Broadway.

With colorful citizens such as Frank Costello, Legs Diamond, Arnold Rothstein, Lucky Luciano, Joe Adonis, Frankie Rizzo, and Dutch Schultz roaming the neighborhood in their patent-leather shoes and bullet-proof Duesenbergs, the first son of old Joe Patrick, the Bible-thumping Methodist who couldn't even abide streetcars on Sunday, was bedded down smack in the middle of Sodom and Gomorrah.

However, it is unlikely that Lester allowed the devil to creep into his soul that first night in Manhattan. The odds are that after seeing that his players were settled into their own nearby hotel quarters that he went straight to bed, little knowing that Jimmy Walker, the playboy mayor, later better known and revered as the most charming crook ever to grace New York City Hall, would soon be courting his favor.

Bright and early on the morning following his arrival, Lester was ensconced in his new Madison Square office, which was just a few doors down the hall from that of the corporation president, Tex Rickard. Lester's office was on the Fiftieth Street side of the building, and from the window, with just a slight crane of the neck, one could see the ticket-speculator's booth occupied by Mike Jacobs, the shrewd hustler who would eventually succeed Rickard as the emperor of the prizefight business, with Joe Louis as his crown jewel.

There were just four days to go before the name "New York Rangers" went up on the marquee for the first time to hail their Garden debut against the league-champion Montreal Maroons.

Rickard was not there for Lester's arrival. He was in Chicago, working on preliminary plans for a rematch between his dethroned heavyweight king, Jack Dempsey, and the new champ, Gene Tunney. Just two months before, Rickard had been one of that huge mob of 75,000 fight fans who had left Penn Station for Philadelphia to witness Tunney's stunning defeat of Dempsey before a mob of 120,757 in Sesquentennial Stadium.

Another prominent absentee was Bill Dwyer, the owner of the Rangers' Garden co-tenants, the New York Americans. Bill was out of town on more pressing business. He was serving a two-year term in a penitentiary, convicted of a bootlegging charge following a sensational trial that had co-featured the prime minister of the underworld himself, Frank Costello. Plus a large supporting cast of lesser hoodlums.

Dwyer, who was said to be the most powerful man in New York, had directed the trafficking of more than $42 million worth of beer and whiskey over a period of little more than two years. He had been nabbed for his part in a spectacular and bizarre rum-running gambit that had involved fake destroyer escorts, the U. S. Coast Guard, the U. S. Navy, shore police, and even a German submarine.

Bribery of U. S. Coast Guardsmen was part of the rap on Dwyer and his chum, Costello. Only Dwyer was nailed.

The fact that one of their owners was a convicted felon seemed to raise not so much as a quizzical eyebrow among the NHL governors, nor for that matter in the office of Bill's new Garden associate, Lester Patrick. The so-called NHL morals code had not yet been invented, and a fellow could still have a friendly beer with "known gamblers or other unsavory characters" without fear of dire punishment.

Lester was a practical man, and he had his own little problems. That morning at breakfast he had come across a newspaper story, about the promising future ahead for the New York Rangers' fine young Italian winger, Oliver Reniccio. This puzzled Lester because he could not recall a fine young Italian winger of that name on his roster. He therefore called in one of the Garden publicity men, Johnny Bruno, for enlightenment.

"Of course, Mr. Patrick," said Bruno amiably. "Oliver Reniccio . . . Oliver Reinikka. Get it?"

Lester admitted that no, he didn't get it.

"Mr. Patrick, perhaps you are not aware that there are nearly 500,000 Italians in New York. Maybe more. They'll just love to see a nice Italian boy out there."

"But," said Lester gently, "I am given to understand that Mr. Reinikka is a Canadian boy of, I believe, Finnish descent."

"Finnish-Canadian?" Bruno sighed. "It won't sell, Mr. Patrick."

"And you can't sell a silly idea like that to me. We are promoting hockey, not flimflam. Good morning, Mr. Bruno."

"Okay," said Bruno. "It's your hockey team. But I've got another idea that's sure-fire stuff, and no phony names. Strictly buildup. The first game is just three days away, okay? So tomorrow we get Bill Cook kidnapped."

"Out!" thundered Lester.

"But of course we locate him in time for him to make it to the game . . ."

"Out!"

So ended Lester's cram course on life as a hockey coach in New York City.

A sellout crowd of 17,000 turned out to watch the Rangers make their bow against the Montreal Maroons, who were the defending Stanley Cup Champions. Led by Nels Stewart and Reg Noble, this was pretty well the same powerhouse team that had buried Lester's Victoria Cougars just a few months before, and there was little money on his band of untested ragtags.

Movie star Lois Moran minced scenically out for the ceremonial face-off, and after dropping the puck between the two rival centermen, Stewart and Frank Boucher, the lady was escorted back to her seat behind the Rangers' bench.

Wrote Ed Sullivan, the young Broadway reporter who chronicled the item in his next day's "Talk of the Town" column: "Miss Moran was in the elegant company of Mayor Jimmy Walker and his beauteous companion of the evening, actress Betty Compton . . ."

That was the first recorded item concerning the romance between the forty-two-year-old playboy mayor and the twenty-two-year-old movie star he had just met backstage at the Broadway opening of *Oh, Kay!*—and who was to become Walker's mistress in the city's most highly publicized love affair. But that night, the publicity-loving mayor was there to be front and center in what had turned out to be a major social as well as sporting event, and his seat right behind the tall, imposing figure of Lester Patrick was the perfect stage. Thereafter, he occupied it frequently.

Mayor Walker's second Broadway opening in a week was a smash hit, as the Rangers upset the Maroons 1–0 in a bruising game, with Bun Cook scoring the only goal in a wild contest that delighted the fans—most of whom had come out of sheer curiosity. As far as the Rangers and New York fans were concerned, it was the start of a long and beautiful friendship.

There was just one sour note in the next day's newspaper raves, and that was from the brilliant and ascerbic creator of Broadway's guys and dolls and Harry the Horse and Nathan Detroit: Damon Runyon. He dismissed the Rangers' sparkling debut with a cryptic note: "Fortunately, hockey is a game I do not fail to misunderstand."

As Lester would discover, several of the veteran New York scribes viewed hockey warily and some never really accepted it. Despite its earlier highly successful incursions into St. Nicholas Arena led by Cyclone Taylor, it was regarded as an interloper on the already crowded Manhattan sports scene.

The New York writers were weaned on baseball, football, basketball, boxing, golf, tennis, and horse racing. They were engrossed with such names of the Golden Age as Babe Ruth, Dempsey, Bobby Jones, Helen Wills, Big Bill Tilden, Red Grange, and the king jockey, Earle Sande. And, across town from Yankee Stadium over on Coogan's Bluff, the lordly figure of John McGraw and his Giants. New Yorkers called the Giants' manager "Mr. McGraw," and the new guy in town, Lester Patrick, paled in his image.

Still, the game was here to stay, as Lester and his Rangers firmly hinted in that first remarkable season, when they finished at the top of their five-team American Division, 11 points ahead of the Boston Bruins. They lost to the Bruins in the Stanley Cup play-offs, but they had made their point in the league, and in Madison Square Garden.

There, vying with Newsy Lalonde's Americans for the affections of the Garden fans, the Rangers dug in as number one and never relinquished their role as house favorites. From the beginning, despite the fact that the Americans were 5–2 victors in the first meeting of the Garden tenants, the Rangers were considered the "class" team while the Amerks were stuck with the "Dead-End Kid" label. Although the capable Tommy Gorman ran the franchise, the Americans may have suffered a little in the unsavory Bill Dwyer image, but there was no doubt that the imposing figure of the man behind the Rangers' bench had much to do with their house rating. Lester's style had rubbed off.

In addition to their impressive first-year performance, and perhaps a good deal because of it, the Rangers also boasted the league scoring champion in the person of Bun Cook, who edged out the Chicago veteran Dick Irvin and the Canadiens' Howie Morenz, who was just approaching his peak as the game's most colorful performer. And in fourth place in the scoring was none other than Lester Patrick's one-time prize Cougar, Frank Fredrickson.

Fredrickson, the only player smart enough to make his own deal as a free agent during the big sale, had signed with Detroit for $6,500, nearly double what Detroit had paid the other Victoria stars. The only trouble with that little coup was that his linemates were so mad when they heard about it that they wouldn't pass the puck to him, so he was traded to Boston. There, he was not only great on the ice but also enlivened the team's train trips with impromptu concerts on his violin, often performed in the middle of the night. Sometimes, just for variety, he switched to the ukulele and sang a little.

The Bruins' fearless defenseman, Eddie Shore, was also musically inclined. He considered himself to be pretty good on the tenor-saxophone, although he was just learning to play the instrument. He occasionally took his sax on the road to practice, and what with Frank on the fiddle and Eddie on the horn, the night rides through the hitherto peaceful wilds of New York, Maine, and Quebec at times became just too much for manager Art Ross. No lover of fine music, Ross banned musical instruments from all road trips, and thus the first brave pioneer road company of the Boston Pops was no more.

While the irrepressible Fredrickson was approaching the end of his fine career as a player (he would shortly and but briefly try his hand at coaching with the Pittsburgh Hornets), his old Victoria manager was getting nicely settled into his long term at the helm of the Broadway Blues.

Lester's manner of handling life in the big town was already well-established. As Tommy Gorman once put it, "Lester didn't adjust to New York. New York adjusted to him."

That would certainly apply to the New York writers, most of whom knew little about the foreign pastime, but soon discovered a very able and willing teacher. Lester's seminars for the press, held in his office, became a popular ritual during the early years.

After a workout, he would summon the attendant scribes to his quarters, get them comfortably seated, and then address them from behind his big desk, much in the manner of a professor at a law school. He would rise and demonstrate the art of the pass and the shot with swift movements around the room, and sprawl on the carpet to illustrate the finer points of goaltending. The lectures were almost Shakespearian in nature, couched in a fine lyrical prose that could charm the most cynical audience. He was a master manipulator.

Said Frank Boucher, the marvelous center who would one day replace Lester behind the bench, "He struck dramatic poses and was in turn kind, sarcastic, pompous, vain, callous, and contrite, depending on the circumstances. He had both a compelling arrogance and a winning humility. By all odds, he was the most knowledgeable hockey man I have ever met."

Said Walter ("Babe") Pratt, a Rangers' star of a later date, "You just couldn't be around Lester without learning something."

What Pratt saw when he arrived in the middle thirties was the same style and philosophy that Lester deployed from day one with his Rangers.

"All that we players ever got from Lester," Pratt said, "was straight common sense. He was a great theorist and believed in doing things the direct and simple way. After we'd win a game and had made mistakes doing it, he'd really get after us, but if we'd been badly beaten he'd lay off.

"He was a disciplinarian, but he left it to the players to police themselves. He'd say, 'As long as you play good hockey, I don't want to hear about any trouble.' There were times when we'd take advantage, but mostly it worked. We respected his attitude.

"He'd come in before game time and chat quietly with us for a while and just remind us to remember the basics. To play our man, play it safe, and 'never make yourself or your team look bad.' After skull sessions between games he'd leave us alone to talk things over for fifteen or twenty minutes. He left a lot up to us, and there was a mutual trust between him and the players. That's why the Rangers' team spirit was always so good, and why there were never any cliques or clubhouse lawyers in Lester's day."

Another perspective of Lester the man and Lester the coach is offered by Michael Francis ("King") Clancy, the artful leprechaun who split a superb sixteen-year NHL career between the Ottawa Senators and the Toronto Maple Leafs. Known as one of the finest and most colorful defensemen in NHL history, King's recollections of Lester date back into the old Pacific Coast Hockey Association days, when all the world seemed young.

"I met Lester for the first time in 1921 and then again in 1923, when I went West with the Senators. I remember after the 1924 series in Victoria Lester took Frank Nighbor and me home to have dinner with his charming wife and family. Mrs. Patrick was an absolutely gracious lady, and I remember thinking what a rare, warm family it was. The kids—Muzz and Lynn—were there, just pip-squeaks at the time, and I had no idea they'd one day be up there belting the hell out of old guys like me.

"I remember Lester bringing the Rangers for their first game against us in Toronto. Before the game, I called out, 'Hey, Lester, how about asking your boys to take it easy on your old buddy to-night,' and he sort of smiled and nodded.

"Well, in the first period, that Ching Johnson hit me a couple of real shots along the boards, and I see Lester grin and I said to myself, 'Lester, I'm gonna nail that big S.O.B. of yours,' and a minute later I got decked in a scramble in front of our net. I see this big bald head looming over me and I said, 'Ching, I got you this time, you big bastard.' I got up and clubbed him with my stick, right across the shoulders. Unfortunately, Ching's hard head got in the way and I hit him on the skull and drew blood. I didn't mean to do that, and felt very sorry about it, but then I saw that Ching was O.K., only bleeding a little but cussing a lot.

"When I came off the ice at the end of the period, Lester leaned over and said, 'King, that was the dirtiest thing I ever saw.'

"I said, 'Why, what do you mean, Mr. Patrick?'

"'You know what I mean, King,' he answered. 'Cracking Ching on the head like that with your stick. It was disgusting.'

"He was all wide-eyed and looked very hurt, even more hurt than Ching, so I thought I should explain. 'I beg your pardon, Mr. Patrick,' I said, 'but you've got this all wrong. I didn't touch Mr. Johnson. Never laid a finger on him, let alone my stick.' And I went off up the chute to the dressing room laughing.

"Then, years later, here we were in Toronto for a play-off game against the Rangers. Lester and league president Clarence Campbell had supervised the selection of the officials. I was through playing then, and I was picked as the referee. It was Easter Sunday morning before a night game, and I was walking across the hotel lobby and Lester was sitting there in an armchair, reading a paper. He got up and called me over in that regal way of his and I thought, 'Oh, oh, what now?' but he smiled and said, 'Good morning, King. It's a beautiful morning, isn't it? Where are you going?'

"I said, 'Why, I'm going to church.'

"'Oh,' said Lester. 'Do you mind if I come with you?'

"'Certainly not,' I said. 'In fact, I'd be delighted.' But I must admit I was a little surprised. I knew that Lester was a real strict Methodist, taking after his old man, and here was I, a good Catholic boy, off to church for Easter Mass, which I know can get pretty heavy for a heathen.

"We walked off into the street, Lester all dressed up as usual, a real Beau Brummel in his beautiful creased pants and gray suit and a stylish gray fedora. We were chatting away as we walked along in the warm sunshine and Lester said, 'King, I've never been to a Catholic Mass before. What do I have to do?'

"I said, 'Lester, don't worry about a thing. Just watch me and do what I do.'

"Well, he followed me pretty good through the first part of the Mass, and then it came time to go to Confession and to receive Holy Communion. Lester didn't follow me to Confession, but did go with me for Holy Communion.

"He watched me, and then when his turn came he genuflected and knelt there for a second, but when he went to get up his left knee was stuck to the floor. The knee of his pants was stuck on a big fresh wad of gum that stretched out as Lester tugged, looking kind of self-conscious. He got up okay, but the gum had made an awful mess of his nice pants. He turned to me and said quietly, 'King, you forgot something.'

" 'What's that, Lester?' I asked.

" 'I think you're supposed to spit out your gum before you take Communion. All the others did.'

" 'Sorry, Lester,' I said. 'I guess we're just not all good Catholics.'

"But he seemed to have something else on his mind, and out again on the street, he said, 'King, did you really confess all your sins today?'

" 'Why certainly, Lester,' I replied. 'How can you ask such a thing?'

" 'Good,' said Lester. 'Now, if I ask you a question, you wouldn't lie to me, would you?' I assured him that of course I wouldn't, certainly not on Easter Sunday.

" 'Good,' he said. 'Now, remember that night years ago in Toronto when Ching got hit on the head? Tell me now, King, you did hit him, didn't you?'

"I said, 'Yes, Lester, I did. I told you a lie. I did hit Ching. It was a pretty good whack, too. I'm sorry about that.'

"Lester stopped, threw back his head and laughed heartily, clapped me on the shoulder, and we resumed the walk back to the hotel. I guess he'd never heard an Easter Sunday confession before. Especially from me. We got back to the hotel all smiles and a lot chummier than a referee and a coach should be. But that was Lester, long on memory, even of little things that others have long forgotten, but just as long on forgiveness and amiability."

There was another memory of Lester that stayed with Clancy through the years.

"It was March 17, 1934, and it was King Clancy Night in Maple Leaf Gardens and they had me all dressed in green, a real bilious green. Stockings, boots, uniform, stick, everything. It was Conn Smythe's idea, and I was a real sickly sight. We were playing the Rangers, and the first time he saw me when I came past the New York bench, Lester said, 'My God, Clancy, what's this?' I think it was the only time I'd ever heard Lester utter a profanity. The effect of my outfit on the Rangers was amazing. They just sort of looked at me and gagged, and for the entire first period not one of them came near me.

"I was having a field day on defense, and when the period was over Lester came to me and whispered, 'King, what are you doing to me? My boys won't go anywhere near you, and you've got the whole building upset. You look awful. Come on now, King, how about taking that ridiculous uniform off so we can play hockey?'

"I just grinned and nodded, but to tell you the truth I did feel a little embarrassed, so I changed between periods. But really I changed out of respect for Lester. We won the game anyway.

"He had a great sense of humor, but the game was always first. He was one of the finest people I have ever met. A real class person, and he raised two fine sons. He fit the New York scene just like a glove. He'd walk to his place behind the bench all immaculately dressed, silver-haired, and with that elegant bearing—he just oozed class. It was written all over him, and the Garden fans loved him for it. In his special way, he was one of them."

It was after one of Lester's press seminars in his Garden classroom that he got the name that stayed with him throughout his career and is now synonymous with his memory.

"Yesterday," wrote Ed Daley, sports editor of the New York *Herald Tribune,* "I spent a fascinating half hour in the lair of The Silver Fox . . ."

After his first triumphant year in the big town, The Silver Fox went back to summer in Victoria, where the youngest brother, Stan, was running the Arena, with the next youngest, Guy, helping Frank over in Vancouver. When he got back to New York in the autumn, Grace was with him, as she would be for the next twenty seasons.

In New York, the Patricks moved into a pleasant apartment in the Alamac Hotel at Seventh and Broadway. It was a sub-let from a Mr. Fred Fitzimmons, better known as Fat Freddy Fitzimmons, a colorful young pitcher who was just starting his outstanding twelve-year career with Mr. McGraw's Giants, and was then on the verge of his first twenty-game season. As Freddy left for his home in Mishawaka, Indiana, early each October and didn't return until springtime, it was the ideal share arrangement.

That apartment remained the Patricks' winter home until a

move to smarter quarters at Park Vendome, a plush apartment building on West Fifty-ninth, four years later.

Meanwhile, in their second season, the Rangers went on to finish four points behind Boston in the league race, eliminate the Bruins in the play-offs, and then whip the Montreal Maroons for the Stanley Cup Championship. It was a remarkable feat for Lester and his sophomore hockey club, and the victory itself was almost anticlimactic in the wake of the substitute-goalie incident that has become part of the folklore of North American sport.

There have been many versions of how the forty-four-year-old coach got the call to go in for his injured goalie in the second game of the final series and what then transpired, and Lester's own version is the tersest and least dramatic of them all.

Asked about the incident—for the millionth time—at his Garden farewell party twenty-one years later, he said, "We thought at first that it was just a mild injury to Chabot's eye and that he'd return shortly, but it was worse than we thought and some of the boys said, 'Lester, you go in there . . .' But I said no; I didn't want to. However, they persisted, so I donned Chabot's uniform, skates, and what have you, and everything fit like a glove except the skates. I took care of that by putting on an extra pair of sox. So, when the game proceeded, the boys went all out to protect me and as luck would have it we won with the extra goal in overtime."

It wasn't all quite that pat, and the newspapers waxed a little more lyrical. A typical headline in the Ottawa *Journal* read: Grizzled Veteran Steps into Breach when Chabot Hurt. Fighting Fury Seizes Rangers, Who Repel Maroons.

A subhead added that Lorne Chabot might lose the sight of his eye, and that "The Heroic Patrick Donned the Pads and Held Off the Reds in Sensational Style."

The background of the extraordinary affair was this: With the entire series booked for Montreal because the Barnum & Bailey Circus had taken over Madison Square Garden for its traditional spring visit, the Maroons had won the first game and after a scoreless first period of the second, Rangers' goalie Lorne Chabot was felled by a hard shot from the stick of Nels Stewart. Chabot was led from the ice with blood pouring from a deep cut over his eye, to await an ambulance.

Play was halted, and Patrick, who didn't carry a spare goalie, requested permission to use the Ottawa Senators' Alex Connell, who was seated in the stands. The Maroons, who did carry a spare goalie, denied the request, and NHL president, Frank Calder, upheld their position. The Rangers had just ten minutes to produce a goalie, or forfeit the game.

Back in the New York dressing room, there was consternation when it became clear that Chabot was too badly hurt to return, and the place became bedlam when well-meaning outsiders burst in with suggestions for ways out of the dilemma. Lester strode the room trying to calm everyone down and work out a solution when Bun Cook and Frank Boucher pulled him aside and talked quietly with him for a moment. Then Lester turned, and with his fine sense of drama he beckoned to Rangers' trainer Harry Westerby and called out: "Harry, I'm going in goal."

There was a stunned silence as he then coolly instructed Westerby to strip off Chabot's gear and get him some fresh underwear and sox.

When he skated out onto the ice minutes later, he was greeted by a curious silence as the puzzled fans pondered this unfamiliar figure. Then, when it finally dawned on them that the new goalie was Lester Patrick there was a ripple of applause that was perhaps more bemused than enthusiastic. As Montreal sports editor Baz O'Mara painted the scene the following day:

> There was "Laughing Lester," who has done everything in hockey and has played a little goal before, sauntering out with a little black cap askew over his whitening thatch, his lanky legs upholstered by brown pads that seemed to fit him like father's old trousers . . .
>
> In any event, a minute later there was Lester in the goal, where he stayed until the bitter overtime end, performing prodigious feats of net-minding, supported by as capable and inspired defensive play as Taffy Abel and Ching Johnson could muster . . .

For Lester, it was like turning back the clock to another such emergency stint for his Victoria Cougars when he was younger, but still considered much too old for the gambit. This one though was a lot tougher, as the Maroons pressed in for the kill. They were staved off by an inspired defense, but still blasted a total of sixteen shots before the ordeal was over.

Lester himself played his big moment to the hilt, pointing a finger at the action and yelling, "Make them shoot . . . make

them shoot . . ." and there was Ching Johnson responding franti-
cally with "No . . . no . . . my God, no . . ."

After Bill Cook had put the Rangers one up early in the third
period, Nels Stewart did manage to hoist the puck over Lester's
prostrate body, but that was it for the Maroons scoring. And as
Lester put it, "as luck would have it, we won by a goal [Frank
Boucher's] in overtime . . ." Luck, maybe. An ageless and un-
quenchable love of the fray and the courage of an old bull seal returned to protect his herd, yes. It was vintage Patrick family stuff.

Lester returned to New York a hero, and nobody embraced him
more warmly than did Mayor Jimmy Walker, who loved heroes
and their company. Walker was still preening in the afterglow of
the colossal tickertape parade he had personally ordered to hail
the return of Charles Lindbergh following Lucky Lindy's epic
flight to Paris. He, of course, was up front with the new American
idol all the way through that incredible parade scene, and he was
also up front a few months later with congratulations and a handshake for Babe Ruth, after the Bambino had hit his record sixtieth
homer for the Yankees. And now here he was on the steps of City
Hall with the Rangers, beaming and embracing Lester as the
crowd cheered and the flashbulbs popped.

Just before the start of the play-offs, newspaper reports repeated "the very strong rumor, from an influential source" that
Lester Patrick would soon be named to succeed Colonel Hammond as general manager, with Hammond reported moving to
Boston to operate a big new arena to be constructed there by Tex
Rickard. "Rickard," said the story, "is very impressed with the
job Patrick has done with the Rangers, and is grooming him for a
top executive position."

Unfortunately, the accuracy of that report was never tested, for
less than ten months later, Rickard was dead.

Accompanied by his now retired ex-champ, Jack Dempsey,
Rickard had gone to Miami in late December to arrange the details of a fight between Jack Sharkey and William ("Young")
Stribling. He was taken to the hospital with severe digestive pains,
and died of acute appendicitis on January 6, four days after his
fifty-ninth birthday. His body was returned to New York by special train in a $15,000 bronze casket that was placed in Madison
Square Garden, where Rickard lay in state as thousands of

mourners filed by. It was a lavish ceremonial of a kind usually accorded only to heads of state, but it was Tex's kind of promotion.

Lester, whose Rangers were due in Ottawa next day for a game against the Senators, visited the arena and sat for a few minutes in the stands, his own small spray of roses buried in the huge mounds of flowers that surrounded the casket. For Lester, that week had marked the end of a brief but mutually profitable friendship.

The next evening he was in Ottawa to watch his Rangers bomb the Senators by a score of 9–2.

The next year saw the close of another chapter in the Patricks' family journal as the Victoria Arena went up in smoke. The building where the family's West Coast odyssey had begun—with that skating party on Christmas Day 1911, with old Joe and his wife watching from the gondola high above the ice—was gone.

It was Armistice Day, November 11, 1929, when Lester received a phone call from the youngest brother, Stan Patrick, with the news that the building had been completely destroyed by a fire that had broken out just before dawn. A milkman on his rounds had seen flames licking through the roof, and within an hour the Arena lay in ashes. The building, which had cost $110,000 to construct nineteen years before, was insured for $50,000. Arson was suspected, but never proved.

Busy with the start of the NHL season, Lester couldn't come West to help, but Frank came from Vancouver to take charge. It was a double blow to him, as apart from his personal stake in the family fortune he was about to start another season as president of his new Pacific Coast League, a four-team minor circuit that included Victoria and his own Vancouver Lions. Emergency plans were made to have Victoria open on the road.

Two years away from hockey had been enough for both Frank and Joe Patrick. Still looking for the big score, Frank had gone searching for gold and silver up in the rolling hills of British Columbia's vast Cariboo country, but none of the claims had been productive. He still had the dream of striking it rich like those two Chinese who had taken more than $1 million gold out of that little mountain stream in the Kootenays, but all that was left after two years of work and $50,000 of his father's money was a bundle of worthless mining stock. But it had been an honest effort, and that's all Joe ever asked for.

So now, back to square one in the business he knew best, Frank was in the process of developing new talent for sale to the NHL, and that for him was the next best thing to being there. It was probably his own fault that he wasn't up there because his records show that he had chances to move up to both Chicago and Detroit, but simply failed to pursue them. He had what he called "a standing offer" from owner Major McLaughlin for an executive job with the Black Hawks, and he had a powerful friend in Detroit in Red Wings' owner, Jim Norris, who was one of Frank's great admirers. It was said that Norris too had left the door open.

There was also, in 1932, a feeler from William A. Carey, who had succeeded Rickard as president of the Madison Square Garden Corporation. Of this, Frank has said, "Yes, Carey did approach me, but the job he had in mind would have made me Lester's boss, and I didn't want that."

For whatever reason, an excess of sensitivity, insecurity, or simply a preference for life with his wife and family and his own modest hockey operation, Frank had declined to walk through the doors that had been nudged ajar.

Back in New York, the economics of survival seemed to be the main challenge for the Rangers as the nation suddenly slid into the depths of the Great Depression. It was just a month before the Victoria Arena fire, on November 13, 1929, when the stock market crashed to herald the Great Depression. It was the apple sellers out on the street corners that gave New York the laconic nickname of 'The Big Apple,' and Broadway was one of the most depressed thoroughfares. Show business suffered badly at the box office and the entertainment industry was in dire shape all over town, except at Madison Square Garden, on hockey nights.

"To me," said Lester, "the greatest compliment New Yorkers paid to hockey was in the way attendance held up during the bad times. The crowds had slipped, certainly, but not much as compared to business elsewhere, and that was a great tribute to the appeal of the game."

Lester tried to brighten up that dark winter of 1929–30 by sporting a jaunty derby hat on the bench. He took a terrible razzing from the players and responded by announcing that he would buy a similarly elegant beanie for every player who wanted one. The next day, twelve players accompanied Lester down to the stylish Brill Brothers shop at Forty-ninth and Broadway, where he bought each of them a derby at the then staggering price of $12 each.

"The next game," recalls Murray Murdoch, "Lester wore his derby on the bench again, and in the second period Harry Meeking came along the boards, stopped, looked at Lester, shouted, 'What the hell's that?' and crushed the bowler with his stick. Poor Lester was out 144 bucks and didn't even have a derby of his own. He laughed as much as we did—but not until a couple of days later."

Although in every play-off and always in contention, the Rangers didn't grasp the brass ring again until 1933, when they won their second Stanley Cup Championship.

By that time, the New York reporters had become increasingly intrigued with the style and substance of the man they called The Silver Fox. They had already conceded that in this courtly and at times imperious man from the wilds of the Canadian West was an uncommon mixture of businessman, impressario, ham-actor, coach, and father-figure. They seemed to agree fully with the surprisingly generous view of the man whose job he had usurped at the Rangers first training camp. When deep in his eighties, the still crusty and belligerent Conn Smythe said, "Lester Patrick was the right man in the right place at the right time. They couldn't have found a better man for the job."

Asked by one writer to explain his philosophy on the handling of hockey games and hockey players, Lester said, "It's very simple. I look for the leaders. Then I let them lead. I give my last instructions in the dressing room just before the game, then I sit and let them think about whatever they like. I see some of the players just sitting there placidly, thinking about nothing much and worrying about less. Then I look along the bench and see Bill Cook. A great player, an outstanding player. He's already made his mark and has nothing to worry about.

"But is he at ease? Not on your life. He sits there rubbing his thighs and rocking back and forth on the bench, a bundle of nerves, just aching to get at it and break the tension.

"The placid player can be depended on for a safe, steady game, but for the kind of inspired hockey needed to win championships, I need the Bill Cooks. The other players, when it comes right down to the crunch, will follow the Bill Cooks. Then I just tag along, and enjoy it."

He had a knack too with the little people around him, the ones outside the Rangers' fold, looking in. One of these was Gerry Cosby, a lively, gregarious man who now operates a large sporting goods store in the new Madison Square Garden rotunda, a popular hangout for the pro athletes who work on the premises. In the early thirties, Gerry was the top goaltender in the New York State amateur leagues, and played for the U.S. team on a European tour. He also had some fine tournaments in the Garden, one of them against the Montreal Royals, the powerhouse amateur team from across the border. One day he summoned up enough nerve to ask Lester if he needed a practice goalie for the Rangers' workouts.

"He told me to report the next day, and I turned up all dressed in my gear and scared to death at the thought of being out there with all those great players. Lester beckoned me onto the ice, called me over, halted the workout and said, 'Gentlemen, I want you to meet this young man. His name is Gerry Cosby, and he is our new goalie.' They knew and I certainly knew I wasn't their new goalie, but Lester made me feel as though I was, even though I was half-scared out of my wits at being there, surrounded by all my idols. But the players grinned, tapped me with their sticks as they went by and I went into the nets and got to work. I still felt scared, but invigorated. In his quiet, gracious way, Lester could have that effect on you."

Bill Chadwick, the American who became the first U.S. official in the NHL and one of the few referees to be named to the Hockey Hall of Fame, had yet another view. "There were some hangups about Americans in the NHL in those days, but not with Lester. He seemed to have a special appreciation for an American in a Canadian game, and always went out of his way to help him. He got me my first officiating job, as a linesman for the New York Americans. Whenever he could he'd watch me and then call me into his office to talk about things I was doing wrong. It was his constructive criticism that got me on my way as an NHL referee.

"He had an amazing grasp of all aspects of the game, including my side of it. He was a great advocate, for instance, of the 'slow whistle.' He used to say, 'Bill, you've got all night to blow that thing, but once you do, you can't call it back. A hasty call often penalizes the wrong team, especially on an off-side decision.' It was his view that a constant flow of play and movement of the puck was not only better for the players and the fans, but also made the game easier to referee. I abided by his advice, and it certainly helped. It changed my whole style and philosophy of officiating."

It was Conn Smythe's Toronto Maple Leafs who were the Rangers' victims in the 1933 play-off final, and all of the original Rangers were there with the exception of Taffy Abel and Lorne Chabot. Chabot had been traded away because of Lester's (mistaken) idea that the eye injury had pretty well finished his career, and poor old Taffy had been traded because of a losing battle with his weight problem.

The fans hated to see Taffy go, and Lester got a polite dressing-down from one of them for peddling Ching Johnson's partner off to the Chicago Black Hawks. The indignant fan was George Raft, who complained that he had won a few dollars on Taffy in the past, and with him gone the odds were now very hard to figure. Raft looked—and sometimes acted—just like the suave mobsters he portrayed on the screen. He was known to bet on anything that moved, or didn't. Between movies, he was a Garden regular along with other showfolks such as Paul Muni, Frederick March, Edward G. Robinson, Humphrey Bogart, and Pat O'Brien. Although Raft was known to put a dollar or two on the Rangers, heavy gambling was not part of the Garden scene on hockey night. The man in charge of keeping the hoodlum element off the premises was Jimmy Broderick, a police detective known as "the toughest cop in New York." He was so tough that no less a hood than Frank Costello had ordered his boys to "lay off Broderick," even though he was a constant harassment and had sent a few of Frank's boys up the river. Broderick was eventually more or less immortalized in a Hollywood movie based on his life called *Bullets and Ballots*. The flick depicted his role in the pinch of Legs Diamond, and other little sagas of the sidewalks of New York.

Lester, who always liked to be on the right side of the law, was one of Broderick's admirers, and could occasionally be seen chatting with him in the rotunda before game time as the scene was scanned for undesirables. The New York players were also fond of Broderick, who had been kind enough to introduce them to the proprietor of a popular spa called the Green Door, which was just a couple of minutes away from the Garden as the thirsty hockey player flies. As those were the days of prohibition, the Green Door was a speakeasy, and patrons with friends in high places, like down at the local police precinct, always got preferred treatment. Being a New York Ranger was just that much better, and the establishment became the players' official hangout after workouts, a social tradition that lasted through the years, long past the repeal of prohibition.

The Americans, better known as the Amerks, also frequented the premises, but as their off-hours rarely coincided, the teams were seldom there together. And only the Rangers had the personal speakeasy sponsorship of the toughest cop in New York.

After their 1933 Stanley Cup triumph, the Rangers were hosted at a sumptuous victory celebration at the Astor Hotel by Garden president Bill Carey and some of his socialite friends. The affair served not only to fete the champions but also to introduce the man who would shortly take over as the new president of the Rangers, General John Reed Kilpatrick.

A World War I officer with a distinguished military record, Kilpatrick had been an All-American football player at Yale. A big, bluff, genial man who loved to socialize, he had craved the post of top man with the Ranger organization, and got it. As he stepped up to the top, Colonel Hammond, the man who had put it all together, stepped down, the unhappy victim of a Garden's stock power play engineered by friends of Kilpatrick.

From their first meeting at the Astor party, Kilpatrick and Lester Patrick got along famously. They were of similarly gregarious natures, and Kilpatrick was very impressed when Lester responded to the request from his boys for one of his *habitant* verses by once again reciting the tale of the poor Quebec farmer boy, "Little Bateese."

One man who would have liked to have been there but couldn't make it was Jimmy Walker. Jimmy was by that time no longer mayor of New York. Caught in a graft scandal that had unearthed secret bank accounts totaling over $1 million and produced

fifteen criminal charges of misuse of his office, Walker had resigned and fled to self-exile in England.

Kilpatrick couldn't take the Rangers to a reception on the steps
of City Hall, but he did take Lester to another imposing function
before he and his wife headed back to spend the summer on the
Coast. A fringe member of the swank theater set, the General had
been invited to a party at the elegant Fifth Avenue apartment of
Broadway's most distinguished tunesmith and playwright, Cole
Porter. Porter was between hits. Having just closed the Ethel Bar-
rymore Theater production of *Gay Divorcee,* he was now working
on the score of his next and possibly best musical, *Anything Goes,*
which would star Ethel Merman. He was famed for his lavish parties, and Lester was properly impressed with his invitation to attend one as Kilpatrick's guest.

Ed Sullivan was there, which is how Lester's and the General's
presence got to be mentioned in the next day's New York
Graphic, along with the names of several other guests such as Irving Berlin, Miss Merman, Gertrude Lawrence, Dorothy Parker,
Robert Benchley, a host of Broadway producers, and the New
York *Times'* theater critic, Alexander Woollcott. But the hockey
coach was not altogether a fish out of water at this cultural gathering, as the host himself had somewhat of a sports background.
While attending Yale University, the young Cole Porter had written two football songs: "Bull Dog," and "Bingo Eli Yale," both
of which are still sung at alumni gatherings.

As usual at his parties, the host entertained at the piano, and
while Porter was running through his brilliant personal repertoire
of compositions, Kilpatrick, who was feeling quite mellow, whispered to Lester that maybe he should do one of his *habitant* verses
as his contribution to the party. Lester, as he put it later, had "the
good sense to decline," although he did admit to a momentary
temptation. For the first and maybe last time, Lester figured that
the competition was a bit too hot for "Little Bateese."

From the party in Cole Porter's swank Fifth Avenue digs it was
then just a 4,000-mile train and boat ride to another major social
event at Cyndomyr, the spacious family home on Victoria's Michigan Avenue. Lester and his wife arrived back from New York just
in time to join the clan there for the celebration of Joe's and

Headline and picture from Boston *Globe*, 1912. (Bill Cunningham)

Frank Patrick and Catharine Porter on their wedding day, 1915, seated on steps of family home with Joe and Grace.

Frank Patrick as player-president of the Vancouver Millionaires (*left*).
(B. C. Sports Hall of Fame)   Ernie ("Moose") Johnson (*right*).

The Vancouver Millionaires, Stanley Cup Champions of 1915. Back row
(*left to right*): Fred Harris, Cyclone Taylor, Pete Muldoon (trainer),
Mickey McKay, Frank Nighbor. Front row: Frank Patrick, Si Griffis,
Lloyd Cook, Hugh Lehman. (B. C. Sports Hall of Fame)

Tex Rickard. (*Ring* magazine)

Art Ross as general manager of the Boston Bruins. (Karanjian Studio)

Lester as he was when he went into goal at age forty-four.

Ching Johnson (*left*). Frank Boucher (*right*).

This cartoon by Burris Jenkins appeared in the New York *Journal* of 1934. (Bill Cunningham)

Coach Lester with Lynn and Muzz, 1938 (*left*).
In 1940 the Rangers were forced out of Madison Square Garden by the circus. They finished the Stanley Cup series in Toronto (*right*).

Lynn with his first child and Lester's first grandchild, Lester, Jr., 1940.

Lieutenant Muzz Patrick's firstborn, Lynda, 1944.

Lynn, Muzz, and Joe Patrick, Jr., at Camp Patrick Henry, Virginia, 1943.

Muzz receiving military commendation from General John Reed Kilpatrick (president of Madison Square Garden) while Lester looks on, 1945.

Art Ross and Lynn Patrick in Boston.

Lynn and son Craig, 1955 (*left*). Lester Patrick at sixty (*right*).

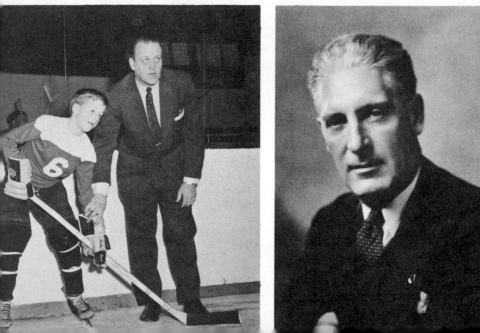

Grace's golden wedding anniversary. They were all there: the eight children, all married, and the grandchildren.

After the toast by Lester, Joe, now seventy-six, took the floor and spoke with moving affection of his family and "the wonderful good fortune" that had brought them all this far. With Grace at his side he said, "When we were married fifty years ago, we had nothing. Now, we have so much."

It is not likely that Joe was thinking about money at that moment, but through shrewd investments he had a good deal of that, too. At the end of his speech he announced that he had willed the sum of $50,000 to each of his eight children, and $30,000 to each grandchild at age twenty-one.

Just two months later, in the July 10 edition of the *Western Miner,* a front-page spread told of a family venture that would eventually have an unhappy effect on that generous bequest. The story read:

> Throwing into their plans the full force of the dynamic energy that has made the Patrick name a household word across Canada and in many parts of the United States, Frank and Lester Patrick have completed the organization of Regional Mines, Ltd., the first public announcement of which is now made.
>
> Known for years for their organizational ability and never afraid to stray off the beaten track, the famous brothers are offering an opportunity to invest in three great British Columbia resources: gold, silver and oil. The gold investment is in the Bridge River country, the silver in the Queen Bess mine near Kamloops, and the oil in a splendidly closed structure in the Cariboo.

There were then details of claims that had been purchased, geological reports, production costs, potentials, etc., and it was obvious that this was a pretty massive program. There was no doubt, according to geological reports, that all the properties were substantial, and some, as in the case of the Queen Bess silver mine which seven years before had been bonded for $750,000, contained "proven reserves." The hundred-ton mill at Queen Bess had been reactivated, diamond drilling had begun, and work crews were already out on the gold and oil properties.

Frank Patrick, who had already lost some of his and a lot of old Joe's money in a previous smaller gamble, was sure that this time he would strike it rich. It was he who had acquired the properties and formed the company. He was personally supervising the huge project and had his son, Joe, Jr., now a sturdy youth of eighteen, working at the silver mine.

But Frank and his partners had not struck it rich. There was some return that summer from the silver property, but not enough to keep Regional Mines, Ltd., afloat. Also, no gold was found, and the "splendidly closed structure" of the Cariboo country refused to relinquish so much as a drop of oil. Still, the *Mining News* report ended on this brave note: "These authorities [quoting a distinguished group of international geological experts] all agree that the Cariboo offers wonderful possibilities, and drilling already completed there has convinced them of the great possibility of oil production in that region."

But the luck of the Irish was not the luck of the Patricks. Four summers later, after abandoning the oil search in the Cariboo, Frank moved further north to drill in what was touted as the even more promising Peace River country. But when a bit broke after drilling to a depth of 3,000 feet, leaving Frank strapped for money to carry on, that property too was abandoned. A few years later, prospectors drilling for oil in the same area tapped one of the world's richest natural-gas fields, and pipeline companies have made enormous fortunes from its vast reserves.

But in that summer of 1933, it was plain financial disaster for Regional Mines, Ltd., and for its principal shareholder, Joe Patrick, who was on his way to losing a total of more than $300,000 on Frank's endless dream of striking it rich. The patriarch's bequest fund was sadly depleted in the process.

Frank still had his Vancouver Lions of the Pacific Coast League and he already had a brilliant young player named Clint Smith just about ready for sale to the NHL, but what otherwise looked like a pretty depressing winter was lightened by a phone call from Montreal. It was NHL president, Frank Calder, offering Frank a job in the newly created league post of managing director. His main duties would be to oversee the NHL officials as Calder's top aide.

The salary was only $7,500, but it was the big leagues, where Frank Patrick on his record certainly belonged. And by now, with nothing much going right on the Coast, he decided that it was time he made the move. In the East, it was believed that the game's master innovator was being groomed as the aging Calder's successor.

So now, with Lester back again in New York City, both brothers were up there where the action was, and it wasn't long before the new NHL managing director was in the thick of it. It was in early December when Frank was called in to adjudicate one of the most sensational cases in NHL history, involving the near death of Toronto's Ace Bailey after being felled by Boston's Eddie Shore.

Early in the second period of a wild game in Boston, Shore was skating back to his defensive post after being boarded by Toronto's trigger-tempered Red Horner when Bailey came wheeling across the rink and Shore suddenly turned and cut him down from behind. The back of Bailey's head hit the ice with a sickening thud. Seeing his teammate unconscious, Horner went after Shore and smashed Eddie square in the face with his forearm. Shore too went down and was carried off bleeding heavily as the Toronto trainer rushed out to tend the stricken Bailey.

Both Shore and Horner were given match penalties, pending any further league action. "League action" meant managing director Frank Patrick, who got a phone call from Art Ross right after the game.

The ugly affair and all its ramifications became progressively more serious as Bailey's condition worsened in the hospital, where he still lay unconscious, suffering from a concussion.

The case, Patrick's first big test, was not as simple as it seemed on the surface. There were a lot of people and a lot of factors involved in this wild night on the ice that had simply gotten out of hand. King Clancy, himself a principal in some of the vicious infighting that had been going on throughout the game, was never exactly sure where the blame lay for the climactic incident involving Bailey.

Here is King's personal version of what happened that night: "It was me, not Horner, who started it because it was me who hit him in the first place. Shore came thundering down the ice and when he wheeled in toward our net I stuck out my knee and upended him just as Red crashed him into the boards. I picked up the puck and raced off with it, and when I looked back I saw

Shore scrambling to his feet and then hit Bailey across the back of his legs.

"It all happened so terribly fast, but as sure as I'm sitting here talking now, Shore didn't know it was Bailey he had hit. I swear that Eddie thought he was retaliating against me, but in the confusion of all the scrambling and turning around he hit Bailey. He was out to get me, but I know he never meant it to be that bad.

"I helped carry Ace off the ice along with Lionel Conacher and some of the other Boston players, and we took him to the Boston dressing room. When I left, Ace looked just awful, and when I got into the corridor Conn Smythe was in a fistfight with a fan. Apparently some of the Boston fans had taken a shot at Conn and he wasn't going to stand for that. But nobody then knew just how bad Bailey was."

The morning after the incident, Frank was deep into the investigation as he interviewed all the players and other principal witnesses and fans who could shed any light on the affair. He talked to Shore and Horner and to doctors and reporters and did what Boston boss Ross praised as an "absolutely thorough job of research and investigation." Red Horner was immediately suspended for six games, but judgment on Shore was withheld. Meanwhile, with Bailey still in a coma and reported near death, Shore was also being quizzed by the Boston police.

Patrick went back to Montreal, and despite pressure for a quick decision on calling for very strong punitive measures against Shore, he refused to make an immediate public statement. He was still deliberating when, after ten days and two delicate brain operations, Bailey was finally reported to be out of danger. Four days after that, Frank handed down his verdict: Shore was given a sixteen-day suspension. Predictably, Conn Smythe, who had beaten an assault-and-battery charge following his post-game fisticuffs, screamed that the penalty to Shore was not severe enough. He tried to form a group to force Patrick's resignation, but got little support.

Of the controversial verdict, Clancy says, "It was a very difficult situation, but the players knew that whatever ruling Frank would make, it would be respected. We knew Shore to be a tough, hard-hitting competitor who was always willing to take as much as he gave, and more. We knew him as a magnificent player who took his chances out there with the rest of us. He was a unique competitor: rough, tough, and mean, but never intentionally dirty. Shore, in a way, with the stigma, was hurt as much as Bailey.

"He was my enemy on the ice, and we never had a game when we didn't have a go at each other. We hit each other hard and enjoyed it. I guess we were sadists. A lot of hockey players are. But as far as Eddie was concerned, we all knew that there would be nothing chippy or cheap. We played hard. That was our way. I personally thought that the sixteen-game suspension was fitting. There had to be a penalty to act as a deterrent, and that seemed penalty enough."

In New York City, Lester Patrick's defending Stanley Cup Champions were having a mediocre year, finishing third in the league race before bowing quickly to the Canadiens in the playoffs. The Rangers, with several of the old originals still around, were plainly getting a little long in the tooth. Lester knew it was time to bring in new legs, time to rebuild.

He may or may not have realized it at the time, but he had the makings of a pretty good start on that rebuilding job right there in his own Victoria household.

7

SEPARATE
JOURNEYS

Even as teen-agers, Muzz and Lynn Patrick were superb all-around athletes, and they looked the part. At seventeen, Muzz was a lean and muscular 6'2", 180 pounds, and Lynn, the elder by just under four years, was a half inch shorter and a few pounds heavier. In both high school and senior city competiton they excelled at everything they tried, and that included baseball, basketball, football, rugby, hockey, track, bike riding, and, in Muzz's case, boxing.

They were two of the best in a truly remarkable Victoria area of athletes who rose to excel at the national and international levels. They all ran in the same pack, and a photograph of nine of the gang, all well over six feet tall, still hangs on the wall of the Victoria YMCA, which was their downtown headquarters. One, a bustling, bruising young giant named Norm Baker, was eventually named as Canada's Outstanding Basketball Player of the First Half of the Twentieth Century. Two others, the Peden brothers, Torchy and Doug, joined Baker in the Canada Sports Hall of Fame, Torchy for his brilliant career as one of the world's best and most colorful six-day bike riders, and the younger, Doug, as a superb all-arounder who led the Canadian basketball team to a silver medal at the Berlin Olympics before joining Torchy on the bike circuit that packed the arenas in New York, Boston, Montreal, Toronto, and Chicago.

Two other members of that unique gang' were the Chapman brothers, Chuck and Art, the twin field generals of a dynasty of national basketball championship teams that came out of Victoria, including the one that also starred the Patrick boys. All seven are in the British Columbia Sports Hall of Fame, and as a group from the same Canadian community at the same time, there has been nothing like them in Canadian sport since.

There is no doubt that the two oldest sons of Lester Patrick were something special in a very special Victoria era, but in the summer of 1933, hockey, the family's bread-and-butter sport, was one of their lesser talents. Nobody, including Lester, could have dreamed that his boys would soon be part of the new breed who would replace the Madison Square Garden old guard and take the Rangers to a third Stanley Cup Championship. But as the family left Victoria that summer to spend the next two years in Montreal, the brothers were on their way.

Their paths first coincided, then diverged, as they traveled the roundabout route to join their father in Madison Square Garden, with Lynn destined to arrive first. Just as they are each separate and highly individual personalties, so are their stories separate and personal, and such stories are sometimes best told by the principals themselves.

Here then are their early stories as told by the two sons in their retirement years; Muzz in his spacious house in the seashore community of Riverside, Connecticut, and Lynn in his converted farmhouse home on wooded acreage in De Peres, Missouri.

LYNN'S STORY

I started skating when I was six. That was back in the days when Lester—we always called Dad that later on—had his Coast League teams, and Grandpa used to take me down to the rink. Grandpa was a great influence on my early life, and when Lester was away coaching the Rangers we used to spend as much time at his house as we did at our own. When we went to school we always dropped in at his place at lunchtime.

I had a much earlier start at hockey than Muzz did, but I really wasn't much of an athlete as a young kid. Muzz was a natural at everything, and I used to sort of hang back and push him into things. Like bike racing. Road races were big on the Coast, and I used to get Muzz up to ride with me every morning at 5 A.M., before breakfast. Torchy [Peden] was out riding every morning too, but he was already one of the best riders in the West, and training for the Olympics.

I was wrapped up in hockey down at the rink long before the basketball days. I played in a commercial league until the night the rink burned down. I was devastated when that happened. I thought it was the end of my life. The fire broke out just before dawn, and we could see the glow from our house, five miles away. When Muzz and I got there, the old arena was just a mass of charred ruins.

Muzz was too young to play commercial hockey then, and the only hockey he ever played in Victoria was in the high school league. I was the one who had pro-hockey ambitions right from the start. It seems that this was all I ever wanted to do in life, although for some reason I never wanted to play for Lester or Uncle Frank. I guess I saw myself doing it on my own. I skated on my own, and got very little teaching.

Muzz got pretty involved in boxing, and even as a little kid he could scrap, and was always very tough. The two of us fought a lot when we were kids, and I guess I must have licked him at least twenty times. That went on until he was about fifteen. One day I accused him of stealing a dollar I had hidden in the basement, and he yelled "I never touched your stupid dollar," and then decked me. I never took him on again.

We both played a lot of rugby and Canadian football and competed in track. One year I held the Vancouver Island record for the 440-yard run.

In 1933 Muzz and I were forwards on the Victoria Blue Ribbons basketball team that won the national championship. That was in the spring, just before Lester came back from New York, and we won by beating the Windsor-Walkerville Alumni in three straight games after losing the first. I missed the first game because of the flu, but Muzz and I and Art [Chapman] finished as the tournament's top scorers.

I was attending Victoria College at the time, but not doing very well with my studies. By that time, both Muzz and I were dedicated to the idea of becoming pro-hockey players, but Mother was dead against it. She thought all hockey players were bums, and we didn't dare mention the idea to her.

One day while we were driving into town Lester asked me what I intended to do with my life, and I said, "Lester, I want to play pro hockey." Well, he yanked the handbrake, pulled the car to the curb, looked me in the eye and said, "That's one hell of an ambition for a young man who has all the opportunities in life that you have." He was to go through the same thing with Muzz a little later.

A week or two after that he called me into the little office he had in the front of the house and said, "Lynn, we're going to move to Montreal, where I can see more of the family during the winter. It's obvious that you haven't any interest in staying at college and studying for dentistry or anything like that, so the move won't hurt you at all."

He made a deal with me that in Montreal I needn't do anything but skate and work on my hockey, and then after a year we'd sit down and talk. If we both agreed then that I couldn't make it as a pro-hockey player, I was to go back to school and study dentistry.

When we arrived in Montreal in the autumn, I went right to work at the neighborhood arena and spent every available minute there until winter came, then moved to the outdoor rinks. I skated until I was blue in the face, trying to make up for lost time. All the other kids, most much younger than I, had far more experience than I, or Muzz. By the time the hockey season rolled around, I was good enough to make the squad of the Montreal Royals of the Quebec Amateur League, and by play-off time I was on a regular line. I still had a lot to learn, but by then Lester grudgingly agreed that I might have a chance.

On the autumn week-ends, I played end for the semi-pro Montreal Winged Wheelers of the Big Four Football League. It was a pretty good team, and our quarterback was a second-team All-American from the University of Pennsylvania named Carl Perina. I played just part of that season as I'd told the coach I'd be quitting early to play hockey, which I did. While I was with the Royals, I also found time to play a season at forward with the

Montreal Nationales basketball team, and we managed to win the
Eastern Canada Championship before being knocked off in the
national final by a Vancouver team called the Province Bluebirds.

But the basketball and the football were just fun things; I was
really serious about hockey, and I got my first big thrill when I
went with the Royals on a U.S. exhibition tour. We played amateur teams in Baltimore and Atlantic City, then in New York, in
Madison Square Garden. I scored the first goal in the New York
game, against a kid named Gerry Cosby, who I got to know a lot
better later on when I was with the Rangers. It was a big thrill
playing in Madison Square, but I had no ambition at that time to
come back some day to play for Lester's team. I had always
dreamed of playing for the Toronto Maple Leafs. I used to listen
to Foster Hewitt's "Hockey Night in Canada" broadcasts from
Toronto, and I thought the Leafs were the greatest team in the
world.

In the autumn of 1934 Lester asked me to report to the
Rangers' amateur tryout camp in Winnipeg. This was the first
NHL camp ever to include amateurs in a full team tryout. I went
to Winnipeg early, lived at the YMCA, and signed to play football
with the Winnipeg Blue Bombers. That's the team that some years
later sent their ex-player and coach, Bud Grant, to Minnesota,
where he built the Vikings into one of the great National Football League powers. There were just two western teams in the Canadian League then, but we played against the eastern clubs and
also exhibitions against U.S. teams such as the Minnesota All-
Stars, the University of North Dakota, and Concorde University.

I guess the play I remember most about that football experience
was a 68-yard touchdown pass I caught from Russ Rebholz to
beat Regina. It was the longest TD pass-play of the season.

Again, it was just a short season of football as I was simply
using the time to keep in shape for the hockey camp in October.

I reported in good condition, and it was a good thing I did because there were some great young amateurs there. Sixteen of the
twenty-five there became professionals and several developed into
really outstanding NHL players. These included Babe Pratt, Mac
and Neil Colville, Alex Shibicky, Bert Connolly, Joe Cooper,
Murray Armstrong, Don Metz, and Bert Gardiner, all real good
ones. And then there was me, with an awful lot to prove. All of

the others had much more competitive experience than I, and one man I did not impress was Lester. He was less than enthused with me as a prospect and told me so. However, Bill and Bun Cook apparently saw something Lester didn't see because they went to bat for me and told Lester he'd be crazy not to sign me. He reluctantly agreed, and I signed a contract for $3,500, plus a $300 bonus. There was nothing much said about it between us, but that was the end of any ideas Lester had of my becoming a dentist.

When camp broke, we took the train to St. Louis to start the NHL season against the St. Louis Eagles, who the year before had been the Ottawa Senators of the NHL Canadian Division. The Senators had gone broke in Ottawa, and wouldn't last long in St. Louis as the Eagles, but they were a pretty good hockey team. In that first game, I played left wing on an all-rookie line with Bert Connolly and Charlie Mason, and we did fairly well.

The Colvilles and Shibicky and some of the other rookies were along, but they left the squad after St. Louis to join the Brooklyn Crescents of the Eastern Amateur League, a Rangers' development team. Babe Pratt was still just eighteen, and he was left behind in Winnipeg to play another year of junior hockey.

There was one incident on that train ride to St. Louis that gave me my first insight into the kind of ship Lester was running. After the train pulled out, the rookies sat down to dinner, checked the menu, and Shibicky said, "Okay, guys, let's order à la carte." I don't think Shibicky knew what à la carte was except that it sounded pretty impressive, but we went along. It was, of course, the most expensive way of ordering, but we really tucked in and just signed the bills afterward.

The next morning, Lester called us into the little compartment he always reserved for the Rangers' train trips and said, "Boys, you might eventually be with us for a while, so there are a few things you should learn. Your meal allowance, for instance, is five dollars a day. That means that your amateur league banquet days are over, unless you happen to be independently wealthy. Now, gentlemen, look at this bill. It's scandalous. I don't want to see anything like it again. While you're with the Rangers I expect you to spend the company's money the way you spend your own— carefully."

But then there was the time a year or so later when we were on the train to Boston, and Shibicky sat down in the dining car and ordered sausage and mashed potatoes, which cost ninety-five cents. After dinner Lester called him into his compartment and said, "Alex, you're in the big leagues now, and how on earth can you expect to play an NHL hockey game on sausage and mashed potatoes?" Poor Shibicky was a little confused, and reminded Lester of what he had said a year before in St. Louis.

Lester laughed and explained that he hadn't meant that he should go on a ninety-five-cent sausage and mashed potatoes diet, and told him to order food with some energy in it. As long as it came to no more than five dollars for the day. That night in Boston, we won 1–0, and it was Shibicky who got the only goal. When we got on the bus for the overnight trip back to New York Lester came around with sandwiches and said, "Alex, my boy, you can eat all the sausages and mashed potatoes you want."

But that was later. On that first train ride out of Winnipeg we were on our way to New York for the season opener in Madison Square Garden, and getting there was a mixed thrill for me. The fans and some of the writers didn't take too kindly to the idea of the boss's son moving right into the lineup, especially with practically no amateur record, and they nearly booed me out of town. But they accepted me after a while, and I stayed around for ten pretty good seasons. And a Stanley Cup Championship.

MUZZ'S STORY

As Lynn says, Grandpa Patrick was a big part of our early years, and he was a lot stricter with us than Lester was. He was a real crank on religion, but he had a very warm and human side and always talked a lot tougher than he really was. He used to pretend anger, and his favorite expression when he was chiding us with a wag of his fist was, "I'll give you an eye," meaning a black eye. He chewed tobacco, and had a big brass spittoon that he could hit from clear across the room. You could hear it go *P'Tinnnnnng*, and we kids were very impressed. He loved all athletics and especially boxing. When I started fighting around Victoria he was always at the ringside. He never missed one of my fights.

We, of course, loved Lester, as everyone did. He was always in demand at luncheons and things to recite verses like "Little Bateese" and "The Curie of Calumet," and he entertained a lot at home, with the family. He loved to sing to us while driving along in the car, mostly the old war songs like "Long, Long Train A-winding," and "Keep the Home Fires Burning." He played piano by ear and was always the life of the party, as he was later with the Rangers at the Christmas gatherings. He always led the singsongs.

I guess Lynn and I were a little rambunctious when we got into our teens. We used to give Lester a pretty bad time, but he always stuck up for us and helped us whenever we were troubled.

Dad used to play golf down at the Victoria Colwood Club, and I remember being told about the time he was putting out on the eighteenth green and Lynn and I went roaring by in our big green Studebaker touring car. One of his foursome said, "Look at those crazy bastards go," and Lester just went on putting and said, "Those crazy bastards are my sons . . ."

Mother was a quieter, gentler person, somewhat like Grandma Patrick, but with a little more warmth. She was a very sweet and gracious lady and the perfect match for my father. Her home had been in the Vancouver Island town of Nanaimo, and she had come from a hard-luck family. Her father had died in a terrible coal-mine disaster that cost thirty-two lives, and her grandmother had been married twice and widowed twice by accidents. One husband was killed by a dynamite blast and the other was drowned. From what I hear, he was a pretty wild one. I think maybe he walked off the Nanaimo dock one Saturday night with a case of beer in each hand, and just wouldn't let go.

I was around sixteen when I started boxing. I got the bug from an instructional series in the Victoria *Times*. The series was written by Gene Tunney, who had just beaten Jack Dempsey for the heavyweight title, and I thought he was just the greatest. I did pretty well in amateur tournaments around Victoria, and when the British West Indies Fleet came to town and staged an Armed Services Boxing Tournament I applied to enter.

I was told that to qualify for the tournament I had to belong to one of the Armed Forces, so I went right down to the Armory and signed up for a short stint in the Canadian Army. That got me into the tournament, and I made it to the finals against Sailor McRae, the heavyweight champion of the fleet. I knocked him out in the second round.

A couple of years later when we were living in Montreal, I went to Lester and asked him for a loan so I could go to the Canadian Amateur Boxing Championships in Edmonton. He was horrified by the request. "Why do you want to spend all that money just to watch a bunch of amateurs?" he asked. I told him I didn't want to watch them, I wanted to fight them. He went with me.

My opponent in the final match for the heavyweight championship was Tommy Osborne, the defending champion. The tournament officials were so sure that he would win that they had his name already engraved on the back of the gold medal. He knocked me down twice in the first round, but I got up and finished him in the second. I've still got the medal, and if you look carefully you can see Osborne's name underneath mine, where they tried to scratch it out.

Lester was at ringside that night, and Neil Colville and Lynn were up in the seats. At the finish, they all came roaring into the ring, thumping me and slapping me, laughing and yelling. Lester was never happier. He, too, like Grandpa, loved the fights.

Before that, I'd had some marvelous times back in Victoria with the Pedens and the Chapmans and those other guys, all terrific athletes, and the salt of the earth. It was a big thrill for all of us when our club, the Blue Ribbons, won the national basketball championship in 1933, just before we moved East.

As for hockey, I was quite a bit behind Lynn, but of course he was a little older and had made a pretty good start at Dad's old arena before it burned down. I began playing a lot more in Montreal, in our high school league and then in the city league. I attended Westmount High, in the same area where Lester and Uncle Frank grew up when they were learning hockey. It took me both of those two years in Montreal before I really dared to start thinking seriously about playing pro hockey, but by the time I left I was rated the best player in the high school league. In Montreal, that's pretty good.

Next to hockey, boxing was my first love, and my mother could never understand that. I remember coming home one night from a fight with a few scratches on my face, and she was appalled. She thought I was permanently disfigured and wanted me to quit boxing right then and there. But when I took five or six stitches home after a hockey game she'd just look at me, shake her head, and say, "Murray, when are you going to get smart and keep your head up out there?"

I did a little bike racing in Montreal too. The local promoter, Harry Mendel, had heard that I used to do some road racing back in Victoria, and he offered me a pro contract to team up with the famous Belgian rider, Gerard Devaets, in a six-day race at the Forum. I accepted, and after the race Mendel said he'd never seen a rider take so many spills and get banged around as much as I did. I know I spent most of the week bouncing around the track like a rubber ball. They rushed me to the hospital afterward, but there was nothing serious and after a few hours I went home.

I was too young and too green to be invited to the 1934 Rangers' camp in Winnipeg, but I followed Lynn to New York at the start of the hockey season and lived there with my parents. I spent all the time I could at the Garden rink, watching the Rangers and working out with some of the local amateurs.

Lester's old boss, Colonel Hammond, watched me play one day and was impressed enough to arrange a tryout for me with the Brooklyn Crescents. The Crescents were an amateur club, but they paid a little pin money and it was step one up the ladder to the Rangers: from the Crescents to the farm-club Philadelphia Ramblers of the American Hockey League and then, if you were good enough, up to the big club in New York. The Colvilles and Shibicky and others had already gone that route.

Meanwhile, I was still doing a little fighting and got into some pretty good amateur cards in the Garden. My first big fight there was in a CYO Championship Tournament, against a heavyweight named Howard Langraf. He was the champion of the Eastern U. S. Seaboard, and as I had been the heavyweight champion of the Pacific Northwest as well as of Canada, there was a lot of interest in the fight and it drew a big crowd.

They didn't get much of a fight because I won by a knockout in the second round. Afterward, Lynn, who had been sitting at ringside with the famous bandleader Abe Lyman, came back and said, "Hey, Muzz, that Langraf had a string of twenty-two straight knockouts!" I said, "Good, now he's got twenty-three."

In another Garden fight I beat a well-known amateur named Bill Gould in another main event. He went the full distance to a decision, but he took a lot of punishment. He never did anything after that fight.

Some of the local promoters and matchmakers were getting interested, so just to make sure I got into the right hands Lester came into the picture. He never interfered with my boxing, but never missed a fight if he could help it, and he had some good friends in the business. One of these was Jimmy Bronson, who was one of the most respected men in boxing. Bronson had helped Billy Gibson manage Gene Tunney to the heavyweight title and was looking around for another prospect. Lester had made an appointment for me to meet him in his hotel-room office at the Forrest, and I was really excited with the prospect of meeting the man who had been so close to Tunney. Gene had been my boxing idol ever since that night in 1927 back in Victoria when we had listened to the blow-by-blow account of his fight with Jack Dempsey, when Gene won the title.

I had a long talk with Bronson about my ambitions and my chances as a pro fighter. He said he'd seen me fight in the Garden and thought I might have something, if I really wanted to work at it. He told me to go to Lou Stillman's Gym down on Eighth Avenue and rent a locker. He said that Lou would be expecting me.

Stillman's was the mecca of pugs in New York. It was a cluttered, gloomy upstairs gym that stank of sweat, but almost all the great fighters went there to train, and a lot of nobodies went there to get their brains bashed in. In between, there were a lot of young fighters who were on their way to becoming great ones. Bronson said that if I was lucky I might be one of those.

I went to Stillman's, paid two dollars for a locker, and Lou told me to start working out on the bags. The gym was full of fighters working out, watched by a lot of fat little gnomes smoking cigars. Leo Lomski, a tough heavyweight of the day, was working one of the heavy bags, and there was a bunch of the little gnomes watching him. A couple of them drifted over to take a look at me.

It was a new world to me, not a bit like the amateur fight racket. Bronson had prepared me and had given me some advice, some of which I thought a little surprising at the time, coming from a guy in the trade. He said, "When you leave here, you'll get a lot of advice from a lot of people. Listen to all of it respectfully, always thank them, and then forget what they said. Some of it might be of value, but not much. It will be up to you to sort it out, carefully." Then he said—and this really surprised me—"Always be a gentleman, and never use profane language."

If he hadn't been who he was, that would have seemed funny, but Bronson was a quiet, scholarly man and much of what he was had rubbed off on Tunney. It certainly hadn't done Gene any harm, for apart from becoming the world heavyweight champion he also became a student of Shakespeare and married a rich intellectual socialite.

Just before I left Bronson he told me that Al Ramo, a well-known trainer, would look me up at the gym, and that he was worth listening to. I was just about to leave the gym when Ramo introduced himself and said, "I'd like you to meet Whitey Bimstein."

Bimstein was a well-known manager and trainer who later became known as the Meat Wagon because he had handled a lot of the third-rate heavyweights that Joe Louis butchered. They both knew of my amateur record—I think it was 35–1, with thirty KO's. Ramo said he'd keep his eye on me, and we'd have another talk later.

There wasn't any "later" because it was about that time that I started having a lot of trouble breathing, and the problem was diagnosed as what they called a "deviated septum." It was apparently the result of an old football injury, and I had to have an operation to remove the obstruction.

That was the end of my fight career, as I was told that there'd be a strong risk of permanent injury if I continued. So I went back to playing defense for the Crescents, and forgot about boxing.

In those years, Torchy Peden used to come through town to ride in the six-day bike races at the Garden, and what an exciting rider he was with that flaming red hair and that reckless don't-give-a-damn style of his! The Garden fans were crazy about him, and I got a terrific kick out of watching one of the guys from back home turn on the fans like that.

Later, my long-time Victoria buddy Doug joined his brother, Torchy, on the circuit, and they won a lot of team races together. One of Doug's winning races became the first sports event ever televised from Madison Square Garden. That, I think, was in 1939. That was the year after I got the call to join Lynn with the Rangers, after doing my time in Brooklyn and Philadelphia.

It was worth the wait.

8

THE NEW
BREED

The year of 1934 that saw the younger generation on the move was marred by the death of Ted, the hapless victim of that sleighing accident in Quebec back in the winter of 1893. The third son, who had never shaken his despondency over the loss of his leg, died at his home in Seattle in November at the age of forty-five.

He had stayed away overlong on a sales trip and had come home very ill, suffering from pneumonia. His wife, Ida, a sweet woman who had two daughters of her own when she married Ted, put him to bed and nursed him, but he had abused his health beyond repair and he sank quickly. Ted's oldest and favorite sister, Cynda, came down from Vancouver to be with him. Although an archetypal teetotaler, Cynda, like the rest of the family, had never rejected Ted. Now, she stayed with him to the end, and he literally died in her arms. Thus ended what from almost the beginning had been a sad, tormented life.

Ironically, that same year had brought good news to the brother who had been so close to Ted, and who for years seemed haunted by the thought that he had somehow been to blame for the Daveluyville sleighing incident. Back in Vancouver following his years as managing director of the NHL, Frank was still brooding over the Shore-Bailey affair and was restless for a challenge that would get him more actively and directly involved with the part of hockey he knew best: that of running a hockey team. Still, there were times when this enigmatic man seemed quite content to settle for what he had, a good job that gave him time to enjoy his family and their beautifully appointed home in the Shaughnessy district.

Frank Miller, one of Cynda's sons and a scholarly man who became a member of the Canadian Parole Board and an internationally respected expert in crime prevention, remembers "Uncle Frank" with great affection:

"To me, he was always that very special and generous uncle who brought the big Christmas present and charmed us with that grand manner of his. He gave me my first bicycle and my first pair of skates.

"He and Catharine loved to entertain, and they were a marvelous host and hostess. When I was attending the University of British Columbia and was president of the Parliamentary Forum there, there was a group of visiting debaters in from England and I very much wanted to entertain them properly. I phoned Frank and Catharine and asked if they'd have us all for supper, and they said certainly. That night was one of the examples of how proud I was of them.

"It was at these affairs where Frank emerged as an erudite person of great charm and wit—after all, he was a graduate of McGill University—and he was more than a match for the boys from Oxford during a highly intellectual discussion of world affairs. Catharine was simply a dazzling lady. Imagine that beautiful woman at one end of the table and Frank at the other, just charming the life out of those Englishmen. I was so proud, I preened like a peacock."

Frank's son, Joe, Jr., now eighteen, was also an active part of the household. A good but not exceptional hockey player in a city industrial league, he had no burning ambition to play pro hockey, and Frank never pushed him. Joe, Jr., who had just finished high school, was with Frank when the telegram came from Art Ross in Boston offering the coaching job there. Art wanted to concentrate on the management end of the Bruins, and offered Frank a salary of $10,500 to replace him on the bench.

The wire came in September, and within a couple of weeks Frank had rented the house, bought a new Buick sedan, and they were on their way: Frank, Catharine, Joe, Jr., and his daughters,

Gloria and Frances. They traveled south through Seattle and Portland and then headed east on Highway 30. It was a nine-day
drive to Boston and a new home at 362 Commonwealth Avenue,
a big house in the heart of town, about a dollar cab ride away
from Boston Garden.

The relationship with Art Ross, for the moment anyway, was
excellent. He and Frank, of course, knew each other from the
days back in Westmount, the years in McGill University, and the
old East-West hockey battles out on the Coast. Ross, tough, ag-
gressive, and at times a pretty crude bullyboy, was not exactly
Frank's style. But they understood each other, and Art did have
the saving grace of a sharp sense of humor to balance Frank's
more somber mood.

At the Bruins' training camp in Quebec City, Frank struck up an
excellent rapport with the players, including the arch-intimidator,
Eddie Shore. They measured each other and liked what they saw.
Eddie was no part of the freeze that would soon descend on the
Patrick-Ross relationship.

Boston was a quiet, cultured, slow-paced community that suited
Frank's style, and he hit it off right away with the Bruins' owner,
Charles F. Adams. Charles F.'s son, Weston, who would inherit
the Bruins, was then still in his twenties.

Frank's first tactical move was soon hailed as a stroke of genius. He moved the newly acquired Babe Seibert, an excellent
winger, to defense, to work with Shore in a combination that
clicked from the start. They became one of the most-feared and
effective defensive duos in hockey history. In Frank's first season
behind the bench, the Bruins finished at the top of their American
Division, and though they were beaten in the play-offs, the notoriously critical Boston press praised the job he had done.

The Bostonians even concerned themselves with the matter of
Joe, Jr.'s future. Learning that Catharine was insistent that her son
should go to college, the Bruins' publicity man, Frank Ryan, a
Harvard University grad, declared that he should go to his old
school. Victor O. Jones, the writer from the Boston *Globe,* was
also a Harvard man, and when he supported the idea, that
clinched it. Joe, Jr., was enrolled in a prep school for a year, after
which he entered Harvard.

There was an interesting twist to this development, for at Harvard Joe, Jr., became the star forward on the Crimson hockey team. He made the College All-American team and set a school record for scoring against arch-rival Yale, with eleven goals in seven games. And the Yale coach was Murray Murdoch, the old original who had taken the Ivy League post after his eleven-year career as the Iron Man of Lester's Rangers.

Joe, Jr.'s most vivid impression of that first winter in Boston is of the time the Rangers first came to town to play the Bruins. "I was simply overcome by the fact that here were the famous Rangers with my Uncle Lester in charge and my cousin Lynn, one of the players, in town to play against my father's Bruins. I forget who won the game, and it doesn't matter. Afterward, we all went back to the house for a late dinner and a family reunion."

For Lynn, half the fun, if it could be called that, was getting there. Press charges of "nepotism" had hailed his debut in New York. A big thing was made of the fact that here was a player who had come straight from nowhere to the NHL, with none of the boyhood training on the frozen outdoor rinks of the Midwest and East that was the traditional route of Canadian hockey players. The "experts" and the fans refused to believe that Lynn had learned enough from his own do-it-yourself kit, and he was immediately derided as "the boss's son."

The boos in the Garden began slowly and then built up and exploded after the third game as Lynn was obviously floundering, unnerved by the pressure, and showing it. It made things worse that he was replacing a very popular and capable winger named Art Somers, who had been benched to make room for him. It also didn't help then that Lynn's special trademark was a beautifully fluid skating style that at first seemed to be more graceful than effective. As he roamed the ice in that smooth style of his, he was pelted with derisive cries of "Sonja . . . Sonja . . ." (as in Sonja Henie, the figure-skating queen who in those days was enchanting Garden fans with her own kind of elfin grace). Just as hurtful were the raucous chants of "We want Somers . . . we want Somers . . ."

Nobody, including much of the press, wanted Lynn, and as a couple of reporters continued to harp on the charge of nepotism, Lester became downright furious. For the first and last time with the Rangers, The Silver Fox lost his cool. He lashed out with a public statement that Lynn was being broken in gradually, and was there entirely on his merits as a hockey player. He labeled the press attack, "Scurrilous, reprehensible, and an irresponsible attack on the integrity of hockey . . ."

But in the end it was the boss's son who came up with the definitive reply to the criticism. After the first four uneasy games, Lynn settled down and began to look like the hockey player that experts like Frank Boucher and Bun Cook—quite apart from Lester—had said he could be. He scored 13 goals in that first season and went on to lead the Rangers in scoring twice after that, with a high of 32 goals in 47 games in the 1940–41 season. He also eventually earned selection to the NHL first and second All-Star teams, and was the playmaker on the Bryan Hextall-Phil Watson line that was rated one of the best in hockey.

In the ten seasons following that cruel welcome to Manhattan, "Sonja" proceeded to do pretty well. By the time the first big shipment of Lester's new breed arrived from the Philadelphia Ramblers the following winter, the boss's son had been accepted for just what he was: an excellent hockey player.

By January 1936 Lynn had been joined by his Winnipeg campmates of the year before: Pratt, Shibicky, the Colville brothers, and also the fiery Henri (Phil) Watson, who had come from the hockey wilds of Quebec. A few others were yet to report, including the ex-boxer, Muzz Patrick, who still had a couple of years' apprenticeship to serve. With this new group, Lester had himself a whole new challenge.

Boucher, the Cooks, Ching, Taffy Abel, and Murray Murdoch were not too many years removed from being his contemporaries, but not so this brash new crop from a different generation. With free spirits like Pratt and Shibicky, and with his own wild one, Muzz, on the way, Lester had himself more than one tiger by the tail.

The first of the new gang to check in was Watson, who was obtained after a boardroom battle with the Canadiens over his playing rights. Then on the ninety-minute train ride up from Philly came Pratt, Shibicky, and Mac Colville. Neil Colville was left behind temporarily to recover from a muscle injury.

The most imposing member of this advance guard was Babe Pratt, a big, strapping, curly-haired youth from Stony Mountain,

Manitoba, where his father had toiled as a prison guard. Pratt, an extraordinarily gifted defenseman who had burned up the Manitoba junior leagues on and off the ice before taking on Philadelphia, had just turned twenty and had already developed a remarkable capacity for the good life. The Babe was ready for Broadway, but to paraphrase an old Tin Pan Alley lyric, was Lester ready for him?

As at least a partial answer, the new boys were no sooner up than they were down again, which was an object lesson in itself. But they weren't down for long.

In the winter of 1979, Pratt remembered that first arrival as though it were yesterday, or at most the day before yesterday. "I knew I'd come a long way from Stony Mountain when we pulled into Penn Station and hopped a bus for Broadway. I looked at all those beautiful bright lights and I said to myself, 'Babe, you are going to look personally behind every single one.'

"We went straight to the Claridge Hotel at Forty-fourth and Broadway and checked in. Then we walked to the Garden with our skates and sticks, got into our Rangers' gear and went right out and played the Montreal Maroons. We won, 3–2. We'd only been in town a few hours.

"Lester hadn't said as much as 'Good evening, boys,' but we got a nice welcome in the dressing room, especially from Howie Morenz, who had just joined the club after spending a miserable season with the Chicago Black Hawks. Howie had long been one of my idols, and I guess I had felt as badly as he had when the Canadiens traded him to the Hawks after his tremendous career in Montreal. He was now thirty-four and past his peak, but it was a great thrill for us rookies when he came over and shook our hands in that warm, shy way of his. He grinned and said, 'I just want to tell you boys that my sister's brother is the greatest hockey player that ever lived.' He nodded at me and said, 'Good luck, kid.'

"Everybody loved Morenz, and of course that night we had no way of knowing what the fates had in store for him. That within a week he would be sent back to his beloved Canadiens and that within a little more than a year he would be dead. But that tragedy was still in the future, and that night in the Garden we were all a mile high. Until right after the game, when us rookies found ourselves back on the train, headed back to Philly. We didn't have much time to brood about it because the next night we were on the ice against the Boston Cubs, and just two days after that we were back on the return run to New York.

"This time, Lester called us into his Garden office and said, 'Well, boys, I think you'll be around town for a while, so you'd better find a nice place to live. Get a nice hotel, and I'll take care of the board money.'

"We moved into a hotel at Broadway at Forty-ninth, two to a room. It cost us forty bucks a month each.

"Lester had instructed Bill Cook, the team captain, to put the rookies in the personal care of Ching Johnson. I felt a little funny about that at first because Ching was the man I'd been brought in to replace, but you couldn't stay uneasy for long around Ching. He was a wonderful guy, with a disposition of a happy schoolboy. He was tough as nails on the ice, but a real panic away from the rink—full of horseplay and practical jokes.

"We'd heard that old Ching knew New York better than Mayor Fiorella LaGuardia, and we really perked up that night when he gave us a sly wink and said, 'Well, I guess you boys would like to go out and have a drink on the town, eh? A nice ice-cream soda, maybe?' And he winked again. We couldn't get into a cab fast enough, and when Ching gave the cab driver the name of a joint off Times Square you could hear our lips smacking all the way to Central Park.

"We got our drinks all right. Ice-cream sodas! Ching left, roaring with laughter. On top of that, he stuck us with the bill. He made it up later, though. He was great to me and taught me a lot about playing defense before I took his job and he left to play out the string with the Americans."

The hotel that Babe and the boys had checked into was just a hop, step, and a hoot from the Green Door, the old speakeasy hangout that had gone more or less legit with the repeal of prohibition but was still the Rangers' favorite spa. The basement bar was then also the favorite midday bistro of show folks like singer Helen Morgan and the great horn-player Bunny Berrigan, but when Pratt arrived, the horizons were broadened to include other such preferred cultural centers as Hogan's Irish Tavern on Eighth Avenue, and once in a while the boys put on the dog and patronized the Mini Bar at the Waldorf.

The first few weeks went by well enough for the rookies, and as the Rangers had won more than they lost in that spell Lester was quite content. Until he discovered where they were staying.

Lester became concerned about the quality of the neighborhood when he saw a spread in the morning paper about the big raid led by New York's crime-busting Governor Tom Dewey, who had sworn to clean up New York. This was quite a challenge for Dewey, but he had started by leading a fleet of paddy wagons into the off-Broadway area around Forty-ninth Street, raiding some of the neighborhood hostels and carting a few wagonloads of ladies of the evening off to the pokey.

Noting that the Pratt & Friends residence was right in that busy area, Lester caught Shibicky in the Garden rotunda, hauled him into his office, shook his finger and said, "Alex, I hear that hotel you're staying at is full of prostitutes. I want you to tell the Babe and the others you've got to check out of there right away."

Shibicky obediently relayed the message to Babe, whose explicit reply was, "You can tell the old man to go and delete himself."

"Babe was safe, though," says Shibicky. "The old man was well out of earshot." And they did check out.

Meanwhile over in Boston, Frank Patrick was having problems. When the Rangers closed out that season in Boston, Lester noted a change in Frank, and remarked on it that night to Ross in Art's office.

"Art," he said, "Frank didn't seem very lively on the bench tonight. We had that run-in with the referee, and he didn't move a muscle. And he left the arena right after the game without even saying hello or good-bye. What's up?"

Ross shrugged. "You've been hearing the rumors, Lester. They're true. To be blunt, Frank's just not doing the job anymore."

Lester was silent for a moment. "Do you let him do the job, Art?"

"You're talking like a coach, Lester. I'm the boss, and this is my hockey club. I like to keep close to things. That's my job. It's my obligation to Mr. Adams."

"What about your obligation to your coach?"

Ross was getting nettled. "For chrissake, Lester, there you go again. Thinking like a goddamn coach. I'm looking at it like a general manager, and I think Frank is too goddamn soft. He's too chummy with the players, and he thinks every referee is his best friend. He protects everybody. He's just too goddamn nice." He paused. "And he's drinking."

Lester knew that to be true. He had seen it starting in Vancouver, shortly after he had taken the job with the Rangers. After practically shunning alcohol for the first forty years of his life, Frank had begun drinking a little after dinner, and a little more so when the mining ventures turned sour. Not to any great excess, but with a growing frequency. It had bothered old Joe, but he had said nothing.

In 1979, Joe, Jr., reminiscing in his Park Avenue apartment that was just a few minutes' walk up Thirty-fourth Street from the new Madison Square Garden, didn't back away from this sensitive family matter. "It is true," he said, "that my father did have a drinking problem in his later years, but he never drank what is normally considered to be excessively. He simply couldn't hold the stuff. What would be a relatively harmless amount to the average social drinker was damaging to him. In his declining years when things were going badly for him, he could and did stay completely away from liquor for months at a time. But when he brooded and slipped back just a little, it hurt him.

"As far as the Boston situation is concerned—and I was playing for Harvard and the amateur Boston Olympics at the time—we could see trouble brewing between Art Ross and my father even in the first year, when the Bruins finished at the top of the league. Frank was a fine coach. You only had to watch him at work to see that, but Art simply couldn't or wouldn't let go of the reins, and my father couldn't abide that.

"It was a drinking indiscretion on the part of my father that apparently precipitated the final break with Ross. In the 1936 playoffs between the first and second teams of each division, the Bruins were pitted against Toronto. Boston won the first of the two-game total-points series 3–0 in Boston Garden, and when they scored the first goal of the game in Toronto, they were 4–0 up on the series. But then the Leafs scored eight unanswered goals in two periods of play, and the Bruins were eliminated.

"A Boston paper alleged that my father had been drinking the day of the game and wasn't in a fit condition to handle the team from the bench that night. It was a terrible thing to happen if, in fact, it was true. The newspaper story was ignored by the club, but the stigma was there, and my father was finished in Boston. It was a cruel personal tragedy because he was a wonderfully warm and loving person, and if he did err that night, he more than made up for it in a thousand other ways."

Ross told Frank that he was through with the Bruins, and that he, Ross, would return to the bench next season. Young Joe remained in Boston to complete his Harvard education as the rest of the family packed up and left to live in Montreal.

It was in that same summer of 1936 that Lynn headed back to the Coast for the off-season. After spending a few weeks in Victoria, he crossed the Straits to Vancouver to visit Guy Patrick and help a little around the Vancouver Arena. It was a trip that Lynn was not likely to forget.

"I took the boat to Vancouver with my girl friend and my cousin Joe was there to meet us. He'd just come West for the summer too, and I think Uncle Guy had sent him to take us to our hotel and make sure we got separate rooms. I spent the day working at the Arena, and stayed over until the following night to watch Max Baer, the ex-world-heavyweight champion, box an exhibition with a local fighter. There was a big crowd in the Arena for the fight card, and I left about 11 P.M. to catch the midnight boat back to Victoria. When we got off the boat the next morning, the paper was out and there was this big black headline: 'Vancouver Arena Destroyed By Fire.'

"I couldn't believe it. I couldn't help but think back to the time seven years ago when Muzz and I came out of our house on Lyndon Street to watch the red glow of the fire that burned down the other arena in Victoria.

"Frank and Lester were both back East, and I went right to Grandpa's house and showed him the paper. He came near to crying, and I'd never seen him like that before. It wasn't just the money, even though the insurance covered just 10 per cent of the Arena's $500,000 value. There was an awful lot of family sentiment tied up in that building, as there had been in the other one."

The fire that at one time threatened to consume the entire residential area of Vancouver's populous West End had started in an adjacent shipyard building around 1:30 A.M. It was just minutes after that time when a billow of flames burst through the roof of the building and was swept toward the Arena by a gusty wind. By 2 A.M. the Arena roof was a mass of flames and the area was bedlam as every available piece of fire-fighting equipment, including the harbor fireboat, raced to the scene. Every road leading to the area was jammed with traffic as people, many still in their night attire, came to watch the firemen fighting to contain the blaze.

By the time the roof collapsed in a cloud of crimson smoke, a mob of more than 20,000 people were at the scene, held back by squads of police. The first of the Patricks to arrive was Stan, the youngest brother, who operated the auditorium that had been built alongside the Arena and was now also doomed. Two other early arrivals with a very personal stake in the disaster were the British Columbia Commissioner of Immigration, Fred Taylor, now fifty-two, and a local insurance man, Frank Fredrickson, Cyclone's adversary in that famous Battle of the World's Greatest Professional versus the World's Greatest Amateur many years ago.

Taylor, an outwardly unemotional man even when generating a brand of excitement unmatched by any other hockey player, seemed his usual stoic self, his true feelings betrayed only by the tears that welled up in his eyes. The volatile Fredrickson wept unashamedly as he watched the north wall crumble, murmuring, "So many memories . . . so many memories . . . !"

The Arena complex was totally destroyed, as were seven industrial buildings, two residences, and fifty-eight small boats. Two lives were lost and three firemen badly injured in the fiery episode that wiped out the last physical trace of the Patricks' West Coast hockey empire.

Lester Patrick's personal loss from his share of the old building was said to have been in excess of $40,000, but unlike Frank, who had taken a similar loss, he was still gainfully and prosperously employed. Taking his dual general manager-coach role into the 1936–37 season, he continued to preside over the inevitable decline and fall of the Ranger originals. The faltering Bun Cook had been sent to play his final year with the Boston Bruins, and both Ching Johnson and Murray Murdoch were now playing their last season in the New York strip. Still, with the heavy transfusion of new blood, the team managed a second-place division finish and were foiled in a bid for the Stanley Cup Championship only in the last game of their final series against Detroit.

There was one poignant memory of that year that none who shared it will ever forget. It occurred in the Garden on the night of March 9, before a game against the Americans, when the fans and the players of both teams stood with bowed heads in memory of Howie Morenz, that magnificent player who in the ebb of his marvelous career was briefly a Ranger. Morenz, after drifting forlornly through his brief spells of exile in Chicago and then New York, had been brought back to play again for his beloved Canadiens, who had inexplicably cast him adrift after eight seasons as the NHL's unchallenged superstar. In January he had broken a leg in a freak accident when the toe of a skate jammed into the boards after a collision there. Complications set in, and on March 8, he died of a heart attack.

Just before the start of the next night's game in the Garden the players lined up at center ice and the lights were dimmed as a lone bugler played taps. Said Neil Colville, looking back through the years, "It was the most emotional, spine-tingling few moments of my life. You had to have known Howie to appreciate the depth of the feeling there on the ice that night."

There was an emotion of another kind the following season when after a decade as the guys from the other side of the tracks, the New York Americans, or Amerks as preferred in the Broadway jargon, finally met and whipped the pampered Blues in a crucial series, for what amounted to the Tenants Championship of Madison Square Garden. They had met several times along the way, these two birds of a different feather, but never in a play-off showdown such as that one in the spring of 1938, after the teams had finished second in their respective divisions. It was the dead-end kids of the bootlegger Bill Dwyer versus the glamorous Broadway Blues of that colorful and beloved archetype of style and integrity, Lester Patrick. At last, before a howling sellout mob of mixed supporters, here was the classic house confrontation.

It was remarkable that the Amerks had gotten that far, but coach Red Dutton—who would later serve briefly as NHL president and, later still, make a fortune in the construction business out in Alberta—had done a masterful job of blending age and youth. Typical of the Americans' teams through the years, this one was packed with retreads and aging castoffs, old gaffers who had come for a last drink at the trough before going to pasture. Among this crop were such as Hap Day, thirty-eight, winding down after eleven outstanding years with Toronto; Hooley Smith, thirty-six, and Nels Stewart, thirty-seven, gnarled throwbacks to that distant age when they had led the Maroons to the Stanley Cup victory that dispatched Lester Patrick's Victoria Cougars to posterity.

And there was also Ching Johnson, now forty. When Ching had been given his ticket at the close of the last Rangers' season, he had just shrugged his shoulders, summoned up a grin, and walked across the hall to the Americans' dressing room. He had asked for and had gotten another year's lease on life.

Of course, the Amerks had some pretty good young players around too to carry the bulk of the load, especially the splendid line of Art Chapman, Sweeney Shriner, and Dave Carr. That was as potent a scoring combo as any in the league. But it was still the blood-and-guts old guys that Dutton, not altogether a sentimental man, looked to for an upset victory in this internecine struggle between the bad and the beautiful.

Opposing these old guys were the members of the rambunctious new youth brigade that now also included Clint Smith and Bryan Hextall, two great young players just up from Guy Patrick's Vancouver Lions.

The Rangers had to fight for their lives to earn a split in the first two games before roaring, jam-packed houses, and then thought they had it all wrapped up when they took a fast 2–0 lead in the decisive third contest. Shibicky and Hextall had scored the New York goals, but Lorne Carr struck back with a goal in the third period and then Nels Stewart beat Davey Kerr to set up what was to be the longest and most punishing hockey game in Garden history.

It was 1:12 A.M. in the fourth overtime period when Carr slipped the puck into the Rangers' net on a pass from Art Jerwa to win the marathon. As soon as Carr stabbed his stick jubilantly into the air, Lester Patrick crossed the ice, hailed Ching Johnson, and shook his hand.

A reporter noted that old Ching didn't know whether to laugh or cry. "Don't you believe it," said Lester, afterward. "Ching was laughing." But then Ching always was, and this was his last hurrah.

The season was over for the Rangers, and it was over for the Americans a week later when they bowed to the Chicago Black Hawks, who then went on to win the Cup.

And then came Muzz.

After serving a three-year apprenticeship with the Brooklyn Crescents (renamed the New York Rovers when they became an official part of the Rangers' farm system) and the Philadelphia Ramblers, the second son got the call from Lester. He went to the New York camp in Winnipeg and came home with them to Madison Square to pair with Art Coulter on defense. With the retirement of Frank Boucher after seventeen superlative seasons of pro hockey, the changing of the guard was now complete.

This time, there were no screams of nepotism from the press or hoots of derision from the gallery. Although Muzz had neither the grace nor the finesse of his older brother, he was eager, strong, and tough, and that was enough for the fans. He was also an instant hit on the Manhattan after-hours social scene, where he immediately began giving that swashbuckling youth from Stony Mountain, Manitoba, Babe Pratt, a run for his stamina.

They were both the same age, twenty-three, and both living proof that 1916 had been a vintage year for Canadian wildlife. As Babe put it during his mellow years, "We gave poor Lester fits."

They were as engagingly handsome a pair of blythe spirits as ever took on Manhattan two-on-one, and Muzz had been with the club barely two weeks when he had his first run-in with the boss over his extracurricular activities.

One morning when Muzz and the Babe walked into Lester's office for the usual team meeting, they got the high sign from Neil Colville that the old man was really steaming. When they saw that Lester had a copy of the morning paper in his hand, they knew what was up. They had already seen the item in Winchell's column that read: ". . . A well known New York Rangers hockey star who is closely related to the manager was observed during the wee hours in a popular niterie, in the exotic company of Miss Lois de Fee, a well-proportioned doll who is touted as the World's Tallest Stripper . . ."

Lester held up the newspaper and tapped the pertinent piece.

"Muzz," he said, "have you seen this in Winchell's column?"

"Sure," said Muzz. "It's well-written, isn't it?"

Just as Lester seemed ready to hit the ceiling, Muzz grinned and added brightly, "Come on now, Lester. Look at it this way. How many Rangers have ever made Winchell's column? Not even Pratt, and you've got to admit that's something."

Somebody started to laugh, then the whole room shook, including Lester.

As for Lois de Fee, Muzz never did forget her, although as Pratt irreverently put it, "How can anybody forget a six-two stripper named Lois?"

Muzz's memory is more reverent, and in fact downright sentimental. "That Lois was one of the greatest gals that ever lived. Oh, she was a big one, and beautiful. With a heart of gold. She'd been a stripper in Minsky's burlesque, and I met her one night in Leon & Eddie's on Fifty-second Street where she was working as a bouncer. She made big money, knew everybody, and everybody just loved her. Years later when I was a First Lieutenant in the U. S. Army I brought her to the base at Norfolk, Virginia, to entertain on show night. I told the boys what a great woman she was, and they agreed. She was a tremendous hit."

Lois was also a tremendous hit with the other Rangers on game nights in the Garden when she appeared as Muzz's guest. The players' wives had seats in a special section along with Lester's wife, Grace, who rarely missed a game. The single players had tickets for their girl friends in another area, and Muzz's guest seat was a good one, right between those occupied by Lynn and Phil Watson's lady friends, a pair of lovely New York models whom they eventually married.

This positioning set up a tableau that is fondly remembered by Muzz's teammates, and especially by the Rangers' brilliant new center, Clint ("Snuffy") Smith, who at 5'7" was the smallest man on the club.

"When they struck up the national anthem before the game," sighs Snuffy from the depths of his fond recollection, "everybody stood up, and there was Lois towering way up there over these two elegant models, all gorgeous show girl, and well over six feet tall. It was a sight to behold, and it used to break us up as we stood watching from the ice. Muzz never could see what was so funny about it. But it was. Lois always got us off to a good start."

Miss de Fee fitted nicely into Muzz's philosophy of life in a big city for a young, fun-loving hockey player. "There were always lots of show people around, but I was never impressed with the stars and starlets, at least not the ones with the big names. They'd only get you in trouble. A fellow could meet all of them he wanted, especially at the six-day bike races. The riders used to race around the clock, and one of the big features was the 4 A.M. sprints. A lot of the big-shot show people used to flock in after the clubs had closed. I remember one time George Raft coming in with this gorgeous young red-headed hoofer, Lucille Ball.

"A lot of the well-heeled socialite ladies were there too, some of them putting up as much as $1,000 as sprint prizes, and big-name jazz groups dropped in to entertain just for the hell of it. There were even song writers there with their own pianos, plugging their songs. But I really wasn't what you'd call a real stayer-outer like Babe and some of the other guys. They'd stay out all night, although it never showed at the rink the next day. Me, I always moved faster than the others and got home fairly early, usually by 2 A.M.

"Babe liked to go out drinking with the newspaper guys, which I never did. Neither of us was married then. I lived at the Alamac Hotel just off Broadway and shared an apartment with Lynn, Neil Colville, Shibicky, and Watson. I was usually home before they were, except maybe Lynn. A reporter once asked me why it was always me in trouble with Lester and never Lynn, and I said that's because Lynn never does anything wrong.

"After games, we used to go to Harlem to the Cotton Club and then maybe back downtown to the Latin Quarter. Cab Calloway played there, and he loved hockey. He often dropped in between shows to catch a period or two, and when any of us Rangers came into the club he'd stop the show and introduce us. Babe and the others used to go there a lot, but I never went except to date one of the chorus girls. Lynn and Phil had a couple of beautiful girl friends, and they were always in love and took their girls to the swanky places. I had lots of girls, then, but I was never in love. It was a lot less expensive that way. Sure, I used to get it in the neck from Lester once in a while, but as long as I produced on the ice he didn't say too much."

Muzz's buddy, Pratt, has his own little collection of folklore from those New York days and nights under the "Benevolent Dictator."

"A lot of the stage and movie people were Garden regulars, and we got to know quite a few of them. People like Cab Calloway, Bill ('Bojangles') Robinson, Joe E. Brown, Edward G. Robinson, Doug Fairbanks, Jr., and Phil Silvers.

"One night, Silvers arrived with a blonde knockout, and after the game he came into the dressing room. We were all out of our uniforms, relaxing on the bench in our long johns before hitting the showers, and Silvers looked around, wrinkled his nose, and said, 'This doll of mine thinks you hockey players are real glamor guys. Boy, I wish she could see you in your underwear.'

"Another night, Bob Topping, the big tycoon who later bought a piece of the New York Yankees, came in with Lana Turner and sat in on the first row of seats next to Jock Sutherland, the coach of the Pittsburgh University football team, and Edward G. Robinson.

"Neil Colville gave Lana the once over and said to me, 'Hey Babe, how about giving me a chance to introduce myself to that Turner doll? Next time we go by, just give me a little bump over the boards, into her lap. The way you're skating tonight nobody will think anything of it anyway.' That was a nasty crack, but next time around I obliged. Afterward I asked Neil how things went and he said, 'Fine, if you happen to be crazy about Edward G. Robinson. Your aim was lousy.'

"Maybe that incident left a permanent scar, because Neil stayed single until he was well past fifty.

"Lester was always a little wary of the show people, especially smoothies like George Raft, who was known to gamble a little. But the nearest I ever got to Raft was one night at the Cotton Club when he was introduced from the audience. He stood up and took a bow, and then the M.C. said, '. . . also with us tonight is that great young star of the New York Rangers, Babe Pratt . . .' I was surprised because I didn't think anyone knew I was there, but just as I stood up to take a bow the spotlight swung to another table across the room. Nobody stood up, and I guess everybody thought I was just too modest, and they all cheered. But this guy at the table was passing himself off as me and having himself a real time, dinner and drinks on the house. I sent him a drink my-self before I left. He was doing a great job."

So, says Pratt, was the high priest of this remarkably permissive hockey society. "Lester let us go our own ways off the ice, but he taught us the meaning of team spirit and knew we'd respond to it. He also taught us all there was to know and more about the basics of hockey: skating, stick handling, passing, and shooting. He was without peer as a teacher. He was a genius at it. And when the puck was dropped, we were always ready to play." And, when the occasion required, to fight.

One such occasion was a late-season game in Boston, with the Bruins running away with the league race en route to a Stanley Cup Championship. Midway through the final period, Phil Watson was in a violent collision mid-ice with Eddie Shore, who was then approaching the end of the line.

Watson, a notoriously uninhibited fellow of Scotch-French-Canadian lineage who was brought up in a Quebec convent, was famed for his colorful pidgin English. Upon scrambling to his feet he waved his stick at Shore and screamed, "You censored peen-head, Shore, why no feenish play this effing game? You so old you got fedders in your effing skates . . . !"

A couple of minutes later, Watson cut past Shore and Eddie let him have it with his stick, right on the skull. Watson was led off the ice, out cold, blood streaming from a cut in his head. Both benches emptied, the Rangers trying to get at Shore, and the Bruins trying to protect him. A wild donnybrook ensued, and when peace was restored the referee gave a five-minute penalty to Watson for "antagonizing" Shore.

Lester Patrick was in a rare rage over what he felt was a gross inequity in the penalty assessments. He filed an official protest with NHL president Calder, and when Calder reviewed the case he found the referee in error and sent him back to work in the Western Canada League, where the poor fellow had learned his craft. The chastened official returned to the big leagues the follow-ing season, and six seasons after that he was appointed to the league's top executive post. Clarence Campbell, the young referee who had run afoul of Lester Patrick, not only survived that expe-rience but also profited by it as he went on to serve a distinguished thirty-two-year term as the league president.

The catalyst of that Campbell episode had another shot left in his barrel before closing off that season. Again, a New York Ranger was involved as the incorrigible Shore took on the tough new kid in town, Muzz Patrick. That brief but bloody battle between this pair is remembered as one of the most devastating one-punch encounters in the history of unlicensed pugilism. The tiff was treasured by no less a person than General John Reed Kilpatrick, who publicly named it as "my greatest thrill in hockey."

The General's choice bemused at least one of the participants. "I heard him say that at Lester's Garden farewell party in 1948," says Muzz, "and I was really shocked. I remember that when I went to the penalty box after the fight the General came down the aisle and patted me on the back. Personally, I wish the fight had never happened.

"It was in the third game of the 1939 play-offs in Madison Square, and the Bruins had us down 3–0. I was back in our zone with the other New York defenseman, Art Coulter, with Lynn, Phil Watson, and Hextall out front. Shore had Watson against the boards and was massaging the back of Phil's neck with his stick. There was no glass then, and Phil's head was jammed up against the screen. I moved slowly toward the action, then grabbed Eddie's shoulder and tried to pull him off. The guys used to look for me at times like that.

"Phil's head was beating a tattoo against the screen, but I managed to pull Eddie away. He turned and threw a punch, and then came at me. I flipped off my gloves and hit him three times with my right hand, square in the face.

"I wish I hadn't. His nose was broken and there was a big gash over his eye. The nose was split and it was spurting streams of blood. Eddie's whole face was crimson, like someone had torn the top off a cherry pie. He was a terrible sight. A photographer got a closeup, and the picture was used on the cover of *Look* magazine. It was a pretty gory photo. Eddie never held it against me, and afterward we were the best of friends. He could take it as well as dish it out.

"Years later when I was general manager of the Rangers, I sent a few players who helped his Springfield team win a couple of American Hockey League Championships, and he asked me down to speak at a luncheon. He introduced me by saying, 'Folks, here's the guy who put me on the cover of *Look* magazine.' He was quite proud of it. What a competitor that Shore was!"

There was no doubt on that point, and in that season of 1938–39, Shore decided to cash in on his talents. He was getting $6,000 a year, demanded $8,000, and when he was refused he became a holdout. NHL president Calder was called in to arbitrate, and after long and stormy negotiations, during which Lester was called in to testify regarding the worth of a bona fide superstar, Eddie capitulated and signed for $7,000. "He deserved more," said Lester, "and I said so, but seven thousand was the league salary maximum. He got the top figure." Three decades later, another pretty good Boston defenseman named Orr was paid almost that much per game, over an eighty-game schedule.

Shore did get an extra bonus of sorts that season when he was called to center ice after the game that had won the Bruins their second Stanley Cup, a 4–1 triumph over Detroit. That contest also marked the end of Shore's thirteenth campaign with the Bruins. He had played a great game on his aging legs, and the Boston fans gave him a tremendous ovation. That ovation wasn't matched until many years later when Bobby Orr stood on his gimpy knees in the same spot as the fans honored his retirement.

Shore had already begun feathering his retirement nest by buying the Springfield club, and apart from playing a few home games the following season, that was his Boston swan song. He was no factor in the campaign that would bring the Rangers their third Stanley Cup, and give Lester his fifth championship in three different leagues, as player and coach.

Before that 1939–40 season began, Lynn married the model he had been dating, a Miss Dorothy Davies, from Winnipeg. It was an ill-fated match. It would last just three years and produce a son, Lester Patrick, Jr.

Shortly after that marriage, the family lost one of its quiet stalwarts when Grandma Patrick died at her home in Victoria. She was seventy-nine. Grace Patrick was the first to be laid to rest in the family plot Joe had bought in the Royal Oak Burial Park, just a short walk from Cyndomyr. Grief-stricken at the loss of the gentle woman he had married fifty-six years before in Drummondville, Joe sold the lovely old home of so many memories and went to live with his youngest son, Stan, in Vancouver.

A sadness of far broader portent loomed on Sunday, September 3, 1939, as England declared war on Germany and the world was cast into six years of bloody conflict. World War II would deeply affect professional hockey, but not yet as the Rangers prepared for the start of their championship season.

The war was still a million miles away as Lester's frisky crew opened with a 1–1 tie against the Red Wings. And it was still a blythe, carefree autumn in New York when Lester got a call from a Hollywood movie company that wanted to make screen stars out of a couple of his hockey players.

Metro-Goldwyn-Mayer planned a movie called *The Great Canadian,* starring Clark Gable as a hockey hero. MGM arranged with Lester to use the Garden rink for location shots, and also got permission to use Phil Watson and Babe Pratt as doubles in the hockey scenes. They wanted Watson to double for Gable, and Pratt was picked to double for the half-breed villain of the piece, whose role had not yet been filled.

As far as the doubles were concerned, Pratt thought it was pretty bad casting, and he was so upset he went to Lester's office to protest. "Lester," he said, "can you imagine Phil Watson as Clark Gable? Why, he's not only ugly, he can't even speak good pidgin English!"

"Babe," Lester replied soothingly, "can't you see that Gable wouldn't dare risk having a handsome young man like you acting as his double? My goodness, Babe, haven't you ever heard of job insecurity?"

Pratt agreed that maybe Lester had something there, and reluctantly agreed to go along.

However, the movie was eventually canceled, and poor Phil never did get to be Clark Gable. Watson recovered from the blow, although he had wasted several weeks working on a pencil-thin mustache and a roguish smile. Gable also survived, turning up a few years later in a pot-boiler called *Gone with the Wind.*

As for Lester, he had more time now to tend wounded egos as he had stepped out as coach to concentrate on the job of general manager. His replacement behind the bench was his trusted old hand, Frank Boucher, who also became Lester's assistant general manager. The players had a great admiration and affection for

Lester, but Boucher was also very popular with them and he was also one of theirs.

The new bench appointment also gave Lester more time to tend his role as keeper of the privy purse, something that he had always considered an important function, and especially so now in an age when, in his words, ". . . players these days just don't know the value of money, especially when it's not theirs."

One of the vexing problems was the matter of expenses on road trips. Unfortunately, only New York had nickel subways, and to help keep taxi expenses under control he appointed "cab captains." One man for each cabful of four was delegated to be in charge of the fares. One of the cab captains was Art Coulter, who was known as a nice guy and a free spender during the social hours, and when the Rangers got back to New York after one road trip, Lester assembled his captains and said, "Okay, boys. What do I owe you for cab fares?"

The chits of the other three captains ranged from $6.00 to $8.75, but Coulter's tab added up to $12.75.

"Art," said Lester, perusing the bill, "why is your bill so much larger than the others?"

"Well, Lester," said Coulter, "you've told us that we're in the big leagues now, so I tip like a big-leaguer."

Lester was just momentarily nonplussed.

"That's very commendable, Art," he said, "but I don't know if the Rangers can afford big tippers like you."

"Okay," Art said, grinning. "You don't have to worry about it. I resign my captaincy."

The big tipper did, however, retain his team captaincy, and was thus a principal party to an unusual meeting held on the eve of the game that was to decide the 1940 Stanley Cup Championship. It could be said that the whole Rangers' season had boiled down to this team meeting held in what the average coach or manager might regard as an unseemly spot: the beer tavern in Toronto's Ford Hotel.

The Blues had finished three points behind Boston in the league race, had ousted the Bruins in the first play-off round, and now had the Toronto Maple Leafs down three games to two in the final round. The superb goaltending of veteran Davey Kerr and a strong defense anchored by Pratt and Otto Heller had been the

principal factors in getting the Blues this far, and now a win in the
upcoming sixth game in Toronto with the Leafs would wrap it up.

With Boucher running the team and doing a great job of it,
Lester stayed aloof and left the closing pep talk to his coach. Except that with the Rangers, in a style set long ago by Lester, there
were never any pep talks per se. When the occasion seemed to call
for a special gathering of the forces, a quiet chat tuned to the idea
that there was a job to do and now was the time to go out and do
it, in the best way possible, always sufficed. It had been Lester's
way, and now it was Boucher's, but Frank figured that this volatile
gang of his needed an extra touch, such as a pint or two with dear
friends in familiar surroundings.

Hence the gathering of the clan in the Ford Hotel beer parlor
the afternoon before game six against the Leafs.

They were all there: the two Colvilles, Shibicky, Clint
Smith (the little center-ice wizard who had gone the astonishing
number of eighty-five games before incurring a penalty), Phil Watson, Pratt, Heller, Bryan Hextall, Alf Pike, Dutch Hiller, Kilby
MacDonald, and the Patrick brothers.

Captain Coulter opened with a toast, Coach Boucher responded
by raising his ale glass, there was a rousing "hear . . . hear . . ."
from the troops, then a reverent silence as the steins were
drained. This, oft repeated, was the extent of the team-meeting
agenda, which was, of course, laced with convivial conversation,
the odd burst of ribald laughter, and even an occasional more or
less scholarly reference to the upcoming game against the Leafs.
"It was," as Coulter, ably seconded by Pratt, later described the
session, "a loosener. The team had been playing great hockey and
wanted no part of a seventh game in Toronto. The only danger
was that of getting a little uptight, and pressing too hard."

By mid-evening, after about four hours of loosening, there
wasn't an uptight pore in the place, and not a soul was seen pressing too hard. Boucher had left a little earlier, already an hour late
for a press conference.

They might still have been loosening by game time but for the
fact that Lester, concerned when the boys didn't show for dinner,
decided to send out a search party. It was the pub-wise club
trainer, Harry Westerby, who located the missing persons. After

just one more beer—this one a toast to Harry—the meeting was adjourned.

The next evening, everybody was beautifully loose and relaxed as the game started. And at the end of the first period the Rangers were down 2–0 after fast goals by Syl Apps and Nick Metz. Lester came into the dressing room, sat down on a bench beside Kerr and said quietly, "Well boys, you've had your fun. Now let's get down to business. I've made arrangements for a victory party in the Tudor Room of the Royal York. I'll see you there. Don't let me down."

They didn't. Neil Colville and Alf Pike scored to tie the game in the third period, and Hextall rapped in a shot off a pass from Watson to win it after two minutes of overtime.

Immediately after the Cup presentation, general manager Lester Patrick posed for an historic picture: that of himself with his two sons, holding the Cup. It was the first and only time that the names of a father and his two sons have been engraved on the old bauble. The sentimental moment provoked by the picture-taking was shared by Frank Patrick, who watched from the stands.

Frank showed briefly at the victory party in the Tudor Room, and afterward he and Lester went out for a quiet supper. The odd-man-out on this special night of family celebration had some good news. Exactly two weeks after that night, on April 27, the Montreal newspapers hailed the return of Frank Patrick to the big league hockey scene. It was announced that he had been signed as business manager of the Canadiens, to act as top aide to general manager Tommy Gorman, and to assist the new coach, Dick Irvin, in rebuilding a team that over the past few years had compiled one of the worst records in the NHL.

Wrote Toronto columnist Jim Coleman: "Frank Patrick, one of the great brains of hockey, has shouldered his way back into the game's high society after five years of unfortunate and needless ostracization . . ."

At $12,000 a year and in a position of responsibility, Frank Patrick was back, and it was freely stated that if anyone could bring respectability to the lowly Canadiens, he could.

He never got the chance. Gorman, a very capable hockey man who had helped Dwyer get the New York Americans off the ground before moving to Chicago and taking the Black Hawks to a Stanley Cup Championship, was very protective of his job in Montreal. He was not exactly enamored with the idea of a man of such experience and popularity breathing down his neck, and a chill quickly set in between the two men.

Although Patrick was given some rein in the rebuilding job and did, in fact, sign such excellent players as Emil ("Butch") Bouchard, Elmer Lach, and Ken Reardon, many of his chores were menial. He was in charge of the team payroll and served as road secretary. As such, he bought train tickets, arranged accommodation, booked practice times, and handled other such monumental executive challenges. Unlike the uneasiness that existed between him and Gorman, Frank got along very well with Irvin, and got some relief from trivia by helping at the team workouts.

Still innovating, Frank experimented with new training ideas. One of these was a conditioning drill, with a sand-filled canvas bag strung from the rafters. Players were sent thumping into the dummy in simulation of a particularly mean but legal body check. There was fair enthusiasm for the idea until three players came up with lame shoulders, and the drill was canceled.

It became clear that the talents of this man who had so much to offer to the then floundering Canadiens were being wasted, and that the bleak partnership with Gorman wouldn't last long. It didn't. It ended by mutual agreement when Frank accepted a position with Canadian Car and Foundry, a Montreal company engaged in the production of war materials. It happened that the Canadiens' owner, Len Peto, was also president of that company, and he had offered Frank a job a little more worthy of his organizational abilities: that of supervising the supply and operation of the huge commissary that catered to the thousands of company employees.

In January 1941, before starting the new job, Frank paid a visit to Vancouver to spend a few days with his father, who had been ailing. Old Joe, still straight and strong at eighty-three, seemed quite all right when Frank headed back to Montreal, but, as Frank related later, he had a premonition that the old man wouldn't be there when he returned in the summertime. When the train stopped the next day in Golden, B.C., high in the Canadian Rockies, there was a wire awaiting him from Stan. Joe Patrick had died that morning in his sleep. The date was January 28, 1941. The patriarch, the anchor, had gone.

Frank was suddenly stricken with an overwhelming feeling of loneliness. He got his bag and paced the platform aimlessly before settling down to await the next train back to the Coast.

On that same morning, Lester was traveling back to New York with the Rangers after a game in Chicago. It was not possible for him, or his sons, to get to Victoria in time for the funeral service that took place just two days later in the little St. James Methodist Church that Joe had served so well since his arrival from Nelson thirty years before.

Frank and the rest of the family were there, along with a great crowd of Victorians who had come to pay tribute to one of their city's best-known and best-loved citizens. The most moving moment in the service came when Cynda, who possessed a magnificent soprano voice, sang her father's favorite hymn: "Some day the silver cord will break, and I will see my Lord face to face . . ."

Cynda's sons, Frank and Dean Miller, remember that hymn as one that began as a terrible ordeal for the daughter who had been closest of all the children to her father. "There were times," said Frank, "when it appeared that she would break down and be unable to finish. But then she gathered strength, and the final notes had a beautiful, strong, soaring warmth. They seemed to light up the church."

Frank Miller had been the first of the family to enlist, joining the Canadian Army. He was followed by Joe Patrick, Jr., who graduated from Harvard in 1939, played two seasons of hockey with the New York Rovers, and then signed up with the U. S. Army Reserve.

By 1942 both Muzz and Lynn were also in uniform. As landed immigrants, they were both eligible for the draft, and they joined the U. S. Army. Lynn was eventually assigned to Camp Custer, Michigan, as a First Lieutenant in the Military Police, and Muzz went from base camp at Norfolk to the Port of Embarkation at Hampton Roads.

There was little left for them in New York anyway. The NHL had been decimated by the departure of players to the Armed Forces, and the Rangers in particular were reduced to a mere shell of their great 1940 championship team. Just before the war exodus, Pratt had been traded to the Toronto Maple Leafs, and a year and a half later half the squad had gone, most of them, including the Colvilles, Shibicky, and Alf Pike, to join Army or Navy Air Force base teams in Canada. Art Coulter, like the Patricks, had enlisted in the U. S. Army.

To add to the somber mood around the Garden, the New York Americans had also joined the exodus, and were gone for good. Dying at the gate, the Amerks tried to stir up interest in 1941 by moving their office across the river to Flatbush and calling themselves the Brooklyn Americans, but nobody fell for this flimsy gambit. After one more sad season, they gave up the ghost of Bill Dwyer and fled the Garden premises, leaving the Rangers as the sole hockey tenants.

Those were grim times for Coach Boucher and his boss Lester Patrick as the Rangers headed into the most abysmal losing spell in NHL history.

9

FAREWELL
TO BROADWAY

The happy bachelor who once said he wasn't the kind of a guy who went around falling in love, finally did, five years after Pratt had taken the plunge. About a year after booking his old Broadway flame Lois de Fee into her boffo appearance at the Norfolk Army base, Lt. Murray Patrick took the marriage vows. He was wed in December 1942 to Jennie Farr, whose father was a professor on the staff at Victoria College. That was where Lynn was to have gone to begin his schooling in dentistry, but never did.

In these wartime years Lynn now went where he was told to go, and that meant spending his war service in the United States, as an officer in charge of Military Police units at Army bases.

Muzz, however, did manage to get in a brief spell of overseas service, as described in his own capsule account.

"My first overseas assignment was in the late spring of 1944, as troop commander aboard the USS *Parker,* bound for Oran, Algeria. I was in command of about 3,000 GI's bound for Africa as part of the buildup of the invasion forces being assembled for the assault on the beaches of Southern Europe.

"Some time after that mission was finished, I was assigned to the Mediterranean Base Sector in Naples, stayed there for a few weeks, and was then sent back to Africa as U. S. Army liaison officer with the First French Armored Division that was training for the invasion of the south of France. This was shortly after the landing at Normandy.

"I was with the French when they moved out, aboard one of the flotilla of about fifty craft for the four-day trip to the French coast. The troops went ashore on the Riviera, between Marseilles and St. Tropez. I went with them, but I never got much beyond the beaches, and maybe that was just as well. As a liaison officer in this action, I had a slight problem: I couldn't speak a word of French. But that's how it was at U. S. HQ in those days. If they found out you were a Canadian, they just took it for granted that you spoke French, and bang, you were a liaison officer. Fortunately, most of the French officers spoke English, some a lot better than I did, so that helped.

"After that landing I went back to Africa with instructions to pick up $9.5 million in invasion francs for delivery to the U. S. Army paymasters in the invasion area. I got the money, which had been printed in Philadelphia, and had it trucked aboard the USS *Panama,* a big troopship that was loading 4,500 men for transport to the battle zone. The bank notes were jammed into fifty-six wooden cases, which I had stored in the ship's hold. I assigned three sergeants and four corporals to stand guard in shifts throughout the voyage.

"Here was I, a poor dumb hockey player from Victoria, heading for the French Riviera with nearly ten million dollars in my possession. I went up on deck and thought about that, and I couldn't help saying to myself, 'Jeez, if Lester could only see me now!'

"We delivered the money, and then when I got back to Africa I learned that my promotion had caught up with me and I was now a captain. Shortly after that, I was shipped back to Virginia. The war was cooling down by this time, and I was home to stay. They made me an athletics officer, and that was my job until I got my discharge in early September 1945. I got out a few months before Lynn because of my battle stars and the points I'd built up overseas."

By early October Muzz was at the Rangers' training camp in Winnipeg, renewing old acquaintances with the other returning vets such as the Colvilles, Shibicky, and Alf Pike, and trying to remember how to skate after four years off the ice. It was a pretty abrupt transition, but he handled it neatly.

Upon his arrival in Winnipeg, he traded his captain's uniform to Hank Goldup for Hank's only good civvy suit. Goldup, who had come to the Rangers in the trade that had sent the reluctant and indignant Babe Pratt to the Toronto Leafs, thought he had a marvelous deal until Frank Boucher told him he had to quit wearing his classy new duds in the downtown pubs.

Boucher was still the Rangers' coach and assistant to general manager Lester Patrick, who was now also a Garden vice-president. They had survived three dismal wartime years together while the Rangers were setting new records for ineptitude, but they hadn't survived them well. Their personal and business relationship was in bad shape. Just as in the bitter Art Ross-Frank Patrick affair in Boston years before, Lester was peering increasingly over his coach's shoulder, and the coach was becoming increasingly resentful.

The Rangers' chronic losing spell certainly hadn't helped.

At one time the harassed Boucher had gotten so desperate that he himself put the skates back on in a vain effort to help. He played ten games, and although he was hardly vintage Boucher he performed as well or better than most of his misfit players, but then that was damning with faint praise. After the mass exodus to the armed services, the Rangers had gone from the best hockey team in the NHL to the worst. They plummeted from first to last place and remained there for three seasons. They had been forced to take whatever players were available, and in the wistful words of the popular wartime ballad, they were either too young or too old.

One of their grab-bag prizes was a goalie named Steve Buzinski who let in fifty-five shots in nine games before being mercifully removed and treated for shell shock. In one season, the Rangers set an NHL record by going twenty-five straight games without winning. In 1943–44, they won only six of the schedule's fifty games. They lost by scores of 15–0, 12–2, and 10–1.

Amid all this embarrassment, it was the general manager and vice-president who suffered the unkindest cut of all. With Boucher called home to attend the funeral of his brother, it was Lester, not Frank, who was behind the bench during the 15–0 hammering that came at the hands of the Detroit Red Wings. That night behind the bench was one of the grimmest experiences of Lester's life. The sadistic Red Wings had seen to that as they poured in eight third-period goals against the stricken Rangers.

At the war's end, the new power in the NHL was the Montreal Canadiens, and the new superstar was Maurice Richard, the swarthy, sleek-haired French-Canadian youth they called The Rocket.

All of this, with the once-mighty Broadway Blues facing the prospect of yet another year in the cellar down among the mushrooms, made for very edgy times at the training-camp reunion in Winnipeg, with most of the veterans back in harness.

Lester, again as in the case of his brother and Art Ross, was accusing Boucher of being too soft with his players, and much of the press seemed to agree.

Lester had never been known as a stern disciplinarian, but in his own quiet way he had commanded discipline. He had been close to his players, but never one of them, and that was perhaps the telling difference between his style and that of his coach. The likable Boucher never ceased to be "one of the boys," and quite naturally the boys liked it that way. They also took advantage of the familiarity.

Later on, when the club was training at a camp in the Adirondacks, Boucher had looked the other way when some of the veterans defied the rule that forbade players to take their cars to camp. Four players became involved in an auto crash, and all four were hospitalized and out of the lineup when the season opened. Three, including All-Star forward Buddy O'Connor, suffered injuries that kept them out for much of the year, and the season was ruined.

This sort of laxity infuriated Lester, and he became increasingly frustrated by his remoteness from the situation. He began lecturing Boucher on the error of his ways, and Boucher responded by accusing Lester of meddling. In return, Lester became snappy and demanding, and complained bitterly of Boucher's refusal to heed his advice.

The widening rift was obvious to everyone in camp, including Muzz. Although his loyalties were divided, he could appreciate the difficulty of Boucher's position.

"By the time I got back, they had just about quit talking to each other, and when they did talk it was usually unpleasant. One day Frank asked Lester to explain some little thing to do with the signing of draft forms, and Lester said, 'Frank, if I've told you once, I've told you a thousand times . . .' You don't talk to Frank like that. He was a very sensitive man, and the two of them were just drawing farther apart."

Muzz went to New York with the club, started the season, and on Thanksgiving Day Lynn got his Army discharge. Lynn's first marriage had ended in divorce, and he was now remarried, this time to a Detroit girl named Bernice Lang. He went right to New York, walked into Lester's office and said, "Well, Lester, here I am. I need work."

As Lynn later wryly observed, "Of course, Lester had no choice, even though I was in no shape to play. I was protected by the G.I. Bill of Rights that guaranteed every returning serviceman his old job back."

Although some of the returning veterans had been playing service hockey, none were anywhere near as sharp or as fit as they had been when they had left to join up. It may have been a fine humanitarian bit of legislation, but the G.I. Bill was a curse on the Rangers' house.

As the season went from bad to worse, Boucher felt compelled to explain his dilemma to the New York press. Some of the writers, especially the New York *World-Telegram*'s Jim Burchard, were castigating the Broadway Blues for their inept performance, so Boucher called a luncheon meeting to talk things over.

"Gentlemen," he said, "these players you are belittling are trying desperately hard to get back the form they had when they left the Rangers to go into the service. The G.I. Bill guarantees them that opportunity. We must give it to them, and we want to give it to them. I hope you fellows will give them a chance too."

The reporters were impressed. They did give the Rangers a chance, but to no avail as far as the league race was concerned, and it was right back to the NHL dungeon.

There were glimmers of hope with the emergence of two fine goalies named Sugar Jim Henry and Chuck Raynor and Boucher's shrewd acquisition of a young winger named Edgar Laprade, but the painful rebuilding process had become too taxing for one member of the organization.

On the cold, cheerless morning of February 22, 1946, Lester Patrick got off the subway two stations earlier than usual and walked the rest of the way to Madison Square Garden through a sleet storm that blanketed the city. He walked slowly, but when he finally got to the Garden, he strode briskly to General Kilpatrick's office and handed in his typewritten resignation.

After reading the brief statement, Kilpatrick looked at his old friend and said, "Lester, I must say that I've been expecting this, but it is still a shock, and I wish it didn't have to happen. I must give you an opportunity to reconsider."

"I'm grateful for that," Lester replied, "but it's final. I've talked it over carefully with Grace. We've been considering it for some time now. It's time I stepped down."

The resignation from an active role with the hockey club was accepted, but when he was asked to remain associated with the club as an advisor and consultant, he agreed. Instead of stepping down, he had merely stepped aside.

This, in Frank Boucher's view, was bad news for Frank Boucher, who had become the general manager in this new arrangement. He had been given full authority to run the hockey operation, but when the next year's camp opened in Winnipeg, the vice-president was also there. Lester did not interfere, but he was around, and that bothered Boucher.

During the last week in camp, Frank got a note from Lester complaining that he was being ignored. Boucher professed to be puzzled by this attitude, claiming that he always acknowledged Lester when their paths crossed, as in the city streets and the hotel elevator. This was obviously not the kind of attention Lester craved. He wanted to be part of the hockey club, but the hockey club was now Boucher's domain, and he guarded it with a zeal that was understandable, if not altogether sensible.

As Conn Smythe has put it, "Any man who would reject Lester Patrick's advice on hockey matters is a fool."

Boucher was certainly not a fool, but perhaps a bit too sensitive, a little too recalcitrant.

Back in New York, General Kilpatrick was quite aware of the situation. He placated Lester when he could but supported

Boucher when it came right down to matters of hard club policy and the general manager's decisions.

One of these matters was a trade Boucher had engineered with the Canadiens for the services of O'Connor and a less-talented winger named Frank Eddols. The deal had to be approved by Kilpatrick, and when the General asked for Lester's advice, Lester vetoed the trade on the grounds that the Rangers would be giving up three good players, including defenseman Hal Laycoe, for two older ones. Boucher countered by threatening to resign unless he was given authority to make the deal. Kilpatrick backed Boucher, and the next season O'Connor finished just one point behind Elmer Lach in the NHL scoring derby and won the Hart Trophy as the league's most valuable player.

Lester had been hurt when Kilpatrick supported Boucher, but when O'Connor turned out to be such a good one, he wrote a note to Frank complimenting him on his acumen, tore it up, and went to Boucher's office to deliver the message in person. It was a terse meeting, but gracious, and it was the first amiable discussion between these two old friends for nearly two years.

After the first shock of the break from the tensions he had thrived on all his adult life, Lester quickly adjusted to the change that he had for a while found too traumatic to handle with his customary élan. He relaxed with Grace in their uptown apartment, attended a few Broadway shows, played the piano at a small party thrown by Kilpatrick, and tried hard to enjoy his new life of leisure. But for Lester, still restless and energetic at sixty-four, New York was now a lonely town. With the exception of Boucher, all the old hockey gang were gone, and so were his sons.

Neither Muzz nor Lynn had been able to get their legs back. Lynn played thirty-eight games of that comeback season and Muzz got into just twenty-four. At season's end, Muzz left to become player-coach of St. Paul in the American Association, and Lynn was sent to coach the Rangers' farm team in New Haven. For Muzz, this was the start of a long and circuitous route through the minor leagues before his eventual return to the Broadway Blues. For Lynn, the stay in New Haven was just a brief pause in an NHL career that still had a long way to go.

And then on the evening of December 3, 1947, the Patricks were together again and all was right with their world as New

Yorkers jammed Madison Square for Lester Patrick Night. They had come to honor his years of service in the Rangers' organization and also his induction into the Hockey Hall of Fame.

The Garden ceremony was preceded by a supper party in a midtown restaurant attended by a horde of celebrities, political dignitaries, and representatives of all the NHL clubs, headed by the new president, Clarence Campbell. Showered with glowing tributes and swamped with gifts, the guest of honor was almost too overwhelmed to respond. One of the gifts was a check for $1,500 from the five teams, with instructions that "it must be spent only by Mrs. Patrick." Fumbling for words, Lester described the occasion simply as "the most wonderful moment of my life."

As noted in the New York *Times* report of the affair: "It finally happened to Lester Patrick—he found himself at a loss for words . . ."

The gentlemen of the New York press, a tough but sentimental fraternity, also paid their tributes, typical of which was that written by columnist Gene Ward, president of the New York Writers Association, in that night's game program:

> There are many tributes which can be paid Lester Patrick. Most of them have been said before and will be said again on other fitting occasions. But the reporters, past and present, who have covered the sport know him perhaps best of all. We have known him as a player, a coach, a manager, an executive, a father, and a man. He has been tops in every category.
>
> Tonight we think of him in terms of a lead for a story, and we simply say: "A great hockey era was celebrated last night before a capacity crowd in Madison Square Garden." And then we'd continue the story . . . that Lester Patrick, the man long known as The Silver Fox and as Mr. Hockey, was heaped with words of praise and with gifts which, when all stacked together, failed by far to measure up to what he himself has contributed to the game of hockey.

There was also a game that night: the Rangers versus the Toronto Maple Leafs. With the Leafs was manager Conn Smythe, the tough little alley fighter who had been elbowed aside by Lester at the birth of the Rangers twenty-two years before. And with Conn was his coach, Hap Day, who had engaged in many a duel with Lester and his Victoria Cougars back in the old Coast

League days when Hap was with Frank Patrick's Vancouver Millionaires.

The last remnants of the Rangers' "new breed" of the late thirties were in the New York lineup that night: Phil Watson and Neil Colville, the team captain, both in their final years as players. One of the new Rangers in the lineup was a defenseman named Fred Shero, of whom hockey fans would eventually hear much more, especially around Philadelphia, home of the Broad Street Bullies.

The outcome of the game (4–1, Toronto) was incidental to the fact that after nearly a quarter of a century in the big town, the man Chicago *Daily News*' sports editor John Carmichael called "by far the greatest Ranger of them all" had cut all ties with the Garden and was headed home.

Still a little loath to leave the sights and sounds of Manhattan, Lester and Grace stayed in New York for another year before finally leaving for the West Coast. They arrived back in Victoria in the early spring of 1948, with the daffodils up and the apple tree in the garden of the house on Lyndon Avenue in bud.

En route, they had stopped briefly in Vancouver to visit with Frank and the younger brothers. Stan was helping Guy with the operation of the auditorium that had been built on the site of the old arena. Guy's Lions were no more, and a new hockey team, the Pacific Coast League Vancouver Canucks, were playing out of a small rink on the east side of town.

After coming home from his war-time job in Montreal, Frank had gone into a restless semiretirement. He was reworking oil and silver claims he still held up in the Cariboo country, but his tentative, poorly financed efforts remained barren. He was also working on other ideas, including a plan for a revolutionary new kind of sports stadium.

He called it a "domed stadium," an arena in which games that are commonly played outdoors could be played the year round, with no threat from the elements. "It is unbelievable in this day and age," he wrote in a précis explaining his idea, "that the scheduling of sports should be governed by the vagaries of the weather." He had prints of his domed stadium plan filed for copyright in Ottawa and Washington. The plans called for a covered stadium with a capacity of 50–60,000, with seats built in movable sections, to fit the needs of baseball and football.

He took the plans to moneyed friends in Chicago and Montreal but could find no takers for an idea that was considered too revolutionary and too costly. There were undoubtedly other millionaires around with both the money and the imagination to take a flyer on this grandiose stadium plan, but Frank did not have access to them.

Fourteen years later, two years after his death, the Houston Astrodome rose on the urban plains of Texas. It had a capacity of 50,000, with movable sections to accommodate football and baseball. Then came the New Orleans Superdome and the Seattle Kingdome. America hailed the marvel of this daring new concept in stadium construction.

Other bold ideas tumbled from Frank's agile brain. Sharing the ageless disenchantment with the operation of the Federal Post Office delivery system, he wrote to the postal authorities in Ottawa with a suggestion for improvement. "Why," he wrote, "can't we have coded areas for mail delivery?" The silence from Ottawa was deafening. In 1963 the United States Post Office adopted what they called the Zip Code for mail delivery. Eight years later, Ottawa stepped boldly in with a prototype called the Postal Code.

Frank developed a detailed plan for the streamlining of hospital administration, with no response from an establishment that is still in dire need of streamlining. He even visited a boys' summer camp on the nearby Sechelt Peninsula and tried to interest sponsors and counselors in ideas for the improvement of the recreation program. "Frank's problem," Lester once said, "is that he just doesn't know how to turn off his brain."

Lester himself was headed for a much simpler retirement lifestyle, although it would not be quite as simple as he planned. Within months of his return to Victoria he had bought and taken over the operation of the Pacific Coast League Victoria Cougars. Lester and his Cougars were in business again, but this was hardly the breed that had humbled the Canadiens to win the Stanley Cup Championship in the sunlit spring of 1925. This return to the hockey wars on a lesser battlefield led directly to a reunion with Lynn that created a furore in the New York press and consternation in the Rangers' organization.

The Rangers had finished next to last in 1947, and following the training camp auto accident that hospitalized four players including MVP Buddy O'Connor and Edgar Laprade, Frank Boucher was in deep trouble early in the season. Forced to spend much of his time finding and grooming replacements, he called Lynn up from New Haven to take over behind the New York bench. Neil Colville was dispatched to replace Lynn as coach of the Ramblers.

Lynn joined the Rangers in December, with the club already far back and headed for the cellar, but the next year, in his first full season at the helm, he took the team to a surprise fourth-place finish and into the play-offs. The only person in the organization not visibly delighted with this performance was Lynn himself.

Long before the start of the play-offs, Boucher had sensed that his coach was not particularly happy with his new job. Frank had heard reports of a job offer from Boston, where Art Ross was preparing to step aside as general manager, but he wasn't too concerned about that. He and Lynn both knew the power of the Patrick name in the Rangers' organization, and that there was a pretty good future right there in the game's richest market. Boucher didn't tax him on the matter.

The fact of the situation was that Lynn had decided before Christmas that he wanted out of the New York operation. More specifically, he wanted out of New York. He had at that time confided solely in Colville and Watson because, in Lynn's words, "Nobody else would have believed me. The plain and simple truth was that I just didn't want to live in New York City anymore. I had a happy marriage and now had three young children to think about, and I just didn't feel that New York was a good family environment. I wanted to get the kids into a different atmosphere with more space, more fresh air. It would have been pretty tough to explain that sort of stuff to the New York writers, let alone Frank Boucher.

"I told Neil and Phil that I was going to quit at the end of the season even if we won the Stanley Cup. I told them that they might as well start bucking for my job because I was sure that one of them would get it when I left, but they didn't believe me."

Later, in Montreal, Lester believed him, after some persuasion.

"We were in Montreal for the semi-final play-off round against the Canadiens, and Dad had come East scouting for players for his team in Victoria. I went to his room at the Royal York Hotel and arrived just as he was unpacking. He sat down in his shirt sleeves and lit a cigarette, and after he'd gotten over a coughing spell I said, 'Dad, you're smoking too much. You'd better give it up.' He smiled, took another puff and said, 'You're right, Lynn. I think I will.' I knew he wouldn't. He'd been a heavy smoker all his life.

"I knew that Lester was looking for a coach as well as players, and after some pleasantries I said suddenly, 'How would you like to have a good coach out there? A real good coach.'

" 'Like who?'

" 'Like me.'

"Lester looked at me kind of funny and said, 'What makes you think you're such a good coach?' and I said, 'Well, we're leading the Canadiens 3–1 in the play-offs. I must be doing something right.'

"He gave me a hard look and said, 'Are you serious?'

"I assured him that I certainly was, and I told him why. He thought about it a minute and then made me an offer. I accepted it. We agreed to keep the matter between the two of us until after the play-offs."

After disposing of the Canadiens in the fifth game, the Rangers faced the highly favored Red Wings in the finals. Despite the disadvantage of having to play the series away from home because of the annual Garden visit of the Barnum & Bailey Circus, the Rangers took the powerful Wings to two overtime periods in the seventh game before surrendering.

This outstanding performance by a team that hadn't been expected to even make it to the play-offs made the news of Lynn's resignation even more of a shock when it surfaced early in May. The fact that a Patrick had quit what many considered to be the best coaching job in hockey to handle a bush-league team out in the wilds of Canada simply added to the general disbelief. But he was gone, and the return of the prodigal son got rapturous play in the Victoria press.

The rapture was short-lived.

Just two months after his return, with his growing family settled into the house on Lyndon Avenue, there was a call from Boston. Art Ross was on the phone. "Lynn," he said, "I want you to coach the Bruins."

Lynn has denied that he had been expecting or even hoping for that call.

"Sure, I'd heard rumors that there might be a job opening in Boston, and that I might be considered, but there are always rumors like that. I wouldn't have taken the job with Lester if I really thought I was in line for the Boston job. Right up to the time Art called me, I had no desire to take another post in the East. After all, I'd just left a pretty good one.

"But Ross was persuasive, and he made me a great salary offer —twelve thousand dollars, which was big money then—and I accepted right there over the phone. Lester understood. I think he was expecting something like this to happen."

By early August, Mr. and Mrs. Lynn Patrick and the three kids were established in a nice house in Boston suburbia. It was to be their home for the next fifteen years. After the first four years of that span, Ross had moved up in the Bruins' organization and Lynn had replaced him as general manager, turning the coaching over to Milt Schmidt, the pivot man of the Bruins' great Kraut Line.

As to Lynn's relationship with Ross, the man who is described by one of his peers as "a tough, mean, hard-nosed sonofabitch . . ." the nephew of the coach he had fired after a long and bitter quarrel has nothing but high praise. "Art Ross," says Lynn, "was the greatest boss I ever had. I loved the guy, and I think the feeling was mutual. He personally groomed me to take over as general manager, and he never at any time did anything to harass me or undermine my authority. The matter of Uncle Frank never came up between us, nor was it broached by anyone else in town."

However, Lynn Patrick's relationship with the Bruins' organization and the Bruins' fans was far from idyllic, and when he took over as general manager in 1954, he had some rough years ahead. The first years were difficult because of declining attendance that plagued the whole league. Television was the new rage, and millions were staying home to watch Uncle Miltie in his funny dresses. The whole entertainment industry was suffering at the box office. Shunned at home, the Chicago Black Hawks went on the road in search of people and were playing in stops like St. Paul, Indianapolis, and St. Louis before crowds of 2–3,000.

Things weren't that dire in Boston, but in the early fifties the

Bruins played to a lot of half-empty houses, and it wasn't until 1955, when Patrick traded to Detroit for Terry Sawchuck, that things improved. Sawchuck's spectacular and colorful play in the Boston net was an instant hit with the fans, and soon the packed houses were back again.

The acquisition of Sawchuck was hailed as a masterly stroke by the new general manager, but as far as the gm's long-term future in town was concerned, Terry was too little, too late.

In the period 1950–58, the Bruins were in the Stanley Cup finals three times, and though they weren't able to bring a sixth Cup Championship to a member of the Patrick family, they were at least contenders. But from there on, for the final six years of Lynn's tenure in Boston, it would be all downhill.

Meanwhile, the other Patrick was going his own route and having his own problems. As Lynn settled down in Boston under the friendly wing of Art Ross, Muzz was making the rounds of the minor leagues, first as player-coach, then as coach and general manager. After two seasons at St. Paul he moved west to Tacoma of the Pacific Coast League, and then, when the Tacoma Rockets folded, he went up to Seattle.

In Tacoma, where he had trouble signing a couple of holdouts, he put the skates back on and lumbered around on defense for a game or two until he had a better idea. He sent out an SOS to Babe Pratt, who had been keeping nimble winning championships and setting records as player-coach of the PCL New Westminster Royals, up near Vancouver. Babe, who was at liberty at the moment, was happy to oblige his old Broadway buddy.

During his three years in Toronto after Lester had traded him to the Leafs, Pratt had managed to help Conn Smythe's crew to a Stanley Cup Championship, set an NHL points-scoring record for defensemen, win the MVP trophy as the league's most valuable player, and get expelled for gambling.

Babe had admitted to putting a dollar or two on various NHL contests, and the gambit drew the ire of NHL president Merv Dutton, who promptly sentenced him to exile. But when a full investigation showed that Pratt had committed the lesser mortal sin of betting against other teams and never against his own, he was reinstated. That was in the season of 1946, and the next year,

Conn Smythe, not exactly noted as one of the great moralists of his time, sold Pratt to Boston, and the Babe was on his way out.

Unlike Lynn, who came along a little later, Pratt, in his own words "couldn't stand that damned, conniving Art Ross." Nor could he stand the knee injury that put him out of action after thirty-two games with the Bruins. Sent down to the Boston farm at Hershey to heal, Pratt scandalized Ross by demanding a full share of that year's Boston play-off money. He got the full share, also another year in Hershey. Then, having been offered the remarkable sum of $17,500 to serve as player-coach of the Coast League New Westminster Royals, he headed West.

It was in 1952, having led the Royals to a pair of league championships and being thwarted in a third bid by Lester Patrick's Victoria Cougars, when he got the call from Tacoma. The sentimental reunion was held in the arena's Heidelberg Room, an after-game retreat where Muzz and his boys went to assuage their thirsts after a hard night on the ice. It wasn't exactly Manhattan's Green Room or Hogan's Irish Tavern, but the malt was of excellent quality and the old friends showed that they had lost neither their zest nor their capacity for the healing potion.

At a meeting called by Muzz to introduce the new defenseman, Babe addressed his new teammates with the words: "Well, fellows, it looks like we've got a pretty good balance here. We've got some hungry rookies, and a couple of thirsty veterans."

Pratt played as the fifth defenseman, and when the team was hit by injuries Muzz pointed to center ice and out Babe went, to get four goals and seven assists in three games.

Lester's Cougars came to town for a couple of league games while Pratt was there, but the owner wisely chose to stay home in Victoria. At the age of thirty-six, his one-time prize hellions were past fatherly counsel.

Babe recalls the time Muzz got into an accident that did several hundred dollars worth of damage to his car. "The insurance man asked him if he had been drinking before the accident, and Muzz said, 'You don't think I'd do this if I was sober, do you?' "

Then there was the time the Saskatoon team came to town and shut out the Rockets as goalie Gump Worsley stopped fifty-five shots. "Worsley used to get a fifty-dollar bonus for shutouts, and the next day I saw him in town with a couple of the other Saskatoon players and he said, 'Babe, I've got fifty bucks in my pocket. How about showing us where to spend it?' When I saw Gump the next day, he looked just awful. He looked at me and groaned, 'Babe, I never ever want to see you again.'

"Saskatoon had a game that night in Seattle, and I told Muzz we should drive up to see this because with Gump in his condition it should be a riot. We went, and Gump was sensational. He blanked Seattle 1–0, and had another fifty bucks to spend."

The 1952 adventures of Gump Worsley, the stocky little man with the paunch and a curious physique that belied his marvelous agility around the net, were of definite interest to Muzz Patrick. Three years later, when Worsley arrived in New York to join the Rangers, Muzz was the coach. His reprieve had come in the winter of 1954 via a phone call from New York.

The Rangers were still on hard times and the general manager was in trouble. Boucher just hadn't been able to get the team moving after Lynn Patrick had turned in his coach's badge. Neil Colville, who had succeeded Lynn behind the bench, had been able to come up with no more than a fifth-place finish and an ulcer. His replacement, Bill Cook, the one-time Ranger hero who had been brought in from pasture in Saskatoon, could do no better. There being little or no place for sentiment in hockey at the top, Cook was fired on Kilpatrick's orders, and Boucher went back behind the bench.

In his desperation he had even tried hypnotists and so-called "magic-potions" guaranteed to cure the Blues, and he was roundly scored by the New York press for resorting to such witchery. Poor Frank's defense was that it was at least "good publicity."

In January 1954 Kilpatrick put through a call to Muzz in Seattle, where he had moved following the Tacoma fold. The timing was excellent, as Muzz had just returned with his Seattle team from a disastrous road trip to Saskatoon.

There are those who say that any road trip to frigid Saskatoon in January is disastrous, but the point here was that Muzz was wide open to any suggestion for a change. When Kilpatrick offered him the coaching job in New York he took the first available flight East.

He arrived with mixed feelings.

"Although he didn't seem too upset about it, I felt badly replacing Frank as coach, even though it was just an interim situation and he was, of course, still the general manager. But with me being a Patrick, the move may have looked like the thin end of the wedge. I really don't think they treated Frank fairly. They paid me as much for coaching as he was getting for doing both jobs."

In May, after the Rangers had floundered to another dismal fifth-place finish, Boucher was summoned back off his Ontario farm for a meeting with Kilpatrick. As gently as such things can be done to an old and faithful servant, Boucher was fired.

He was deeply hurt, but gracious. When asked by Kilpatrick if in his considered opinion he thought he had been given ample time and opportunity to build a winner, Boucher agreed that yes, he had. Muzz, the son of the man who had once so reluctantly relinquished the post to him, was named to replace him as general manager.

With that involuntary exit from the Rangers' organization, Boucher walked out of hockey forever. That same month, 3,000 miles to the west, Lester Patrick had also closed the book on his hockey career.

It had finally happened.

Lester had sold his Victoria hockey club, retaining just one token share for each of his sons, and had gone into full retirement. He was seventy-two.

The baton had been passed to the next generation.

10

THE LAST CHALLENGE

Back in New York, in one of his first acts after moving into the general manager's office that had been occupied for so many years by his father, Muzz hired himself a coach. He picked Phil Watson, the Ranger who had almost got to double for Clark Gable. Fiery Phil responded by taking the team to the play-offs in each of the next three seasons, but in 1958 that prosperous string ended as abruptly as it had begun. The Rangers plunged from second place in 1958 to fifth in 1959, and then back down into the cellar in 1960.

Curiously, that sudden return to hard times coincided with the end of a similar streak of respectability in Boston, where Lynn's Bruins were also headed into troubled times. For the next seven seasons, the brothers were doomed to fight it out for last place in the league standings. They took turns shuttling from fifth to sixth place and back, but never higher. And while the dwindling fifties saw the family fortunes on the wane in the East, another era was drawing to a wistful close in the West.

There, the twilight years of Lester and Frank Patrick were marked with the same sense of contrast that had remained constant for most of their adult lives: Lester's life, orderly, fulfilled and serene; Frank's, disordered, troubled, plagued by disappointments and frustrations. And bedeviled by a weakness for drink. The weakness was never outwardly chronic, and there were long spells when he would abstain completely, but it gnawed at him, and in the end it destroyed his dignity.

For a man of Frank's intense pride, that was the ultimate humiliation, although only he and his wife, Catharine, knew the depth of the hurt. To his nephews, he was still the kind, gentle, and considerate Uncle Frank they had known as children. But nothing had worked out: The oil, gold, or silver strikes never happened; none of the ideas that had poured from his brilliant and restless mind over the years of struggle since his departure from hockey had borne fruit.

To help with the bills, Catharine had gone to work, employed as a saleslady in the fur department of the Hudson Bay Department Store. Lester helped out financially, as much and as discreetly as he could. "Uncle Lester," says Frank's son, Joe, Jr., "was fantastically generous."

In those lean years, there was also help from another source: the National Hockey League. President Clarence Campbell and the league governors were well and gratefully aware of hockey's debt to Frank Patrick, and a check for $300 arrived each month from the league office.

Frank was still trying to make it on his own almost right up to the end. His last try was with an unbreakable hockey stick he had developed and tested in his workshop. Produced through a then unique lamination process, the stick passed all tests and looked like a winner. Here at last was a practical idea with commercial possibilities, but Frank's bad luck held. It had come too late. Before his new stick could be merchandised, fiberglass was in and lamination was out.

In the meanwhile, Guy Patrick had gone to live in the balmier climate of California, where he dabbled in various modest promotions. One of these was the bottling and sale of a "healing" concoction of mud that had been dug from the riverbanks of the Queen Charlotte Islands off the northern B.C. coast. Although it was claimed by the Indians of the region to possess magic healing qualities, Californians weren't impressed enough to buy, and Guy was stuck with a lot of imported mud.

The fourth brother, Stan, was still in Vancouver, retired on a modest income.

Then, in the summer of 1960 Lynn, in Boston, got a phone call from Victoria. It was from his mother, with the news that Lester was very ill. He had been taken to the hospital, and cancer had been found in one of his lungs. Lester, now seventy-seven, had been ailing for some time, and Lynn had been out to Victoria a few months before to visit with him. At that time, Lester had had a touch of pneumonia, but now it was more than that.

Lynn telephoned his brother in New York and asked if he would go to the Coast right away to see just how serious it was. Muzz went, and a few days later he called Lynn and told him that if he wanted to see Lester alive he'd better get out there right away. Lynn was sitting out in his garden writing out the monthly checks when that call came. He pushed everything aside and got the next flight out of Boston and was in Victoria on the afternoon of May 30.

The two brothers were with Lester in his hospital room the morning of the day he died. Recalling the last moments, Lynn says, "He was conscious off and on while we were there, and he spoke to me during that last visit. He said he was glad to see me, and when I went to his bedside he smiled and made a feeble motion with his hand, as if to take a punch at me. He still had his great sense of humor. We'd just arrived back to the house after that visit when we got word that he had died."

The date was June 1, 1960. It was exactly fifty-nine years and four months since Lester had arrived in Victoria with Joe, Frank, and the rest of the Patrick brood to start a new life in the West.

The huge crowd that attended the funeral service in the old family church spilled out into the street, and in the words of a Victoria reporter: "The world of hockey seemed to have converged in front of the flower-laden Communion table, to pay homage to the memory of a man and an era."

Ned Irish, the new president of the Madison Square Garden Corporation, was there, with Boston's Walter Brown, the chairman of the NHL board of governors and president of the Boston Bruins, and Toe Blake, the coach of the Canadiens. From the days when Lester and all the world was young, there were Fred Taylor, Frank Fredrickson, Moose Johnson, and Frank Foyston. There were the old Rangers, Frank Boucher, the Cook brothers, and Taffy Abel and Art Chapman of the old New York Americans. The pallbearers were Boucher, Bill Cook, and four of Lester's "new breed" of the roistering thirties, Babe Pratt, Neil Colville, Clint Smith, and Alex Shibicky. Among the huge mass of flowers that blanketed the church entrance was a floral wreath formed with two crossed hockey sticks.

In all the thousands of tributes that poured forth from across North America, none was better nor more simply stated than that of the Reverend A. I. Higgins, Minister of the First United Church with which the Patrick family had been so long associated: "Some men have played greater hockey, but no greater man ever played the game."

A little later, family and friends stood in the bright, warm sunshine under a sky pocked with puffy white clouds as Lester Patrick was laid to rest beside his father and mother.

Frank Patrick wasn't there that day. It was reported that he had been too ill to come, but his was not a sickness that could be diagnosed as a physical ailment. Frank was simply too distraught by the news of his brother's death to make the trip to Victoria. And exactly twenty-eight days after Lester's death, on the morning of June 29, 1960, he too passed away.

He had been suffering from what had been vaguely described as a heart condition. "Frank," said old friend Fred Taylor, "simply died of a broken heart."

Frank's funeral was attended by another large delegation from the NHL and a distinguished gathering from hockey's past and present. The crowd overflowed Vancouver's largest church, and the eulogies befitted the stature of the man who must certainly be ranked with his brother as one of sport's illustrious pioneers and hockey's most inventive genius. Still, his passing evoked far less publicity and international attention than that of Lester. Even in death, Frank lay in the shadow of the brother who was the first son beckoned off the logs by Joe Patrick during that long-ago siege on the Columbia River.

Lester left an estate of $287,000. His widow, Grace, received a lifetime pension from his investments, which included a few shares of Madison Square Garden stock. Lynn and Muzz got $20,000 each, and $5,000 each was willed to Frank, Guy, Stanley, and Lester's three sisters.

Ironically, that year of 1960 also saw the passing of Lester's old friend and admirer, General John Reed Kilpatrick, and another link with the past had been severed.

With Kilpatrick gone, Muzz had lost an influential friend at a time when the whole Garden scene was undergoing an upheaval. The Graham-Paige Corporation, an investment company, had bought majority control, and their board chairman, Irving Felt, was the Garden's new top executive. Admiral John J. Bergen had been named president of the Rangers, although he would be replaced very shortly by a city-smart New York lawyer, Bill Jennings.

Felt wasted no time making his first major pronouncement regarding the future of the Garden and its employees. On November 3, 1960, as Muzz's Rangers were losing a 2–1 game to his brother's Boston Bruins, Felt announced plans for the new Madison Square Garden, a vast $116 million sports and convention complex that was to rise into the airspace above Penn Station. The demolition work was to start in 1963, with the whole daring project scheduled for completion five years later. Whether or not Muzz Patrick would be there to lead the Broadway Blues into their opulent new premises was a moot point.

As speculation grew over his future with the Rangers under the tough new ownership, there were reports that he was safe for a few years yet as he had signed a ten-year contract. Muzz denies this. "In all my years with the Rangers," he says, "I never signed a contract of any kind. Every contract was verbal, running from year to year."

The way things were going, a formal long-term pact might have been a good deal more comforting, for after struggling to a fifth-place finish in 1959, the Rangers sank to the bottom in '60 and then climbed back up a notch in '61. Phil Watson was gone from behind the bench, to be followed by Alf Pike and then the aging but still magnificent ten-time All-Star defenseman from Montreal, Doug Harvey. Next came an ex-Ranger of recent vintage, Red Sullivan.

Between coaches, Muzz himself shuttled back and forth between his office and the bench, but, as in the case of the long-departed Frank Boucher, nothing worked. With the exception of the 1961–62 season, when they managed to finish fourth, the Rangers continued to bounce in and out of the cellar.

As is usual when things are going badly, Muzz was having trouble with some of his players, sometimes demanding more than they were willing to give. A hard-liner like his father on the matter of salaries, Muzz had more than one run-in with players on that sensitive point.

One such encounter was with Rod Gilbert, the talented winger who arrived in 1961, destined to succeed Andy Bathgate as the Rangers' all-time scoring leader and crowd favorite. Gilbert, who after his retirement joined the Rangers' staff as assistant to the president, recalls that squabble.

"I took my father with me to help negotiate my first contract, and we'd just sat down when Muzz said, 'You want to play in the National Hockey League?' I nodded. 'Okay,' said Muzz, 'your salary is $7,000 for the first year, and $9,000 for the second.'

"I knew my father was thinking of a lot more than that, but I was overcome by just the thought of the NHL contract. My father haggled awhile, but Muzz was tough. And in those days there were only six teams in the league. There was nowhere else to go. I signed.

"The third season, after I'd had a couple of pretty good ones, Muzz offered me the same money: $9,000. I told this to Doug Harvey, who was the coach then, and he said that if I settled for anything less than $16,000 he'd never speak to me again. I went back to Muzz and he asked me what kind of money I had in mind. I was afraid to say I was thinking of $16,000, and just asked for another offer, and he said, 'Okay, you've had a pretty good year, I'll make it $9,500.'

"I told him I could make more than that back in my father's blacksmith shop in Montreal, but that didn't impress him much. So I left training camp and went to see Clarence Campbell at the NHL office in Montreal. I told him I thought I was worth $16,000 and after we talked for a while he agreed. He got Muzz on the phone and told him he thought I was worth $16,000 and should get it, and Muzz said okay, he'd go along with that if he had to. I went back to camp and there was a new contract waiting for me— for $14,500.

"I said, 'Muzz, I was promised $16,000.' His reply was that it was Campbell who promised me that figure, not him. He sent me out on the ice to work out and after a while he called me over and said, 'Gilbert, you're grossly overpaid.' I signed for the $14,500."

Muzz himself has a terse summation of this and other dealings with the slick winger who was known to be just as cagey off the ice as he was on. "Gilbert," he says, "was a prima donna."

Four years later, the NHL establishment was stunned when Gilbert and his mates on the so-called GAG (goal-a-game) line, Jean Ratelle and Vic Hadfield, signed for a reported $200,000 each. But there was another general manager then, and with the birth of the World Hockey Association, another league. And with the WHA firing the first shots in an all-out talent war, it was now a players' market and it was no world for old-fashioned hard-liners.

By the 1963 season, Muzz Patrick had problems beyond "outlandish" salary demands. It was no secret around town that his fondness for the cocktail hour was placing a strain on his relationship with club president Bill Jennings. He was also in trouble with the fans when in 1964 he traded Andy Bathgate to Toronto. The immensely popular veteran who held the club's all-time scoring record went to the Leafs along with Don McKinney in exchange for five veterans including Dick Duff and Bob Nevin plus the rights to a highly touted young amateur, Rod Seiling. "Muzz Must Go" banners were hoisted in the Garden balcony, and although Jennings gave his general manager the usual vote-of-confidence, word was out that Muzz was about to be sacked.

One man who professed to be disturbed by all this was Émile Francis, the nimble little goalie who had earned the nickname of "The Cat" during his four years with the Rangers before the arrival of Worsley. Muzz had brought Francis up from a coaching job in Guelph to become his assistant gm, and Émile was grateful for that gesture.

"Muzz," he said, "if you go, I go too."

"Don't be crazy," answered Muzz. "Just stay put and say nothing, and I think you'll get my job."

Francis stayed put, kept quiet, and, at the end of the '64 season, got the job. The end for Muzz had come at a press conference called to probe Montreal goalie Jacques Plante's public criticism of the Rangers' operation. In confronting Plante, Muzz lost his cool and got into a shouting match, causing the embarrassed Jennings to walk out.

Muzz was dismissed as general manager shortly after that incident.

As in the case of his father before him, he was elevated to a Garden vice-presidency, if elevated is the proper word for this gruff nudge upstairs. With the hockey operation now in the hands of Francis, Muzz, who was tremendously popular with the Garden staff, was assigned to assist in the preparations for the move into the new building that was now under construction. The job also included the transfer of bookings and the supervision of the complex's huge 42-lane bowling center. It was a decent enough challenge, but it wasn't hockey.

In Boston, Lynn was approaching the crossroads as boss of the Bruins. And in the continuing pattern of strange coincidences that follow the Patrick story, he too was about to lose a valued ally during difficult times.

It was in that summer of 1964, the year of Muzz's exit from the Rangers' organization, that Lynn attended the funeral of the man who had brought him to Boston, Art Ross. The "Mr. Big" of the old Westmount neighborhood gang of more than six decades ago was in his eighty-first year. Lynn went to the funeral with the aging Boston Bruins' president, Walter Brown, who also owned the Boston Celtics of the National Basketball Association. One month later—echoes of the Vancouver summer of 1960—Walter Brown too was dead.

C. F. Adams, the man who had hired Ross in 1925 and backed him in his support of Frank Patrick's $300,000 player deal had gone years before. Just as in New York, it was now a clean sweep of the Boston old guard, and Lynn on his recent record had little to offer the new.

In the 1964–65 season, with Milt Schmidt behind the bench, the Bruins set an NHL record by finishing last for the fifth straight time. The era dominated elsewhere by such young giants as Gordie Howe, Jean Beliveau, Doug Harvey, Bill Gadsby, Pierre Pilote, Terry Sawchuck, and Jacques Plante had been a bad one for the Bruins' general manager.

It was no surprise when in the spring of 1965 Weston Adams brought in a new man, Hap Emms, as his general manager. Lynn was offered a vice-presidency to work as assistant to the president, but he had other ideas. "I knew that expansion was coming, that franchises would go to the West Coast to widen the television market, and that Los Angeles was considered a prime location. I knew Dan Reeves, who owned the Los Angeles Rams and also the Los Angeles Blades of the Pacific Coast League. Dan wanted an NHL franchise, and with the Blades' operation as a beginning, he had an excellent chance of getting one. I had decided that Los Angeles was a good place for me in those circumstances, and I told Reeves I was available. I got the Los Angeles coaching job, but Jack Kent Cooke finessed Reeves and got the NHL franchise. I coached the Blades for just one season, but with Reeves out of the expansion picture, so was I.

"Late after the season I got a phone call from Bill Jennings in New York. St. Louis had been awarded an expansion franchise, and he and Émile Francis had recommended me to the owners there for the general manager's job. I said I was interested, so I then got a call from Sid Solomon, Sr., the head of the family that had bought the St. Louis franchise. He asked me to come to St. Louis for an interview. I went right after the season ended, and had a long meeting with Sid Solomon, Jr., Sid III, and Bob Woolfson. They had already talked to other people including Keith Allen and Max McNab, and they didn't seem too sold on me.

"I went back to L.A., and a couple of days later I got a call telling me I had the job. I got a three-year contract at twenty-five thousand a year."

That signing, as they might say around St. Louis, marked the birth of the Blues as an instant hockey power. Whoever may have been responsible for the remarkable events that ensued, Lynn was certainly the beginning and the catalyst, and he had picked the right man as his top aide. That man was William ("Scotty") Bowman, a once promising winger in the Montreal system whose playing career had been ended by a severe head injury.

Lynn knew him to be an astute young hockey man with a sharp eye for talent and lots of drive and ambition.

"Scotty had come to me while I was in Boston and told me he wanted to leave Montreal, where he was coaching the Junior Canadiens. I told him that I was heading for Los Angeles to work for Reeves, and that if we got an NHL franchise, I'd hire him as my assistant. During the winter I spent with the Blades, Scotty was

on the phone constantly, checking on the situation. When Cooke
got the franchise, he was pretty upset.

"As soon as I got the St. Louis job I went to Montreal, talked
to Scotty and signed him as my coach and assistant. The Solomons
wanted me to go behind the bench because of my name, but apart
from my stint in Los Angeles I hadn't coached for years and I
wanted no part of it. I sent Bowman to Europe to scout a couple of
Czech players I'd heard about, and to see what else he could find.
He went along with the Canada National Hockey Team on their
trip across Europe to the World Hockey Championships in
Vienna, and stopped in Prague along the way. He didn't have any
luck signing the Czechs, but we did eventually get a couple of the
National Team players."

Despite his misgivings, Lynn started the Blues' first season behind the bench, but it was a dismal beginning for the expansion
team. Crowds were poor, and they got worse as the Blues lost
seven glames in a row. That was enough for the reluctant coach.
He turned the reins over to Bowman, and the two of them looked
around for help. A week later, veteran Ron Stewart, the Blues'
leading scorer, was traded to the Canadiens for a little-used forward named Red Berenson.

That move, soon bolstered by the addition of veteran defensemen Doug Harvey and Dickie Moore, triggered the explosion
that rocked the league as the Blues soared to the top of their six-
team division and then all the way to the Stanley Cup finals.
There, they were finally halted by the powerful Canadiens in a
four-game series, but the amazing Blues had already made their
mark on hockey history. It had been an incredible beginning by an
expansion team that had to be built from scratch.

To show that their heady rise was no fluke, the Blues soared to
the play-off finals again in each of the next two seasons. The imperious and slightly incredulous Canadiens again stopped them in
four games, and the next year it took the Boston Bruins to cut the
brash upstarts down to size. It was Scotty Bowman who took the
bows for this brilliant run, and rightly so, but Lynn Patrick stood
tall in the background. The family name was back in business, and
back at the top.

Lynn had his own ideas regarding the key to the spectacular
emergence of the Blues as a winning hockey club. "The key was

the acquisition of goaltender Glen Hall, who had been put into the expansion draft after his ten great years with the Chicago Black Hawks. He'd been around the NHL for fifteen seasons, and we needed his experience. Scotty and I knew that we'd live or die in the net, and that's where we needed the experience most. Hall had the cool and the poise a young team has to have back there to win.

"Our other two top choices in the expansion draft were also goalies: my old Boston netminder, Terry Sawchuck, and Bernie Parent, an outstanding young prospect with what looked like a great future. But our future was now, and we wanted Hall. We drew straws for the draft pick, and Los Angeles got first selection. When Philadelphia got the second pick we thought we were out of luck.

"Hall and Parent seemed sure to go first, and we figured to have precious little chance at either of them. But Los Angeles picked Sawchuck, and when Philadelphia called Parent's name, Bowman and I were out on the floor doing cartwheels.

"There is no doubt that Hall was the glue that held us together that first season, and it was his colorful style that helped pull in the crowds.

"The fans didn't start packing the building until one week-end in the opening season when we beat Chicago and New York at home in consecutive games. From then on, they fought to get in. I wish they'd been in Philadelphia the night Berenson ran wild and scored six goals, four of them in one period. The last player I knew who had scored that many goals in a game was my Uncle Frank, who got six for his Vancouver Millionaires a hundred or so years ago." (It was actually a mere fifty-five years ago.)

Life wasn't quite as exciting for Muzz Patrick in New York City in that wildly successful St. Louis winter of 1967–68, but there were some interesting moments. Such as on the evening of February 11, when the new Garden was formally opened. With Mayor John Lindsay heading a glittering delegation of the city's social and political elite, the grand opening featured a show headlined by Bing Crosby and Bob Hope and a parade of many of the great athletes who had made history in the old building.

For those with long memories, there was a particularly nostalgic moment when Jack Dempsey, seventy-two, climbed into the ring to shadowbox with Gene Tunney, the sixty-nine-year-old ex-Marine who took Dempsey's heavyweight title in the early autumn of 1926. That added up to forty-two years since the afternoon when Tex Rickard, the old Garden's first president, left Penn Station with that huge mob of fight fans to watch his boy get whipped by Tunney in the rain in Philadelphia.

The only physical reminders of that day and Rickard's special place in Garden history were the trains that still rumbled along the tracks beneath the new Garden.

Muzz was there for the opening after a busy afternoon at the old plant on Eighth Avenue, where he had assembled dozens of the top NHL stars of the past for a hockey game and farewell bash before the jackhammers moved in. After the requiem, he and a gang of the old Rangers attended the Irving Felt spectacular, watched the show, and then adjourned to a more intimate Manhattan establishment where the ale flowed as freely as the nostalgia.

The rest of the roving vice-president's benevolent exile was spent in the sprawling innards of the gleaming new Taj Mahal, where he was involved in various activities, none of them to do with the Rangers. He became sort of ambassador-at-large to various enterprises, such as the operation of the huge bowling center, indoor soccer, and the ill-fated World Hockey Association New York Raiders, a sad-sack team that hoped to challenge the Rangers for the affection of the fans. The Raiders, a pallid imitation of Bill Dwyer's Americans, never came close, and it was Muzz who gave them their eviction notice partway through a terrible second season. They got the heave-ho when the management was unable to meet the team payroll, a fact that jeopardized the whopping $20,000 per game rental fee Muzz was authorized to collect.

Muzz was also in charge of Garden security, an establishment that had changed a bit since the days when Jimmy Broderick, the toughest cop in New York, was a one-man patrol in the old arena lobby, on the lookout for hoodlums. Muzz's security force ran from a basic staff of around sixty to as many as six hundred for rock concerts.

His eviction of the Raiders was the first hockey decision Muzz had made since the Rangers days, and it was his last. In 1974 the expected happened. As Muzz puts it, succinctly, "Bill Jennings called me in, told me to retire, and I did."

He cleared out his desk, locked the office and caught the evening train for the sixty-minute ride to his home in Riverside, Connecticut, his long association with the Garden behind him for good.

He had a family of four, but they were all grown, and his two sons had no ambition to follow the old man into the hockey business. The youngest of the four children was Lori, eighteen, and the oldest was the other daughter, Lynda, twenty-six and married. Of the sons, both of whom had played high school and college hockey, Dick had his eye on a law career, and Paul was headed for a job in a New York brokerage house.

Muzz was neatly tucked into a life of retirement, but back in St. Louis, Lynn still had a few years to go. He had been promoted to the position of senior vice-president, and the direct operation of the St. Louis Blues hockey club was in the hands of the new general manager, Al Arbour. Scotty Bowman, who had become hot property after taking the Blues to three straight play-off finals, had returned to his native Quebec, as coach of the Canadiens.

Lynn himself was doing little more than easing gracefully into retirement, content to rest on his record with the remarkably successful Blues' organization that he had put together from scratch. Then, on the morning of April 1, 1972, he left his house in De Peres for the thirteen-mile drive to the St. Louis Arena, taking his youngest son, Dean, 17, with him. Lynn spent a couple of hours checking on preparations for that night's game against Chicago, the last contest of the regular schedule. Dean spent the time skating on the rink.

They got back to De Peres just after noon to find Bernice Patrick lying unconscious on the floor of the master bedroom. She had been perfectly well and happy when she had seen her husband and son off just a few hours before, but had been suddenly stricken by a cerebral hemorrhage. She died seven days later.

The tragic end to his happy marriage of twenty-seven years to the girl from Detroit was a cruel blow to Lynn. He considered retirement right then, but decided to stay on awhile longer. His family numbered five: a daughter, Karen, and four sons, Lester, Jr., Craig, Glen, and Dean.

All of the sons played hockey, three of them quite well, and two years after their mother's death, history turned full circle as Craig came to St. Louis to join his father's hockey club. It was exactly forty years since another son had arrived in New York, to join his father with those other Blues—of Broadway.

Lynn wanted no part of the player trade that had brought Craig to St. Louis after his three moderately successful years with the NHL Oakland Seals. He had recorded one good twenty-goal season, and Al Arbour went along with the Solomons' suggestion that another and younger Patrick would look good on their hockey team.

Lynn was outspokenly opposed to the deal. "I remembered my own experience when I joined my father in New York. It took a long time for that 'boss's son' stigma to wear off, and in the meanwhile it was pretty rough on both me and Lester. I don't think the New York fans ever really accepted me. I didn't want this to happen to Craig, or to me, in St. Louis. However, in St. Louis all trade decisions were made by committee, and Sid Solomon III had a pretty powerful voice. I didn't want Craig, but I was outvoted."

So at the age of twenty-eight Lynn's boy had come to play in the city that had been his father's first stop as a professional, en route to that stormy debut in New York in the autumn of 1935. In St. Louis, Craig Patrick had no problem with the fans, but he did have a problem that his father never had: a limited ability as a National Hockey League player. In Lynn's own words, "He was too defense-minded for a winger."

After one season with the Blues, Craig was traded to Kansas City, and then went from there to the minors, to Tulsa of the Central League. He had gone as far as any of his generation of Patricks would go as a player. The younger brother, Glen, was also playing in the Central League, at Salt Lake City, and would likely go no higher. Dean had played as an amateur, but had no ambitions to be a professional.

As for Lester, Jr., Lynn's first-born, his only fling at the trade had been in 1972, as a general manager of the World Hockey Association franchise in Miami that more or less boasted a team called the Screaming Eagles. When that venture failed to get off the ground and the Eagles screamed off to roost awhile in Philadelphia, Lester, Jr., was not with them. Next seen, he was in Brussels managing a professional basketball team in a European league. That was his last job in sport before settling in Los Angeles as a "head-hunter," the trade name for recruiters of promising young junior executives for hire by big corporations.

"Lester," said Lynn, "is a mover and a promoter, just like his grandfather."

In February 1977, after one last brief and luckless return to action behind the bench with the Blues on a bad streak, Lynn bowed out. He left the Blues voluntarily, picking his own time.

"I was just two days away from my sixty-fifth birthday. I was tired, and I was over the hill. I had run out the string."

For the first time in seventy years, since that Saturday afternoon in Montreal when the young Lester Patrick had taken the ice for the first time with the Wanderers, there was no Patrick in big league hockey.

Said the Montreal *Gazette* of Lynn's exit from St. Louis: "Like the story of the Ten Little Indians, there goes the last of an illustrious NHL breed of Patricks."

As players, yes, but otherwise that wistful statement may have been just a little premature.

Although Dean had settled for a job on the fringe as a public relations employee and P.A. announcer for the Blues, two other brothers would soon be making at least a tentative move up: Glen as coach of the Northeast Professional League team at Hampton, and Craig as assistant general manager and assistant coach of the United States team at the 1980 Winter Olympics in Lake Placid. It was still a stubborn, die-hard dynasty.

There was no pressure from Lynn for his boys to stay in or out of hockey. He was content in his retirement, the first year of which was marred by another of those tragedies that continued to dog the family. His niece—Muzz's young daughter, Lori—was badly injured in an auto accident in Corvallis, where she was attending the University of Oregon, and the crash left her without the use of her lower limbs. When she was well enough, Lori was flown home to Riverside, Connecticut, to spend her days in a wheelchair, uncertain that she would ever leave it.

There was already a great strain on the Riverside household, as Muzz had brought his mother to live there after Lester's death in 1960, and for the past several years she had been a helpless invalid.

"Murray and Jessie," said Lynn, "were just marvelous to Mother all those years."

A few months after Lori returned home after her accident, Grace Patrick passed away. She had been preceded in death by Lester's brothers Guy and Stanley, and by two of Lester's three sisters. Of that generation of Patricks, only Myrtle, the youngest, was still living.

Of that sturdy lot, only memories now remained, and they were kindled in mid-February 1979 by the man who is acclaimed as the greatest hockey player of his time, Bobby Orr. Orr was one of the large gathering in the Starlight Room of the Waldorf-Astoria, where media people and hockey celebrities had assembled for lunch. They were there to honor the players of the NHL-Soviet Challenge Series that was due to begin that evening in Madison Square Garden.

The squads of the NHL and Soviet teams were there, but it was Orr who was the center of attention. He was the star guest, as he was to be presented with the Lester Patrick Award trophy, symbolizing "outstanding service to hockey in the United States." The award was instituted in 1976 by the New York Rangers Hockey Club, and Lester Patrick himself, whose bronze statuette depicting him in a classic coaching pose stood in the foyer, would not have quarreled with the choice of this year's recipient.

When called forward to receive the trophy from NHL president John Ziegler, Orr moved gingerly to the microphone on those gimpy knees of his, surveyed the audience for a moment, and then, speaking softly in his earnest and engaging manner, he said, "This award is a very special honor for me because of the name it bears. I really don't know as much as I should know about the Patricks, but I do know of the tremendous contribution they have made to hockey. As I accept this award, I humbly acknowledge that contribution."

As he spoke, a Russian official was bent over the team table, whispering an interpretation, and when Orr finished speaking they were on their feet with the others in the room, applauding Bobby as he held the trophy aloft.

The Russians undoubtedly knew a good deal less than Orr did about the Patrick family's place in hockey and in the legends of sport in North America, but they sensed that it was something very special.

EPILOGUE

A soft summer wind ruffled the leaves of an ancient arbutus tree, letting the sun glint through the branches and dapple the double row of headstones that lay in a neatly tended patch of green. Just behind the burial plot rose a tall, clipped evergreen, and two miles beyond that lay the placid waters of the Pacific. Only one of the headstones was raised above the ground, and that just a few inches.

This simple gray slab was etched with the names of Joe Patrick and his wife, Grace. Alongside, beneath the other stones, lay the third son, Ted; Lester and his mate, Grace; Frank and Catharine; and the youngest son, Stanley.

The only sound that intruded on the peace of this landscape was the whisper of the wind, but if you were to listen very carefully, the distant murmur of children's laughter could be heard on that gentle breeze.

In the rolling hills of Missouri more than a half-continent away to the east, the Patricks were gathered at Lynn's place for the family reunion they now held once every two years. There were twenty-nine of them there: Joe, Jr., Lynn, Muzz and Jessie, their nine children, and sixteen grandchildren.

In the spacious garden behind the old farmhouse, the youngest grandchild, Karen's four-month-old son, Gregory, lay asleep in a crib tucked into the shade of the big brick patio.

Out on the lawn, some of the grown-ups were defying the sultry heat of the afternoon with a languid game of volleyball, watched by a pretty brown-haired woman in her twenties. This was Lori, who was walking again after more than two years of therapy and painful surgery. She had helped put up the volleyball net, and even played a little. It was a remarkable recovery, and the doctors were now predicting that she would regain 90 per cent of her mobility.

Nearby, the grandchildren had found their own way to beat the heat, squealing and chattering as they splashed and frolicked in the pool. The squeals turned into merry peals of laughter as Grandpa Muzz hoisted son Dick's four-year-old Christopher aloft and tossed him far out into the water.

A few hours later, they all sat down for a barbecue supper, after which the parents began packing for home.

This was the fourth and last day of the reunion, but there would be others. The clan had already agreed to meet again in the summer of 1981, at Muzz's place in Connecticut, just off the beaches of Long Island Sound. But, as the fates would decree, one of them, the senior member, would not be there.

On the night of Saturday, January 26, 1980, Lynn Patrick left his seat in the St. Louis Checkerdome with ten minutes still left to play in the game between the Blues and the Colorado Rockies. It was a dull game and Lynn was not enjoying it, but apart from that he was anxious to get home to tend the collie pup that son Dean had given him just two days before.

Ten minutes later, Lynn pulled up at a cross-section on Oakland Avenue three blocks from the arena and slumped over the steering wheel, suffering from a heart attack. The car moved forward and nudged to a halt against a stop sign, and moments later police arrived on the scene. Dean was brought immediately from his official's seat in the Checkerdome penalty box, and he accompanied his father to the hospital. Lynn died barely an hour after arrival, without regaining consciousness.

In yet another of those strange strokes of irony that haunt the family story, as Lynn lay dying in St. Louis, Torchy Peden, his friend and boyhood idol from the early days in Victoria, was also dying at his home in Northbrook, Illinois, just 290 miles away. Torchy, the flame-haired hero of those epic six-day bike races in the old Madison Square Garden, had succumbed within the same hour following a brief and painful bout with cancer. He was seventy-four, six years older than Lynn.

Lynn had missed another great family adventure by just twenty-nine days.

It was in the late afternoon of Sunday, February 24, when Craig Patrick emerged from the tumultuous scene on the ice in the Olympic arena at Lake Placid, stood by himself for a moment and murmured, "God, I wish Dad had been here."

It was just moments after the U.S. hockey team had beaten Finland 4–2 for the Olympic Gold Medal to climax the most stunning upset in the history of international sport, and the place was utter bedlam. Here, without doubt, was a very special piece of hockey history, and it was proper, nay, perhaps inevitable, that a Patrick had been part of its making.

Craig, the modestly talented winger who had joined his grudging father's St. Louis Blues six years before at the ebb of his brief NHL career, had just concluded his services as the U.S. team's assistant manager and assistant coach. He was at his post on the bench during that climactic win over Finland, and of course during the incredible triumph over the U.S.S.R. just two days earlier.

His job on the bench was to relay messages from the spotter's booth to the coach, Herb Brooks, and also ride herd on team morale. The latter, on and off the ice, was his special job. And if any one single quality had been paramount during that historic week in Lake Placid, that quality was team morale. It was never higher on any team, any time.

The next day, along with the rest of the nation's instant heroes, Craig had lunch with the President of the United States, in the White House. Here was a fitting setting for a scion of hockey's royal family. Lynn, and all the Patricks clear back to the patriarch, Joe, would have been proud. But not surprised.

INDEX

Abel, Taffy, 156, 157, 161, 163, 176, 182, 207, 251
Adams, Charles F., 143, 152, 157, 158, 205, 210
Adams, Jack, 140–41
Adams, Weston, 205, 256
Allan Cup, 135
Allen, Keith, 257
American Hockey League, 200
Apps, Syl, 226
Arbour, Al, 261, 262
Armed Services Boxing Tournament, 198
Armstrong, Murray, 195

Bailey, Ace, 187–88
Baker, Norm, 191
Barnett, J. G., 65, 66, 67
Bathgate, Andy, 254, 255
Battling Nelson, 154
Beech, Bert, 52
Beliveau, Jean, 256
Benedict, Clint, 151
Berenson, Red, 258, 259
Big Four Football League, 194
Big Jack, 91
Blimstein, Whitey, 202
Blachford, Cecil, 37
Blake, Toe, 251
Boer War, 21
Borden, Sir Richard, 122
Boston Arena, 89
Boston Bruins, 7, 17, 91, 143, 167
  New York Rangers and, 175, 220–22, 224

Patrick (Frank) and
  as coach, 204–5
  Ross and, 205, 210–12, 233, 234
Patrick (Lynn) and
  as coach, 242–43
  as general manager, 243–44, 256
  troubled seasons for, 249, 256
Ross and, 143–44, 152, 153, 157, 169, 204, 205, 241, 242–43, 245
St. Louis Blues and, 258
Boston Celtics, 256
Boston Cubs, 209
Boston Garden, 205
Boston *Globe*, 7, 10, 93, 100, 124, 205
Boston *Post*, 27
Bouchard, Emil, 227
Boucher, Billy, 145
Boucher, Frank, 141, 144, 157, 161, 167, 251, 252, 253
  New York Rangers and, 223–24, 225, 229, 241, 246–47
  Patrick (Lester) and, 233–37
  on Patrick (Lester), 170
Bowman, William, 257–58, 261
Bradshaw, Joe, 91–92
Brill Brothers, 180
British Columbia, University of, 204
British Columbia Sports Hall of Fame, 192
Broderick, Jimmy, 182–83, 260
Bronson, Jimmy, 201–2

Brooklyn Americans, 229
Brooklyn Crescents, 196, 200, 216
Brooks, Herb, 267
Brown, Walter, 251, 256
Bruno, Johnny, 166–67
Buchard, Jim, 235
Buzinski, Steve, 233

Calder, Frank, 157–58, 176, 186–87,
    220, 222
Campbell, Clarence, 172, 220, 238,
    250, 254
Canada Sports Hall of Fame, 191
Canadian Air Force, 136, 137
Canadian Amateur Boxing Cham-
    pionships, 199
Canadian Amateur Hockey Associa-
    tion, 14, 26
Canadian Army's 196th Battalion,
    135
Canadian Car and Foundry, 227
Canadian Hockey Association,
    64–67, 72
Canadian National Hockey Team,
    258
Canadian Rubber Company, 26
Carey, William A., 179, 183
Carmichael, John, 239
Carr, Dave, 215
Cavanaugh, N.J., 58
Chicago Blackhawks, 158, 179, 182,
    208, 216, 226–27, 243, 259
Chicago *Daily News,* 239
Chicago Stadium, 158
Chabot, Lorne, 157, 161, 175–76,
    182
Chadwick, Bill, 181–82
Chapman, Art, 192, 193, 215, 251
Chapman, Chuck, 192
Clancy, Michael Francis ("King"),
    171–74, 187–89
Cleghorn, Odie, 17, 124
Cleghorn, Sprague, 17, 124, 145
Coal-Oil Johnny, 43
Coleman, D'Alton, 159
Coleman, Jim, 226
Colorado Rockies (hockey team),
    266
Colville, Mac, 195, 207, 225, 229,
    232
Colville, Neil, 195, 199, 207, 214,
    216, 218, 219, 225, 226, 229,
    232, 239, 241, 246, 252

Conacher, Lionel, 188
Connell, Alex, 176
Connolly, Bert, 195, 196
Considine, Bob, 155
Cook, Bill, 144, 157, 161, 167, 177,
    180–81, 196, 207, 209, 246,
    251, 252
Cook, Bun, 157, 161, 167, 169, 176,
    196, 207, 213, 251
Cook, Thirza, 122–23
Cooke, Jack Kent, 70–71, 257
Cooper, Joe, 195
Corbett, Young, 51
Cosby, Gerry, 181, 195
Coulson, Art, 30
Coulter, Art, 216, 221, 224, 225
Crescent Valley, 1–3
Cutting, Frank Alexis, 25
Cyclone Taylor: A Hockey Legend
    (Whitehead), 113
Cyndomyr (family home), 114, 222

Daley, Arthur, 129
Daley, Ed, 174
Dandurand, Leo, 145
Darragh, Jack, 113
Davies, Dorothy, 222
Day, Hap, 215, 238–39
Dempsey, Jack, 154, 166, 167, 177,
    198, 201, 259–60
Denenny, Cy, 149
Desireau, Sid, 95
Detroit Red Wings, 47, 107, 141,
    179, 233–34
    New York Rangers and, 233–34,
    242
Detroit Tigers, 67
Devaets, Gerard, 200
Dey's Arena, 31
Diefenbaker, John, 79, 80
Donovan, Ivan, 161
Duff, Dick, 255
Duggan, Frank, 155
Duggan, Tom, 152
Dunderdale, Tom, 105, 107, 111
Dutton, Merv, 144, 244
Dutton, Red, 214, 215
Dwyer, Bill, 143, 147, 152, 155, 166,
    169, 214, 226, 229, 260

Eagleson, Alan, 35, 152
Eastern Canada Hockey League, 27,
    30, 47, 48, 64

East-West All-Star challenge series (1912), 111–13
East-West Stanley Cup series, 122
Eddols, Frank, 237
Elliott, Chaucer, 36
Emms, Hap, 256
Empress Hotel, 115, 140, 146

Farr, Jennie, 231
Felt, Irving, 253
Fitzimmons, Fred, 174
Ford Hotel, 224
Fort Garry Hotel, 136, 163
Foyston, Frank, 130, 144, 251
"Franchise," the, 68, 99
Francis, Émile, 255–56, 257
Fredrickson, Bea, 142
Fredrickson, Frank, 134–37, 141–43, 144, 146, 152, 169, 213, 251
    Patrick (Lester) and, 134–37, 141–43

Gadsby, Bill, 256
Gans, Joe, 154
Gardiner, Bert, 195
Gardner, Jimmy, 105, 107
G.I. Bill of Rights, 235
Gibson, Billy, 201
Gibson, Doc, 36
Gilbert, Rod, 254–55
Gilmour, Larry, 70
Glass, Pud, 31, 35, 100
Gloucester, Duke of, 122–23
Goldup, Hank, 233
Gone with the Wind (film), 223
Gorman, Tommy, 147, 169, 170, 226–27
Gould, Bill, 200
Graham-Paige Corporation, 253
Grange, Red, 167
Grant, Bud, 195
Great Canadian, The (film), 223
Great Depression, 179
Green Door (speakeasy), 183, 209, 245
Grey, Governor-General Earl, 31, 34, 62
Grey, Sybil, 62
Griffis, Si, 28, 38, 105, 110, 127, 129
"Gunnar from Galway," 43, 44

Hadfield, Vic, 255

Hagen, Walter, 154
Hainsworth, George, 144, 148
Hall, Glen, 259
Hall, Joe, 28, 78–79, 134
Hamilton Tigers, 146
Hammond, Colonel John, 152, 153, 156–57, 160, 161, 162, 164, 177, 183, 200
Hardwick, "Tack," 157
Harris, Fred, 105, 110
Hart Trophy, 237
Harvard University, 27, 205, 211, 212, 228
Harvey, Doug, 253, 254, 256, 258
Hearn, Riley, 28, 35, 49, 98
Heller, Otto, 225
Henie, Sonja, 206
Henry, Sugar Jim, 235
Hewitt, Foster, 195
Hextall, Bryan, 207, 215, 221, 225
Higgins, Reverend A. I., 252
Highland, Harry, 105, 107, 111
Hiller, Dutch, 226
Hockey Hall of Fame, 28, 127, 144, 181, 238
"Hockey Night in Canada" (radio program), 195
Hod Stuart Memorial Match, 51
Hogan's Irish Tavern, 209, 245
Holden, Barney, 78
Holmes, Hap, 130, 139
Horner, Red, 187, 188
Hotel Vancouver, 106
Houston Astrodome, 240
Howe, Gordie, 256
Hudson Bay Department Store, 250
Hughes, Charles, 157
Humphries, Joe, 51–52
Hyland, Mayor, 156

Icelandic Aero Company, 136
International League, 36, 65, 67, 72
Ion, Mickey, 139
Irish, Ned, 251
Irish, Mike, 95
Irvin, Dick, 130, 144, 169, 226
Irving, W. P., 106

Jacobs, Mike, 165
Jeffries, Jim, 82, 83, 154
Jennings, Bill, 253, 255, 257, 261

Johnson, Ching, 156, 157, 161, 163, 171–72, 173, 176, 177, 182, 207, 209, 213, 215, 216
Johnson, Ernie ("Moose"), 28, 29, 30, 31, 32, 34, 35, 37, 47, 62, 83, 90, 98, 100, 251
   New Westminster Royals and, 105, 107–8, 111
   Portland Rosebuds and, 125, 130, 137
   Victoria Cougars and, 137–40
     last game of, 140
Johnson, Jack, 83, 86, 154
Joliat, Aurel, 145
Jones, Bobby, 154, 167
Jones, Victor O., 205
Jordan, Herb, 66, 70

Keats, Duke, 144, 152
Kennedy (referee), 78–79
Kennedy, George, 116–17, 134
Kenora Thistles, 38–39, 46, 47, 105
   Ross and, 38–39
Kerr, Davey, 215, 224, 226
Kilpatrick, General John Reed, 221, 236–37, 246, 247, 252–53
King Clancy Night, 173
King Edward Hotel, 51
Klondyke Hotel, 44
Kokanee Glacier, 1, 41
Kootenay Lake, 1, 2, 39, 41
Kootenay League, 46, 56

Lach, Elmer, 227, 237
Lake, Fred, 100
Lakeside Park, 44
Lalonde, Newsy, 49–50, 65, 72–73, 79–80, 105, 110, 111, 114, 117, 130, 131, 133, 134, 144, 167
   Patrick (Frank) and, 73–74
Langraf, Howard, 200
Laprade, Edgar, 235, 241
Laurier, Sir Wilfrid, 21
Laurier Arena, 50
Laval University, 22
Laycoe, Hal, 237
Leasowe Castle (troop ship), 135
Lehman, Hughie, 105, 107, 110, 124, 127
Leipzig (cruiser), 125
Leseur, Percy, 32, 34, 74, 100

Lester Patrick Award trophy, 264
Lester Patrick Night, 238
Lichtenhein, Sam, 101–3, 112, 115, 116, 123, 137
   Pacific Coast Hockey Association and, 131–32
Lincoln Hotel, 164
Lindbergh, Charles, 177
Lindsay, Bert, 47, 66, 70, 72, 105, 107
Lindsay, John, 259
Lindsay, Terrible Ted, 107
Linn, Grace, *see* Patrick, Grace Linn
Lomski, Leo, 201
London Illustrated, 128
Look, 221
Los Angeles Blades, 257
   Patrick (Lynn) and, 257
Los Angeles Forum, 70
Los Angeles Kings, 70
Los Angeles Lakers, 70
Los Angeles Rams, 257
Loughlin, Clem, 148
Louis, Joe, 165, 202
Lou Stillman's Gym, 201
Lunny, W. P., 65

McBride, Sir Richard, 122, 125
McCourt, Bud, 29
McDonald, Jack, 134
MacDonald, Kilby, 225
McDonald, Ran, 107
McDonald, Sir William, 17–18
McGee, Frank, 33
McGill University, 5, 21, 24, 26, 39, 204, 205
   Patrick (Frank) and, 26–27, 29, 39, 48, 52–53
   Patrick (Lester) and, 22–23
McGovern, Terry, 51–52
McGraw, John, 82, 167
Mack, Connie, 71
Mackay, Mickey, 125, 126, 135, 141, 144
McKinney, Don, 255
McLaughlin, John, 35
McLaughlin, Major, 179
McLean, Archie ("Sue"), 107
McNab, Max, 257
McRae, Sailor, 198
Madden, Ownie, 164

Madison Square Garden, 5, 15, 52,
    85, 143, 147, 152, 154–55,
    164, 168, 175, 177–78, 181,
    192, 195, 197, 202, 236, 264
  new sports complex, 253, 259–60
Madison Square Garden Corpora-
    tion, 162, 251
  Patrick (Muzz) and, 256, 259–61
Mallen, Ken, 107
Manhattan Saloon, 42, 95
Manitoba, University of, 135, 163
Manitoba Amateur League, 135
Manitoba League, 24, 38
Maple Leaf Gardens, 164, 173
Marshall, Jack, 35
Martel, George, 66, 67
Mason, Charlie, 196
Masson, Charlie, 29
Mendel, Harry, 200
Metro-Goldwyn-Mayer, 223
Metz, Don, 195
Metz, Nick, 226
Miami Screaming Eagles, 262
Millar, Hay, 70
Miller, Dean, 228
Miller, Frank, 204, 228
Mining News, 186
Minnesota All-Stars, 195
Minnesota Vikings, 195
Minsky's Burlesque, 83
Mitchell, Thomas, 9, 11
Mitchell, William, 11
Mix, Tom, 23
Montreal Arena, 38, 46, 131
Montreal Canadiens, 71–72, 116,
    130, 131, 133–34, 144–46,
    155, 156, 234
  New York Rangers and, 189, 242
  Patrick (Frank) and, 226–27
  Renfrew Millionaires and, 73–74
  St. Louis Blues and, 258
Montreal Forum, 146, 149
Montreal Gazette, 17, 263
Montreal Herald, 124
Montreal Maroons, 143, 146, 149,
    151, 152, 157, 165, 167
  New York Rangers and, 175–77,
    208
Montreal Nationales, 195
Montreal Royals, 181, 194, 195
Montreal Shamrocks, 14, 19, 22,
    78–79
  Renfrew Millionaires and, 78–79

Montreal Star, 36, 37, 106, 121, 132
Montreal Victorias, 5, 18, 19, 38
Montreal Wanderers, 5, 14, 27, 28,
    30, 31–38, 46–49, 98, 124
  disbanded, 131
  first signed players to professional
    contracts, 35–36
  game against first All-Star Team,
    51–52
  O'Brien and, 64–65
  Ottawa Silver Seven and, 31–34
  Patrick (Lester) and, 27–30,
    31–34, 35–38
  Renfrew Millionaires and, 72
  Ross and, 47–48, 49, 98, 102–3,
    124
  Stanley Cup and, 74, 81
Montreal Winged Wheelers, 194
Moore, Dickie, 258
Moose Johnson Night, 137–40
Morenz, Howie, 145, 146, 155, 156,
    169, 208, 214
Muldoon, Pete, 125, 139
Murdoch, Murray, 162–63, 180,
    206, 207, 213

Nanooskin (stern-wheeler), 45, 62
National Basketball Association, 256
National Football League, 195
National Hockey Association
    (NHA)
  Pacific Coast Hockey Association
    and, 115, 116, 117, 121, 130
  Patrick (Frank) and, 104–6
National Hockey League (NHL), 5,
    71, 104, 111–12, 135, 146,
    163, 244, 252
  goes international, 143, 146
  Patrick (Frank) and
    financial assistance to, 250
    as managing director, 186–89,
      203
NHL-Soviet Challenge Series, 264
Nelson Light Opera Society, 56
Nelson News, 1, 56, 59, 61, 62, 65
Nelson Victorias, 46
Nevin, Bob, 255
New Haven Ramblers, 237
New Orleans Superdome, 240
New Westminster Royals, 107–8,
    109, 110, 114, 244, 245
  failure of, 122
  Johnson and, 105, 107–8, 111

New York Americans, 147, 155,
     156, 166, 167–68, 182,
     214–16, 226, 229
  New York Rangers and, 214–15
New York *Evening Telegram,* 82
New York Giants, 82, 167, 174
New York *Graphic,* 184
New York *Herald Tribune,* 174
New York Raiders, 260
New York Rangers, 17, 50, 82, 85,
     127, 141, 154, 162, 165, 167
  Boston Bruins and, 175, 220–22,
     224
  Boucher and, 223–24, 225, 229,
     233–37, 241, 246–47
  Detroit Red Wings and, 233–34,
     242
  Montreal Canadiens and, 189, 242
  Montreal Maroons and, 175–77,
     208
  New York Americans and,
     214–15
  Ottawa Senators and, 178
  Patrick (Lester) and
     Boucher and, 233–37
     as coach, 160–61
     defends nepotism charges,
       206–7
     first game with, 167
     as general manager, 223–24
     Lester Patrick Night, 238
     new groups of replacements,
       207–8
     New York press and, 170, 174,
       180
     nicknamed "The Silver Fox,"
       174
     1939–40 season, 223–26
     relationship with players,
       163–64, 166–67, 170–74,
       180–82, 220
     resignation from, 236
     Stanley Cup and, 226
     substitute goalie incident,
       175–77
  Patrick (Lynn) and
     first experiences with, 195–97,
       206–7, 221
     postwar season with, 237
     rejoins as coach, 241
     resignation from, 242
  Patrick (Muzz) and, 202, 207,
     234–35
     as coach, 246–47
     first experiences with, 216–17
     as general manager, 249, 256
     postwar season with, 237
     problems with players, 254–55
     Shore and, 220–22
  Pratt and, 207–9, 223, 224, 225
  Stanley Cup and, 175, 180, 183
  Toronto Maple Leafs and, 182,
     224–26, 238–39
  troubled times for, 249, 253
  World War II and, 228–29, 233
     postwar problems, 235–36
New York Rangers Hockey Club,
     264
New York Rovers, 216, 228
New York *Times,* 80, 86, 100, 129,
     184, 238
New York *World-Telegram,* 235
New York Writers Association, 238
New York Yankees, 219
Nichols, Sibby, 110
Nighbor, Frank, 127, 171
Noble, Reg, 167
Norris, Jim, 157, 179
North, John Ringling, 155
North Dakota, University of, 195

Oakland Seals, 262
O'Brien, Ambrose, 64, 70–71, 74,
     81, 82, 98–99
O'Brien, M. J., 63–64, 70–71, 73, 74,
     81, 90, 98–99
  Montreal Wanderers and, 64–65
  Renfrew Millionaires and,
     66–67, 70–71, 99
O'Brien, Stella, 72–73
O'Connor, Buddy, 234, 237, 241
Oliver, Harry, 144
Olympics Gold Medal (1980), 267
O'Mara, Baz, 176
Ontario Professional League, 48
Order of the British Empire, 86
Oregon, University of, 263
Orr, Bobby, 24, 222, 264
Osborne, Tommy, 199
Ottawa *Citizen,* 50–51
Ottawa *Evening Journal,* 66–67
Ottawa *Free Press,* 51, 122
Ottawa *Journal,* 175

Ottawa Senators, 37–38, 48, 50, 74,
    81, 98, 122, 127, 155, 164,
    171, 196
  New York Rangers and, 178
  Taylor and, 99–103, 105, 121
Ottawa Silver Seven, 14, 24, 27, 30
  Montreal Wanderers and, 31–34
Ottawa Victorias, 28, 29, 48
  Patrick (Frank) and, 48

Pacific Coast Hockey Association,
    111, 127
  East-West All-Star challenge
    series, 111–13
  final season of, 147
  formation of, 106
  franchises of, 106
  Lichtenhein and, 131–32
  merges with WCHL, 143
  NHA and, 115, 116, 117, 121,
    130
  opening game of, 107
  Patrick (Frank) and, 118,
    151–60, 178
  sale of, 151–60
  as Stanley Cup contender, 121
Parent, Bernie, 259
Park Vendome (apartment build-
    ing), 175
Patrick, Bernice Lang, 235, 261
Patrick, Catharine, 129, 130, 204,
    205, 250, 265
Patrick, Christopher, 266
Patrick, Craig, 261–62, 263, 267
Patrick, Dean, 261, 262, 263, 266
Patrick, Dick, 261, 266
Patrick, Dora Carmel, 12, 42, 114,
    252
Patrick, Edward Feather (Ted),
    12–13, 42–43, 90, 114–15,
    265
  death of, 203
  drinking problem of, 43
  leaves home, 61–62, 103–4
  marriage of, 146
  Patrick (Frank) and, 12–13,
    103–4
  Patrick (Joseph) and, 20–21, 43,
    90
  Patrick (Lester) and, 43–44
  Patrick Lumber Company and,
    60, 62

right leg amputated after sleighing
    accident, 13
  skating attempts of, 19–21
Patrick, Frances, 160, 205
Patrick, Frank Alexis, 265
  Boston Bruins and
    as coach, 204–5
    Ross and, 205, 210–12, 233,
      234
  Canadian Car and Foundry and,
    227, 239
  death and funeral of, 252
  disappointments and frustrations
    of later life, 250
  drinking problem of, 211–12,
    249–50
  family background of, 9–10
  on first league All-Star team,
    51–52
  game improvements initiated by,
    127–30
  as hockey referee, 28–29, 48–49
  innovative ideas of, 240, 250
  introduction to hockey, 14–16,
    18–19, 20
  job offers turned down by, 179
  Lalonde and, 73–74
  at McGill University, 26–27, 29,
    39, 48, 52–53
  Montreal Canadiens and, 226–27
  NHL and
    financial assistance from, 250
    as managing director, 186–89,
      203
  Nelson hockey club and, 57–59
  oil, gold, and silver mine ventures
    of, 178–79, 239, 250
  Ottawa Victorias and, 48
  Pacific Coast Hockey Association
    and, 118, 151–60, 178
  Patrick (Ted) and, 12–13, 103–4
  Patrick Lumber Company and,
    53–55, 60, 90, 91–92
    Crescent Valley log spill, 1–7,
      62, 69
  plans to develop hockey league on
    West Coast, 93–98, 104–6
  plans for "domed stadium,"
    239–40
  receives first skates, 12
  Regional Mines, Ltd. venture of,
    185–86

Renfrew Millionaires and, 62–90
  exhibition game in New York
    City, 83–86
  romantic imagination of, 57
  San Francisco ice palace project
    of, 119–21
  social life in Nelson, 55, 56
  at Stanstead College, 24–26
  on Taylor, 75–76
  Vancouver Lions and, 178, 186
  Vancouver Millionaires (Ma-
    roons) and, 109–10, 113–14,
    122, 127, 131, 157, 239
  exhibition games in New York
    City and Boston, 122–24
Patrick, Frederick Murray (Muzz),
    114, 130–31, 139, 160–61,
    171, 197–202, 252, 265, 266
  as amateur boxer, 198–99, 200–2
  early sports activities of, 193–94,
    199–200
  New York after-hours social life
    of, 216–20
  New York Rangers and, 202, 207,
    234–35
  as coach, 246
  first experiences with, 216–17
  as general manager, 249, 256
  postwar comeback season, 237
  problems with players, 254–55
  Shore and, 220–22
  as player-coach with St. Paul, 237
  Patrick (Joseph) and, 197
  Patrick (Lester) and, 198, 201
  Tacoma Rockets and, 244, 245–46
  vice-president of Madison Square
    Garden Corp., 256, 259–61
  World War II and, 228, 231–32
Patrick, Glen, 261, 262, 263
Patrick, Gloria, 160, 205
Patrick, Grace, 10, 11, 42, 55, 58,
    61, 62, 90, 125, 129, 185,
    222, 265
Patrick, Grace Linn, 59–60, 61, 91,
    92, 98–99, 103, 130, 173,
    217, 236, 237, 238, 239,
    252, 264, 265
Patrick, Guy Waterson, 39, 42, 125,
    174, 212, 215, 239, 250, 252,
    264
Patrick, Ida, 203
Patrick, James, 9
Patrick, Joseph, 1–2, 265, 267

as alderman, 131, 146
death and funeral of, 227–28
decision to develop hockey league
  on West Coast, 93–98
early business ventures of, 10–12
family background of, 9–10
golden wedding anniversary of,
  184–85
marriage of, 10
opening of Victoria Arena, 106–7
Patrick (Lynn) and, 192
Patrick (Muzz) and, 197
Patrick (Ted) and, 20–21, 43, 90
Patrick Lumber Company and
  Crescent Valley log spill, 1–7,
    62, 69
  formation of, 39, 40, 45–46, 54,
    55
  lumber camps destroyed by fire,
    69–70
  sold to English syndicate,
    92–93
  success of, 59, 90
Pennsylvania Wood and Coal
  Company and, 16, 18
provides money for Nelson's new
  hockey rink, 57, 58
Quebec coal-and-lumber company
  of
  expansion of, 13–14, 16, 24
  formation of, 12
  liquidation of, 26
Regional Mines, Ltd. venture and,
  185–86
semi-retirement activities of,
  115–16
Vancouver Arena destroyed by
  fire, 212
wife's death and, 222
World War I and, 124–26
Patrick, Joseph, Jr., 130, 160, 185,
    204, 205–6, 211–12, 228,
    250, 265
Patrick, Karen, 261, 265
Patrick, Lester, 2–7, 25, 265
  arrival in Nelson, B.C., 41–46
  Boucher on, 170
  with Brandon hockey club, 24
  death and funeral of, 251–52
  with Edmonton hockey club, 46–
    49
  estate of, 252
  family background of, 9–10

Fredrickson and, 134–37, 141–43
full retirement from hockey ca-
    reer, 247
game improvements initiated by,
    127–30
as hockey referee, 101
introduction to hockey, 14–16,
    18–19, 20
at McGill University, 22–23
Montreal Wanderers and, 27–30,
    31–34, 35–38
with Nelson hockey club, 57–59
New York Rangers and
    Boucher and, 233–37
    as coach, 160–61
    defends nepotism charges,
        206–7
    first game, 167
    as general manager, 223–24
    Lester Patrick Night, 238
    new groups of replacements,
        207–8
    New York press and, 170, 174,
        180
    nicknamed "The Silver Fox,"
        174
    1939–40 season, 223–26
    relationship with players,
        163–64, 166–67, 170–74,
        180–82, 220
    resignation from, 236
    Stanley Cup and, 226
    substitute-goalie incident,
        175–77
Patrick (Muzz) and, 198, 201
Patrick (Ted) and, 43–44
Patrick Lumber Company and,
    46, 55, 60, 90
    Crescent Valley log spill,
        1–7, 62, 69
plans to develop hockey league on
    West Coast, 93–98, 104–6
as a ranch hand in Calgary, 23
receives first skates, 12
Renfrew Millionaires and, 62–90
    exhibition game in New York
        City, 83–87
Ross and, 210–11
social life in Nelson, 55, 56
on survey gang of Canadian
    Pacific Railway, 23–24
Vancouver Arena destroyed by
    fire, 213

with Victoria Aristocrats (Sena-
    tors), 107–8, 113–14, 118,
    122
    failure of, 131
    wins Stanley Cup, 130
Victoria Cougars and, 148–49,
    238
    sells club, 247
    takes over operation of, 240,
        245
with Westmount hockey club, 26
Patrick, Lester, Jr., 222, 261, 262–63
Patrick, Lori, 261, 263, 264, 265–66
Patrick, Lucinda, 9–10, 13
Patrick, Lucinda Victoria (Cynda),
    12, 42, 60, 90, 114, 203, 238,
    252
Patrick, Lynda, 261
Patrick, Lynn, 110, 114, 160, 161,
    171, 191, 192–97, 199, 212,
    217, 218, 252, 265, 267
    Boston Bruins and
        as coach, 242–43
        as general manager, 243–44,
            256
        troubled seasons for, 249, 256
    as coach of New Haven
        Ramblers, 237
    death of, 266
    early sports activities of, 193–96
    Los Angeles Blades and, 257
    New York Rangers and
        first experiences with, 195–97,
            206–7, 221
        postwar comeback season with,
            237
        rejoins as coach, 241
        resignation from, 242
    Patrick (Joseph) and, 192
    St. Louis Blues and, 257–59
        departure from, 263
        as senior vice-president, 261
    World War II and, 228, 231
Patrick, Margaret, 9, 11
Patrick, Myrtle Eleanor, 39, 42, 114,
    252, 264
Patrick, Paul, 261
Patrick, Thomas, 9–10, 12, 13
Patrick, William Stanley, 39, 42, 61,
    174, 178, 213, 222, 227, 239,
    250, 252, 264, 265

Patrick Lumber Company, 1–7, 40
  Crescent Valley log spill, 1–7, 62, 69
  lumber camps destroyed by fire, 69–70
  Patrick (Frank) with, 53–55, 60, 90, 91–92
  Patrick (Joseph) and
    formation of, 39, 40, 45–46, 54, 55
    sold to English syndicate, 92–93
    success of, 59, 90
  Patrick (Lester) and, 46, 55, 60, 90
  Patrick (Ted) and, 60, 62
Patterson, Lt. Governor, 107
Peden, Doug, 191, 202
Peden, Torchy, 191, 193, 202, 266
Pennsylvania, University of, 194
Pennsylvania Wood and Coal Company, 16, 18
Perina, Carl, 194
Peto, Len, 227
Philadelphia Athletics, 71
Philadelphia Ramblers, 200, 207, 216
Phillips, Tom, 38, 47, 48, 105, 110
Pickell, J. B., 164
Pike, Alf, 225, 226, 229, 232, 253
Pilote, Pierre, 256
Pitre, Didier, 47, 72, 134
Pittsburgh Hornets, 169
Plante, Jacques, 255, 256
Porter, Cole, 184
Portland Rosebuds, 125, 130, 131, 152, 157
  Johnson and, 125, 130, 137
Poulin, Skinny, 107
Povey, Fred, 76
Pratt, Walter ("Babe"), 170, 195, 196, 229, 231, 233, 244–46, 252
  New York after-hours social life of, 216–20
  New York Rangers and, 207–9, 223, 224, 225
Presse, La, 21
Province Bluebirds, 195
Pulford, Harvey, 33

Quebec Amateur League, 194
Queen Bess silver mine, 185

Queen's University, 30, 164

Ramo, Al, 202
Ramsey, Mrs. John, 93
Ratelle, Jean, 255
Raynor, Chuck, 235
Reardon, Ken, 227
Rebholz, Russ, 195
Redband's Stanley Cup Championship (1906 and 1907), 5
Reeves, Dan, 257
Regional Mines, Ltd., 185–86
Relief of Ladysmith celebration, 21–22
Renfrew Creamery Kings, 64
Renfrew Journal, 89–90
Renfrew Mercury, 78–79
Renfrew Millionaires, 66–67, 79–80
  failure of, 98–99, 101
  Haileybury and, 76–77
  Montreal Canadiens and, 73–74
  Montreal Shamrocks and, 78–79
  Montreal Wanderers and, 72
  O'Brien (M.J.) and, 66–67, 70–71, 99
  Patrick (Frank) and, 62–90
    exhibition game in New York City, 83–86
  Patrick (Lester) and, 62–90
    exhibition game in New York City, 83–87
  Taylor (Fred) and, 70, 74, 77, 78, 80–81, 90, 98–99
Reniccio, Oliver, 166–67
Richard, Maurice, 234
Rickard, Tex, 86–87, 153–56, 162, 165–66, 177–78, 179, 260
Rizzo, Frankie, 165
Robinson, Bill, 219
Roosevelt, Kermit, 155
Ross, Arthur Howie, 17, 18, 19, 21–22, 25, 64, 74, 76, 77, 112, 113, 123, 128, 133, 187
  Boston Bruins and, 143–44, 152, 153, 157, 169, 204, 205, 241, 242–43, 245
  death of, 256
  with Kenora Thistles, 38–39
  with Montreal Wanderers, 47–48, 49, 98, 102–3, 124
  Patrick (Lester) and, 210–11
  with Westmount hockey club, 26
Ross, Hugh, 133

Rowe, Bobby, 66, 70, 80, 83, 105, 107
Royal Flying Corps, 135
Royal Oak Burial Park, 221
Royal York Hotel, 226, 241
Russell, Ernie, 29, 31, 52, 72, 79, 98
Ruth, Babe, 154, 167, 177
Ryan, Frank, 205

St. James Methodist Church, 228
St. Louis Blues, 266, 267
   Boston Bruins and, 258
   Montreal Canadiens and, 258
   Patrick (Lynn) and, 257–59
   departure from, 263
   as senior vice-president, 261
St. Louis Checkerdome, 266
St. Louis Eagles, 196
St. Nicholas Arena, 81, 89, 98
Sande, Earle, 167
San Francisco *Chronicle*, 119–20
Saskatoon Sheiks, 144, 148–49
Sawchuck, Terry, 244, 256, 259
Schmidt, Milt, 243, 256
Seattle Arena, 133
Seattle Kingdome, 240
Seattle Metropolitans, 129, 133–34, 143
   Stanley Cup and, 131
Seibert, Babe, 205
Seiling, Rod, 255
Sesquentennial Stadium, 166
Sharkey, Jack, 177
Sherman Opera House, 44
Shero, Fred, 239
Shibicky, Alex, 195, 196–97, 200, 207, 210, 215, 218, 225, 229, 232
Shore, Eddie, 144, 148, 152, 158, 169, 187–89, 205
   Patrick (Muzz) and, 220–22
Shriner, Sweeney, 215
Simpson, Bullet-Joe, 144
Smaill, Walter, 17, 30, 49, 98, 100, 105, 107
Smith, Alf, 37, 38
Smith, Clint, 186, 215, 217, 225, 252
Smith, Don, 79, 107
Smith, Harry, 33, 34, 37, 38–39
Smith, Hooley, 215
Smythe, Conn, 153, 156, 161–64, 173, 180, 182, 188, 236, 238, 244, 245

Solomon, Sid, Jr., 257
Solomon, Sid, Sr., 257
Solomon, Sid, III, 257, 262
Somers, Art, 206
Spittal, Baldy, 37, 38
Spokane Canaries, 131
Spokane *Spokesman Review*, 65
Sporting News, 34, 132
Sportsmen's Battalion, 125
Stallings, George, 82
Stanley, Barney, 127, 144
Stanley Cup, 14, 24, 30, 31, 38, 64, 72, 98, 112, 126, 130
   Montreal Wanderers and, 74, 81
   New York Rangers and, 175, 180, 183
   Pacific Coast Hockey Association as contender for, 121
   Seattle Metropolitans and, 131
   Vancouver Millionaires (Maroons) and, 146
   Victoria Aristocrats (Senators) and, 130
   Victoria Cougars and, 144–46
Stanley of Preston, Lord, 14, 65
Stanstead College, 24–26, 28, 43
Stewart, Nels, 151, 167, 175, 177, 215
Stewart, Rod, 258
Strachan, Billy, 30
Strachan, Jim, 35
Stribling, William ("Young"), 177
Stuart, Bruce, 98
Stuart, Hod, 35, 36, 37–40, 51, 52, 98
Sullivan, Ed, 167, 184
Sullivan, Red, 253
Sutherland, Jock, 219

Tacoma Rockets, 244
   Patrick (Muzz) with, 244, 245–46
Taylor, Fred ("Cyclone"), 50–51, 62, 65, 67–68, 73, 135, 146, 167, 213, 251, 252
   becomes highest paid team player in sports, 67–68
   in East-West All-Star challenge series, 112–13
   exhibition games in New York City, 81–82, 83–86
   last game played by, 140
   marriage of, 122–23

Ottawa Senators and, 99–103,
105, 121
Pacific Coast Hockey Association
attempts to get, 106, 112–13
Patrick (Frank) on, 75–76
Renfrew Millionaires and, 70, 74,
77, 78, 80–81, 90, 98–99
Vancouver Millionaires and,
117–18, 121–22, 126, 129,
137
Taylor Flip, the, 75
Tilden, Bill, 154, 167
Toronto, University of, 164
Toronto Arenas, 134
Toronto Maple Leafs, 164, 171, 182,
195, 229
New York Rangers and, 182,
224–26, 238–39
Toronto St. Pats, 164
Tunney, Gene, 166, 198, 201, 202,
260

U. S. Army, 228
U.S. hockey team, 1980 Olympics
Gold Medal Winner, 267

Vancouver Arena, 109–10
destroyed by fire, 212–13
Vancouver Canucks, 239
Vancouver Lions, 178, 186
Vancouver Millionaires
(Maroons), 99
name change of, 141
Patrick (Frank) and, 109–10,
113–14, 122, 127, 131, 157,
239
exhibition games in New York
City and Boston, 122–24
Stanley Cup and, 146
Taylor (Fred) and, 117–18,
121–22, 126, 129, 137
Vancouver *Province*, 111
Vezina, Georges, 131, 145
Victoria Arena, 18, 97, 131, 137
destroyed by fire, 178
opening of, 106–7
Victoria Aristocrats (Senators)
name change of, 107
Patrick (Lester) and, 107–8,
113–14, 118, 122
failure of, 131
wins Stanley Cup, 130

Victoria Blue Ribbon, 193
Victoria College, 194, 231
Victoria Colwood Club, 198
Victoria Cougars, 134, 144–49, 151
Johnson and, 137–40
last game of, 140
Patrick (Lester) and, 148–49, 238
sells club, 247
takes over operation of, 240,
245
Stanley Cup and, 144–46
Victoria *Times*, 108, 152, 198
Victoria YMCA, 191

Waddell, George Edward ("Rube"),
71
Waldorf-Astoria, 82, 123, 209, 264
Walker, Jack, 130, 144
Walker, James J. (Jimmy), 156,
165, 167–68, 177, 183–84
Walsh, Marty, 66
Ward, Gene, 238
Washington Redskins, 71
Watson, Phil, 207, 217, 218, 220,
221, 223, 225, 239, 241, 249,
253
Westerby, Harry, 176, 225–26
Western Canada Hockey League
(WCHL), 143–44, 156
Western Miner, 185
Westmount High, 199
Westmount hockey club, 26
Westwick, Harry ("Rat"), 33, 39
Whitcroft, Fred, 47, 70
Williams, Bert, 83
Wills, Archie, 152
Wills, Helen, 167
Winchell, Walter, 215, 216
Windsor Hotel, 152, 154
Winnipeg Blue Bombers, 195
Winnipeg Falcons, 135–36
Winnipeg Victorias, 18
Winter Olympics (1920), 135–36
Winter Olympics (1980), 263, 267
Woodman, Allan ("Huck"), 136
Woolfson, Bob, 257
Woollcott, Alexander, 184
Woolworth Tower, 85
World Hockey Association, 255,
260, 262
World Hockey Championships, 258

World War I, 121, 124–26
World War II, 223
  New York Rangers and, 228–29,
    233
  postwar problems, 235–36
  Patrick (Lynn) and, 228, 231
  Patrick (Muzz) and, 228, 231–32

Worsley, Gump, 245–46

Yale University, 183, 206
Yankee Stadium, 167

Ziegfeld Follies, 83
Ziegler, John, 264